THE HISTORIC TRAGEDY OF THE ISLAND OF CEILAO

THE HISTORIC TRAGEDY OF THE ISLAND OF CEILAO

CAPTAIN JOAO RIBEIRO

TRANSLATED FROM THE PORTUGUESE BY

P. E. PIERIS

GYAN

Published by

Gyan Publishing House
5, Ansari Road
Daryaganj, New Delhi-110002
Phone: 011-47034999, 9811692060
E-mail: books@gyanbooks.com

Distribution Network
gyanbooks.com
India, USA, Canada, UK, Australia, France

ISBN : 9788121234894 (PB)
First Published, Colombo, 1909

2nd Impression 2020

Printed at: Gyan Press, Delhi.

The Historic Tragedy of the Island of Ceilao
Author: Captain Joao Ribeiro

The Historic Tragedy

OF THE ISLAND OF

CEILĀO

DEDICATED TO HIS MOST SERENE MAJESTY

DOM PEDRO THE SECOND

KING OF PORTUGAL, OUR LORD

WRITTEN BY

CAPTAIN JOÃO RIBEIRO

TRANSLATED FROM THE PORTUGUESE BY

P. E. PIERIS

DERANIYAGALA SAMARASINHA SRIWARDHANA,

LITT. D. (CANTAB.)

Fourth Edition

INTRODUCTION

TO THE THIRD EDITION

In March 1640 João Ribeiro started from the mouth of the Tagus in the fleet which conveyed João da Silva Tello, Conde de Aveiras, who was on his way to assume the duties of Viceroy of India ; and he was still a boy of fourteen years when he reached Ceylon the following October, one of a body of four hundred *soldados*. Except for an interval of a few months, he continued on service in the Island till 1658, and rose to the rank of Captain in the Army. In that year the last of the Portuguese possessions in Ceylon surrendered to the Hollanders, and Ribeiro was transferred to India, where he served for another nineteen and a half years. In October 1680 he returned to his own country, and shortly after commenced to write his *Fatalidade Historica*, which was dedicated to King Dom Pedro II on the 8th of January 1685.

In 1701 a greatly abbreviated and curiously garbled French translation of the work was published by the Abbé le Grand at Paris, Treves, and Amsterdam, and of this an English version was issued in 1847 by Mr. George Lee of the Ceylon Civil Service. In the meantime the Academia Real das Sciencias of Lisbon had in 1836 published the original Portuguese, and it is from this edition that the present translation is made.

We know from the great work of the Jesuit Fernão de Queiroz that there were several Portuguese who had recorded the narrative of their experiences in Ceylon ; some of these memoirs have at last been traced but none has so far been made available to the public. To Ribeiro therefore belongs the credit of being the first European who has left to us a detailed account of the country from personal knowledge. A hundred years of pitiless warfare, the terrible details of which have been set out in full in another work,* had reduced

*Ceylon, the Portuguese Era. 2 vols., Colombo Apothecaries Company, Limited.

the Sinhalese who still maintained their independence, to a small handful concealed among the forests of the mountain highlands. The effort however had cost the Portuguese dear, and they had not the strength to resist the onslaught of the Hollanders who now appeared on the scene under the guise of the mercenaries of the Sinhalese King.

The details of this last struggle as narrated by Ribeiro are of interest, though they are found to be somewhat coloured by the imagination of the veteran soldier, and marred by lapses from accuracy due no doubt to the distance of time at which they were committed to writing. The chief value of his work however, arises not from his account of the military operations, but from his delightful observations on the life and customs of the Sinhalese, and the internal conditions of the country as he saw it. To him Ceylon was always "the loveliest parcel of land the Creator has placed upon this earth"; and as he painfully toiled at his indictment of the mad folly which had robbed his country of this beautiful land, the glamour of her loveliness grew more and more on him. He painted her as the Portuguese who had revelled in the comfort of the obsequious East had seen her; he could not see those horrors by which his countrymen had brought a curse upon themselves. None the less his work is equalled by that of de Queiroz alone in the knowledge which it has preserved to us about the conditions of life in Ceylon in the middle of the seventeenth century.

In the present Edition the Third Book, with Ribeiro's valuable comments on the colonial policy of his country, has for the first time been translated in full, while the interpolations from other authors, which appear in the second Edition, have been omitted as being no longer required for the guidance of students of the period.

P. E. P.

A Note to the Fourth Edition

Senhor Frazão de Vasconcellos in his Subsidios Ineditos sobre O Capitão João Ribeiro (Lisboa, 1927) which are the fruit of his researches among the Lisbon Archives, has supplied further information about Ribeiro. He was born at Lisbon and was baptised on the 17th of May, 1622. His parents were Domingos Ribeiro, a native of Viseu and a "barreteiro" or cap maker by profession, and Gracia, the daughter of Gaspar Alvares, also a "barreteiro", and Teresa de Aragão, who were married at Lisbon on the 15th of November, 1620. So that when Joao landed in India in 1640, he was eighteen years of age and not fourteen as asserted by himself. In 1658 he was sent with the other Portuguese who were taken prisoner at Jafanapatam to Batavia, from where he returned to Portugal the following year. A few years of active service in Europe, in the course of which he was severely wounded in the head, followed, and in 1667 he was invested with the Order of Christo, and despatched to Madeira as Captain of the garrison at Funchal. While there he married Dona Felipa, daughter of Pedro Catanho, a member of a noble family of that Island. Her brother Matias had been João's companion during his campaigns in Ceylon and his imprisonment in Batavia, and had been burnt to death in his vessel while chasing some Turkish frigates. In 1680 João returned to Lisbon where he died in November, 1693. His Testament, which was begun on the 22nd of June, 1688 and completed five months later, is preserved at the Torre do Tombo. After invoking the Mother of God and various Archangels and others to intercede for the Repose of his Soul, he directed certain religious and charitable bequests, including the provision of a silver lamp for the Church where he was baptised. He appointed his widow, by whom he had no child, his sole heir, at the same time giving her much godly counsel. Above all he advised her "to occupy herself for such portion of life as still remained in praising God our Lord." She however elected to seek consolation with a second husband.

Here it might be added that three signed copies of Ribeiro's manuscript are known, of which one is in Ceylon.

Nugedola, Pasyala.
Sept. 1947.

DEDICATION

Senhor,

Time may dull the vigour of my limbs, after forty and a half years spent in fighting for Your Majesty ; but it cannot deaden the enthusiasm with which I have pursued my task. Love is as a fire and needs must burn so long as it is not quenched. The constancy of my love will endure within my heart so long as life does last. To-day the flame still burns as best it can, though it may not burn as it would.

Nineteen and a half years have I served Your Majesty in the State of India ; eighteen successive years were spent in Ceilão. The various events which occurred there were of a verity beyond the ordinary, and had they not befallen in places so remote and consequently little known, they could demand their share of wonder with the most memorable in Europe. These and other reasons which some day may be of use to our policy, have induced me to commit my recollections to writing in such periods and with such rugged style as befit a soldier who has no other lessoning or schooling than the books of his powder and the teachings of his sword. The same love which sent me out on service and forced me to undertake this little work, now gives me courage to place it at the Royal feet of Your Majesty from whose greatness I hope for pardon for this my presumption.

May God preserve the Most High Person of Your Majesty for the safety and glory of your subjects.

João Ribeiro

Lisbon, 8th January 1685.

INDEX TO CHAPTERS

BOOK I

BOOK II

Book III

PROLOGUE

THESE memoirs cost me more to acquire than to commit to writing, because they were obtained not from hearsay, but from toil and experience. To commit them to writing I had not to steal the time from any other occupation. They are not published for the display of rhetoric or style, for such should not be expected from a soldier who has spent the best years of his life in war. They are due to my regret that there is no one willing to occupy himself in placing on record the greatness and the events of Ceilão so that they may reach the notice of everyone. They deserve to be engraved on plates of bronze to be preserved for ever in the recollection of man, not only for the benignity of its nature, its wealth, and other circumstances, but also for the different and varying incidents which we encountered there against two such powerful enemies. This course therefore seemed to me convenient, and it might some day be of advantage to show what that Island is and the reasons why our arms could not be maintained there. Of this at least I am sure, that my memory has not played me false, nor has boastfulness led me to deviate from the truth. It was open to me to dilate on the attending circumstances, but as this was not absolutely necessary I was unwilling to give cause for offence without some clear advantage.

To prevent confusion, I have divided this little treatise into three books. In the first I point out what Ceilão is, and the title of our Most Serene Kings, a title obtained by legacy and not by force, to this beautiful Island. In the second is detailed the progress of that war. In the third I state some reasons to prove that it was to our advantage to have occupied Ceilão alone with everything we had in the State of India.

May God grant that in view of these examples there may arise on these ruins a structure more solid. Such was the purpose with which I undertook this little work. If I fail in my object, and cannot interest the reader, censure can well be spared the soul which has no other aim in view but this desire.

CHAPTER I

In which is described the position of the Island of Ceilão by Polar elevation

The beautiful Island of Ceilão* stretches from the sixth to about the tenth degree of north latitude, that is, from the Point of Galle to the Point of the Rocks†. Its length is seventy-two leagues‡ and its breadth forty-seven, which is the distance from Chilao to Trequimale§; while its circumference is one hundred and ninety leagues, and it lies forty-five leagues to the East of Cape Comorim. Owing to its position it is the Mistress of all those regions which are commonly named India, embracing the kingdoms and provinces lying between those two handsome rivers, the Indus and the Ganges, which are separated from one another by more than six hundred leagues of coast line.

From Cape Comorim the Coast of the Fishery** runs inland, forming a gulf between Ceilão and the mainland, similar to the Adriatic. This has a length of fifty-seven leagues and a breadth of thirty-six, with its centre in the Islands of Ramanacor†† and Manar, between which lie twelve leagues of shallows. The only means of approach at this centre to the Coast of Xoromandel is afforded by two very narrow channels, the one at Ramanacor and the

*From the Arabic *Selon dip*, a corruption of *Sri Lanka dvipa*.

†Ponta das Pedras was the name applied by the Portuguese to Paritti Turai, the most northerly point in Ceylon. The Portuguese name still survives in the English form of Point Pedro.

‡A Portuguese league was identical with the Sinhalese, being approximately four English miles.

§The Portuguese form of the native name, Trikuna Male, of the loftiest of the headlands commanding the finest harbour in Indian waters. The English name for the town is Trincomalee.

**That is, of the South Indian Pearl Fishery.

††The Portuguese form of Ramana Kovil, the Temple of Rama. This is the Island of Ramesvaram, the centre of the Indian pearl fishery, which contains one of the most famous temples in India.

other at Manar, through each of which only a small *sumaca** can make its way, and that too when the sea is high. All vessels sailing those seas, whether from South to North or from North to South, must go past the Point of Galle, since it is the most Southerly among those lands ; wherefore Ceilão is by her position the Crown of the whole of India, and God would appear to have created her to be the Mistress of that great world, dowering her with a healthful and benign climate, with the greatest treasures which he has distributed over the whole earth.

For a clearer understanding it will be reasonable to describe the provinces ; their nature, wealth and products ; our fortresses therein ; the title of our Monarchs to this beautiful Island ; and the laws and customs which we have preserved among the natives together with their rites and ceremonies. All this will be done with the accuracy possible to one who has spent eighteen years there, and lived from the age of fourteen† in those forests, amidst the miseries and ceaseless anxieties of a war so terrible, that one scarcely knows how to relate them so as to be understood.

*A sailing vessel of shallow draught.

†He was eighteen when he came to Ceylon.

CHAPTER II

IN WHICH WE SHOW HOW MANY KINGDOMS THE ISLAND CONTAINED

THEY say that this Island had seven Kingdoms, and I am not surprised at this ; for even to-day on the Coast of India the Gentiles of each small Province form a separate Kingdom, as we see on the Coast of Cannara and Malavar*. Now this is a strip of land one hundred and forty leagues in length, which is the distance from the Rio do Sal† to Cape Comorim, and fifteen to seventeen in breadth—since the distance from the sea coast to the Gauts is not greater ;—and yet some fifteen Kings are found therein, such as the King of Cannara, of Lala, of Cananor, the Samorim‡, the King of Cochim, of Pallur, of Mangatte, of Chinota, of Porca, of Coulao, and others. This is the reason why the Moors§ have conquered all the Gentiles of India ; as each King by himself was so petty, he was not strong enough to repel invasion. But these same Gauts have preserved the others ; they form an impregnable range of mountains stretching along the coast of India and Xoromandel** at a distance of fifteen to seventeen leagues at most from the sea, as already stated, and have to be crossed by a few difficult passes, which too do not extend to the coast of Cannara and Malavar, for that side is entirely precipitous.

I have crossed from the Coast of Xoromandel by land to Goa, when taken by the Hollanders to Negapatão, where they sent me in 1656 with the others who had surrendered

*The Malavar Coast commences from Cape Comorin and runs along the western side of the Indian promontory. The name Malavar is derived from Malai, a mountain. Canara is to the North of Malavar.

†This must be the Chundragherry river.

‡The powerful ruler of Calicut, who was for so many years a thorn in the side of the Portuguese.

§In the light of their experience at home, the Portuguese called all Mohammedans by the name Moor, and that name is still applied in Ceylon by the English to the followers of Mohammed.

**The Coromandel Coast extends north from Point Calimere along the Bay of Bengal.

at Columbo. Advancing inland from the Gauts, which have an altitude of two leagues, the elevation does not diminish to any extent, but a plateau, from which one can only see the sky and horizon, stretches for more than two hundred leagues. In all this region there are no springs of water or wells, and on our journey we only found three rivers, and these at a distance from each other. Though the lack of water is so great, the land is extremely rich in grain, vegetables and cattle ; the villages are numerous and very large, and by the side of each there is a tank, either artificial or natural, in which is collected during the rainy season the water which the people and cattle use in the hot weather.

Turning to Ceilão, the chief King and Kingdom there were those of Cotta* ; this King the others reverenced with the respect due to an Emperor His Capital was at a distance of half a league from Colombo, and there its ruins and the foundations of buildings, all overgrown with forest, can be seen today. This Kingdom stretched along the sea from Chilao as far as the Grevayas, a distance of fifty-two leagues, and embraced the best districts of the Island, *viz.*, the Four Corlas†, the Seven Corlas, Salpiti Corla, Reigan Corla, Pasdum Corla, the Galle Corla, Beligan, Corna Corla, Cucuru Corla, Atagan Corla, Mature, the Pagoda of Tanavare‡, the Grevayas, the whole of the Kingdom of Dinavaca, which

*The Portuguese form of the Sinhalese *Kotte*, a fort. The correct name of the Capital at this time was Jayavardhana Kotte.

†The King who ruled at Kotte was the Suzerain of the entire country. Tributary Kings ruled over the Tamil district of Jafanapatam in the North, and the Kanda Uda Rata in the centre. This last name, which means the Country above the Mountains, has been corrupted into Kandy by Europeans. The Sinhalese Kingdoms were divided into Disavas, each under its Adipati, Chief appointed by the King. These represent the numerous "Kings" and "Princes" whom the early Europeans discovered. A Korale (Corla) is the sub-division of a Disava.

‡The Portuguese form of the Sinhalese Devi Nuvara, the City of God, the Dondra of to-day. The majestic temple of Vishnu which was described by Ibn Batuta in the XIV century, was destroyed by the Portuguese in 1587.

is the name given to the District from the Two Corlas as far as Adam's Peak* and the frontiers of Candia and Uva.

The Kingdom of Uva stretched from the skirts of Adam's Peak to the frontiers of Batecalou and Candia. The Kingdom of Candia adjoined the Kingdom of Uva and stretched from the skirts of Adam's Peak to the frontiers of Trequimale, the Bedas† of the Kingdom of Jafanapatão, and the Four and Seven Corlas, as it is in the centre of the Island. The Kingdom of Ceitavaca‡ adjoined the frontiers of the Four Corlas and Dinavaca, and included the territories of Sofregam. The kingdom of the Seven Corlas adjoined the frontiers of Candia, the Four Corlas, Chilao, and the territory of Mantota. The kingdom of Chilao stretched from Negumbo as far as the mountain of Grudumale§, and adjoined the Seven Corlas.

These were the seven kingdoms which were usually said to make up the island of Ceilão without including the kingdom of Jafanapatão although it is in the same island ; for this does not consist of Chingalas, but is a settlement of the Malavars ; and also the other kingdoms which used to exist there in ancient times, such as those of Batecalou, Trequimale and Jaula,** which have not been considered as such for many years. Besides these there is a stretch of land lying between the kingdoms of Jafanapatão and Trequimale where there live a race of people known as the Bedas, of whom we should speak in their own place.

*Such a name is not known to the natives of Ceylon, who call the mountain Samanala Kanda, and the footprint (See Ch. XXIII) Sri Pada. The Mohammedans consider the footprint to be that of Adam, and the Buddhists that of their Founder.

†The Veddas, see Ch. XXIV.

‡This was a fief created about 1521 for the brother of the King at Kotte.

§The Portuguese form of Kudira Male, the Horse Mountain, the Hippouros of the Greeks.

**Yala, see Ch. XXIV.

CHAPTER III

In which we describe the riches of Ceilão

The King who allowed us to enter the Island was the King of Cotta ; as already stated he was styled Emperor. Almost all his territory, which stretched from Chilao to two leagues beyond the Temple of Tanavare, consisted of cinnamon forests ; these are so dense that a man cannot walk through them a stone's throw. In shape the leaves of the cinnamon resemble those of the plantane in that they have three ribs, and in texture the laurel ; when crushed between the fingers their smell is as of the best cloves of Rochella. The trees are not very tall, for they do not exceed two *bracas** at the most ; and as there is rain here daily they do not shed their leaves, and most of them bear two crops of fruit, which is similar to the laurel berry, in the year. When this falls on the ground, it immediately starts growing in consequence of the heat and moisture ; and it is for this reason that the inhabitants have a law that they should clear their roads frequently; unless they do so, they would be all thick forest in one year. None the less their roads are only broad enough to admit of one person going at a time, and therefore our armies could not march except in single file.

Various precious stones are also found in great abundance in the kingdoms of Ceitavaca, Dinavaca, Candia, Uva and Cotta, within a circumference of sixty-seven leagues. Here all the valleys and mountains are full of them and they are obtained with little trouble; such as rubies, the finest that can be found anywhere within our discoveries, all in separate crystals ; sapphires, topazes (some of them of extraordinary size) cat's eyes (some have been found worth 20,000 cruzados†), garnets, beryls, jacinths, tourmalines, and various others which are held in no account there, since they are the stones with which the river beds are furnished.

*A *braca* is a fathom.

†In 1510 Alboquerque issued a gold cruzado of 420 reis, a rei being worth .268 of a penny in 1513, and .16 in 1600.

There is an abundance of cardamons in the Kingdom of Candia, and they are of such a great size that six of the Cannanor kind do not equal one of the Candian; throughout the Island there is plenty of Brazil wood, which is called Sapan in India, where it fetches a high price. Every year there is exported from the Kingdom of Cotta up to a thousand *champanas* of areca* (a *champana* is like a *sumaca* of forty tons); for this article is largely consumed over the whole of India. There are also many elephants and much pepper, both of which are considered the best in the East. The earth yields much iron and also two kinds of resin; the varieties of timber are so numerous that the choice of them will cause confusion; and there are several other products which I shall for greater clearness describe each in its own place.

*In Portuguese times arecanut took rank next to cinnamon in point of importance among the vegetable products of the country. The boom in the arecanut trade led to a state of things which almost rivalled the doings in the Belgian Congo and the rubber forests of Brazil. A *Champana* is the well known *Sampan*, from which are derived the place names Sampanturai and Hambantota. For details about Portuguese vessels see Ceylon and Portugal: Kings and Christians, Note 2. Marinharia. (Pieris and Fitzler, Leipzic 1927, pp 331—364)

CHAPTER IV

THE FORTRESSES WHICH WE HAD IN THAT ISLAND

WE begin with the city of Columbo, because it is the Emporium of the whole Island. It is situated on the coast which runs from North to South facing Cape Comorin, and lies spread round a bay which can hold a large number of small vessels. Seven leagues to the south, on a hill at the mouth of a river of the same name, stands the fortress of Caliture. Thirteen leagues beyond is the fortress of Galle built on a rocky promontory, and from here the coast runs a distance of forty-six leagues from West-South-west to East North-East. On a point of land we had the fortress of Batecalou where there is good anchorage for vessels with high sides. From here the coast runs from South to North twenty-four leagues, and at its extremity on a tongue of land we had the fortress of Trequimale, which adjoins the famous Bay of the Arches. From here the coast runs South-East to North-West thirty-six leagues, which is the distance to the Point of the Rocks : thence with an interval East to West twenty-four leagues as far as Manar, having behind it the kingdom of Jafanapatão and its fortresses. From Manar it stretches North to South ten leagues to the mountain of Grudumale, and from there fourteen leagues to Chilao. From Chilao the distance to Negumbo, a fortress where we kept a garrison, is ten leagues, and from Negumbo to Columbo about six.

We have thus shewn the fortresses which we possessed in Ceilão and their distances from each other ; and before we relate the particulars of each, with its inhabitants and garrisons, it is reasonable to explain the right by which our Most Serene Kings held this beautiful Island as their undoubted heritage, and this will be seen in the subsequent chapters.

CHAPTER V

Our arrival in Ceilão and the Building of the Fortress of Columbo

A few years after we entered the Orient we obtained information of this Island*, but as we were busy with many other enterprises it was not possible for us at the time to put its greatness to the test. As soon as our affairs were properly settled, in the year 1517, when Lopo Soares De Albergaria was Governor of the State, he set sail with an Armada and reached Columbo, the principal port in the Island, where many ships from Bengalla, Persia, the South and the Red Seas used to assemble to take on board cinnamon and elephants ; and here was carried on the trade of the Island in other commodities which they brought.

The Governor was well received by that Emperor, from whom he demanded the pareas† which he on his part had promised to Dom Lourenco de Almeida when he first discovered the Island in 1505, as well as a site on which to erect a wooden palisade for the better protection of a mercantile store where they could stock those goods which the country needed, and also receive her own products : great profits would thus accrue both to the Emperor and to his subjects. The Emperor, who was styled Boenegabo Pandar‡, was favourably disposed, and it did not escape his knowledge that according to report we obtained whatever we desired ; he gladly conceded both our requests, despite the protests of the Moors who were there and who were suspicious of us ; for

*The Portuguese first reached India in 1498, and at the time they had knowledge of *Zelon* from maps published in Europe.

†This was the payment which the King had promised the Portuguese for guarding his coast. For details of this period see The Portuguese Era, 1. and Ceylon and Portugal : Kings and Christians,

‡Bhuvanaika Bahu Bandar, who certainly did not ascend the throne till several years later. It is not certain who was the King in 1505, though it was probably Dharma Parakrama Bahu ; he at any rate was the King de Albergaria treated with. The correct date is 1518.

the result of our arrival would be the destruction of their trade ; and in this they were not mistaken.

In spite of them a stockade was at length erected, strong enough to resist any attack, as it was on a rocky headland which the bay throws out into the sea. Here he left João da Silva* as Captain of the Station, with two hundred soldiers, a Factor, a clerk and a priest to administer the sacraments ; and after providing everything that was necessary, the Governor himself sailed away, leaving behind four *fustas*† for the defence of the place.

In 1520 orders were given that some ships should proceed to that Fort with men and material with which to begin a building of stone and mortar. With this new fortification the Emperor's attitude towards us underwent a marked change with the result that he laid the Fort under very close siege, which continued for some time ; but when assistance arrived the Emperor, in view of the loss which he had sustained, was compelled to make peace. This state of things continued for some years when various events occurred which forced us to increase our garrison in consequence of the Emperor's own brother Madune‡ King of Ceitavaca ; for he maintained a fierce and tyrannical war against the Emperor because he saw that the latter was showing himself too favourable to us. We, to show our gratitude, assisted the Emperor with all our power; and because he had no one save a daughter to succeed him on the throne, he gave her in marriage to a young kinsman of his named Tribuly Pandar.§ The offspring of this union was a grandson, Parca Pandar** by name; and his grand-father was so devoted to him that he sent ambassadors to Portugal to beg King Dom João the Third to crown the child, and for this purpose they took with them a

*Or rather Silveira.

†A *Fusta* is a pinnace ; Ribeiro's details are very incorrect

‡Vijaya Bahu succeeded Dharma Parakrama Bahu, and was deposed as the result of a successful plot. He was succeeded by Bhuvanaika Bahu, who created the fief of Sitavaka for his brother Mayadunne.

§This appears to be the Portuguese form of the Tamil rendering of the Sinhalese Vidiye Bandar, the correct name of the prince.

**A misreading of the Portuguese Mss for Perea Pandar, the Prince, whose name was Dharmapala, being known by that Tamil honorific.

figure of the Prince. This ceremony was solemnly performed by the King in 1541 in his Capital, and he thereby guaranteed to the Prince the Crown of the Isand.

After the Emperor's death* this Prince succeeded to the throne ; shortly after Madune in turn was succeeded by his son Raju†, whom his father had trained in arms in the long warfare which he had carried on against his Emperor and brother Boenagabo Pandar ; in fact the son was a worse tyrant than his father, for not only did he inherit the kingdom of Ceitavaca and his policy, but he was also determined to drive the Prince entirely out of the Island. He steadily seized on all the provinces appertaining to the Empire of Cotta in such fashion as to compel the Emperor Parca Pandar to throw himself into our arms and to seek refuge in the Fortress of Columbo.‡

Next he turned on the Kingdom of Candia and compelled its King to flee with his wife and only daughter to Manar§, where we extended to him the hospitality due to a persecuted and fugitive King. The tyrant King Raju took away their arms from the inhabitants of this Kingdom and imposed the penalty of death on their use ; and he similarly continued his war against the King of Cotta and pressed him hard. The troubles of the Emperor caused great loss to the Portuguese, for as a neighbour and friend he received every assistance at our hands. So the war was furiously pressed against us too and our fort repeatedly besieged, but each time the enemy had to retire with considerable loss.

While the King of Candia remained at Manar with his wife and daughter, being well treated and looked after by us ; in view of his misfortunes, or, which is the more probable, by the blessed illumination of God, he with his wife

*He was murdered in 1551 by the mulatto slave of the then Viceroy of India, with whom the King had had a quarrel.

†Raja Sinha, the Kingly Lion, the last of the great Sinhalese rulers, was vested with the Royal power by his father about 1578.

‡Kotte was abandoned in July 1565, as the hostilities waged by Mayadunne and his son rendered the position no longer tenable.

§As a matter of fact the King and his wife died at Trincomalee of small pox, and his infant daughter was taken to Manar by her uncle.

and daughter received the water of the sacred baptism, himself taking the name of Dom Phelipe, and his daughter that of Dona Catherina. The Queen died shortly after, and the King with his burden of trouble drew near his appointed time. In making his Will he nominated his daughter Dona Catherina his universal heir, entreating the King of Portugal to take her, with his kingdoms of Candia and Uva, under his guardianship and protection. He also enjoined on his daughter not to marry except some one who was selected and approved by His Majesty or his Viceroy, for thus his kingdoms would be freed from tyrants and the affairs of the Portuguese placed on a footing which would best serve the interests of His Majesty.

As soon as news was received of the death of the King of Candia, the Emperor of Cotta and the Captain of Columbo discussed what action should be taken to release these kingdoms from the tyranny of Raju, for their affairs were in a desperate condition owing to our numerous campaigns; at the same time the Emperor took on himself to sound the nobles of those kingdoms. They embraced his proposals both with the object of freeing themselves from tyranny, and aslo induced by the many promises of the Emperor; but as they had no arms and none were to be procured without grave risk, they prepared with great secrecy in the forests a large quantity of bows and arrows of wood hardened in the fire; and filled with them several stores which were hidden in the thickets.

When the Emperor was informed of the disposition of the people and how they had prepared weapons, he communicated with the Captain of Columbo and advised him that matters had reached a stage which would not admit of delay; it was desirable to send some person of discretion and judgment to head the movement; for it would not be suitable to invite Dona Catherina to those kingdoms until they had been re-subdued. After consulting with each other as to a suitable person, they agreed upon a certain Apuame* of the Emperor, a favourite of his, a man of talent, high birth and sound judgment, a devoted friend of ours who had become a Christian

*An Appuhami is the son of a Sinhalese nobleman, but the honorific is now applied to most high caste men of good position.

under the name of Dom João ; in a word, a man well adapted for an undertaking of this nature. They gave him two hundred Portuguese to accompany him on his expedition with the title of Modeliar*, a rank corresponding to that of *Mestre de Campo* among us.

In a few days he reached Candia, where he was well received and found the people glad of his coming. With his arrival all equipped themselves with those weapons which as stated they had prepared, and they pressed on with such vigour that they not only released those kingdoms from their yoke, but, encouraged by the association of the Portuguese, they entered and ravaged the territories of Raju. With this revolt and the hostilities which we waged against him from Columbo, the fortunes of Raju reached such a low ebb that our men entered Ceitavaca his Capital, and gave him battle in which he was defeated ; while retreating he ran a splinter into his foot from which he came by his death.†

The Emperor being thus relieved by the death of Raju, King of Ceitavaca, was immediately acclaimed King by those people : just as he was King of the Seven Corlas, Dinavaca, Chilao, Candia and Uva, which were subject to him. As he was now advanced in years without any sons to succeed him, he began to think about the mysteries of our sacred religion, and frequently conversed about them with pious and devout members of the Order of St. Francisco ; and through the great love which he owed to the Portuguese for delivering him from his enemies, he resolved to become a Christian. In carrying out his decision‡ he was baptized with such pomp and rejoicing as the importance of the event and the position of the chief personage demanded. His example was followed by the bulk of the Nobles of his Court ; for, as is often the case, the example of the Prince could effect more than the force of arms. He took the name of Dom João Parea Pandar, and showed himself in his lifetime worthy of so great a blessing from the Lord our God ; for he was in every way a devoted Christian, kindly, pious, gentle and very liberal to all.

*Originally a high military rank among the Sinhalese.

†In 1593 in his 59th year.

‡He was actually baptised in 1557.

CHAPTER VI

THE REVOLT OF THE APUAME DOM JOÃO WITH THE KINGDOM OF CANDIA AND UVA; AND THE FIRST CONQUEST

THE Apuame Dom João who was in Candia, seeing himself master of the armies of those kingdoms, set about seizing them for himself. His first step was to destroy the Portuguese whom he had in his power, blinding some with a hot iron which he passed over their eyes, and cutting off the noses and ears of others whom he distributed over the country; and to win over the people to his designs, he apostasized from Christianity and offered sacrifices with the rest of the Gentiles. As however he was not a member of the royal caste, he assumed the title of Defender of the Kingdoms; and he acted so skilfully that he won the affection of the people and obtained as much power over them as if he had been their rightful Sovereign. At the same time he waged every act of hostility which he could against our territories and subjected them to great damage which we were not in a position to repair.

Now it chanced that Pedro Lopez de Sousa touched at Columbo on his way from Malaca, and landed to take on board provisions and water, of which he stood in need; he was well received by the Captain of the fortress Francisco da Silva, and entertained with all ceremony, for Pedro Lopez was one of the chief fidalgos who were serving in the State and was held in great respect. He informed Lopez of the war which Dom João was waging against us, how with no regard to his being a Christian, he had reverted to the rites and ceremonies of the heathen and how he had treated the Portuguese; he urged that it was to the advantage of His Majesty that an expedition should be sent from Goa as speedily as possible, to quench the flame which this rebel had kindled before the mischief grew beyond remedy; and he further begged Lopez to suggest to the Council of State that the Captain himself should be placed in charge of the expedition, as he knew more about the matter and the country than any other person to whom they could entrust the command. Pedro Lopez promised to do everything in his power in order to obtain for him his desire; he went on board and, after saying farewell, reached Goa in a few days.

His first step was to visit the members of the Council and to point out to each one of them in turn the importance of expelling from Ceilão the tyrant at whose hands we had received such great loss ; if we did not stem the force of the tide as quickly as possible, there was grave risk of our losing the Island and being compelled to conquer it over again, which would not be an easy task ; there was no person better qualified by his great experience and intimate knowledge of the country to be entrusted with this mission than the Captain of Columbo ; moreover by his intelligence, his services and high birth, he had deserved well at their hands ; any other nominee of theirs who did not have the requisite knowledge might prove our undoing rather than our salvation; for in enterprises of this nature it is experience rather than courage which leads to success.

Every one approved of the proposal of Pedro Lopez de Sousa, and they promised him their support whenever the matter came before the Council for determination. He was well pleased, for he appeared to have obtained what he wanted both to redeem his word and also to serve his King.

The Council met to discuss the question, and it was there resolved to organise an expedition with the least possible delay ; and it was further unanimously voted that Pedro Lopez de Sousa himself should go as Captain-General of the Conquest*. When informed of his selection he was greatly vexed and urged many reasons why he should be excused, but none of them were admitted, and their request was repeated and his acceptance urgently demanded as being in His Majesty's interests. He replied by putting forward two requests of set purpose,—requests which it appeared to him that it would be impossible for them to grant—solely with the object of ridding himself of the offer : since they were so anxious, he demanded two concessions : first that he should take with him one of his two nephews as Captain-Major of the Field, a post corresponding to that of the General-Master of the Field in Portugal ; and secondly, as the Queen Dona Catherina had to marry with the consent of His Majesty or of his Viceroy, that she should be given in marriage to that nephew.

*He was the first Conquistador in Ceylon.

The Council met to consider this proposal and his request ; various opinions were expressed, and after the matter had been well discussed, they recognised the necessity of securing a Christian Prince, and the impossibility of obtaining such an one of her own race ; the intrusion of a stranger had its dangers, and there was always the necessity that the Princess should marry at some time or other ; moreover the interests of His Majesty would always be better looked after by one who was his subject, than by some Prince to whom they should give these two kingdoms as a dowry ; they further took into consideration the fact that he was a fidalgo of high birth, who had served with satisfaction in that State ; such a connection might attract the natives to a comprehension of the true Faith and they might learn, as the result of such marriages*, to serve His Majesty with love and fidelity.

The Council accordingly resolved that the conditions demanded by Pedro Lopez were expedient, and they granted to him either request ; they however stipulated that his nephew should not marry the Queen until she was placed in possession of the two kingdoms of Candia and Uva ; that he should remain faithful and loyal to the interests of His Majesty, and that after he became King he should be his vassal ; that he should do homage, but in every other respect be the independent King of those kingdoms.

*This at any rate was the policy of Alboquerque, but it was not very successful in Ceylon.

CHAPTER VII

In which is Recounted the Result of the War of this First Conquest

In a short time an armament of several vessels driven by oars and some galleys conveying one thousand two hundred Portuguese soldiers in excellent condition, and everything else that was necessary, had been prepared. Leaving Goa with good weather it reached Manar where the Queen was immediately taken on board ; and sailing from here with a favourable wind, it anchored at Negumbo.

The arrival of Pedro Lopez with this large armament and in company with the Queen was reported to the Captain of Columbo, who was frantic with rage ; for it appeared to him that what Pedro Lopez had promised for him he had obtained for himself, the fact being however the very opposite ; for the faculties of man are such that his own language it is which drives him into wrath without any consideration of what the truth may be ; and merely for the gratification of a burst of passion he converts into a crime what is an act of good service, and obedience into an offence. Such were the feelings of the Captain of Columbo towards Pedro Lopez de Sousa, that not only did he not treat him as a friend, but he even forgot his duty towards him as a subject of the King ; he gave him neither men nor any other aid to assist him in the enterprise with which he had been entrusted by the Lords of the Council of the State of India.

Three days after his arrival a Modeliar*, a noble man among the Chingalas, came over to render him obedience and to assist him in his undertaking with twenty thousand men of war ; he had grown estranged from Dom João because he saw that though he was only a private gentleman, he let himself be treated as a King, (and this is a matter which this people will not tolerate) ; and the arrival of Pedro de Sousa with his great force furnished him with the desired

*Jayavira Bandara, who had deserted the Court of Sitavaka after the death of Raja Sinha, and had acquired a great reputation by his achievements in the field on behalf of Dharmapala. See Port. Era I.

opportunity. When the kindly politician received him with all affection and good faith, he vowed that he would die in the service of the Portuguese; at the same time, acknowledging Dona Catherina as his Queen and Mistress and kissing her hand, he offered to devote his person and property to assist her against her enemies.

This Modeliar was so brave, courteous and gentle, that he was beloved by all his people. Pedro Lopez set great store on his arrival, and with such help he promised himself a successful issue to his enterprise: and he was a man of such great intelligence that he held him in the highest esteem and never began anything without his advice and without revealing to him his plans and his designs; for he found in him so much wisdom, and in everything his opinion was sound.

The arrival of the Queen and of Pedro Lopez with this large force, as well as the defection of the Modeliar, were all reported to Dom João, and he gave himself up entirely for lost; but he was shrewd and bore himself in his words and actions as if he considered all these forces as naught. To prevent his people losing heart he rapidly collected all the fighting men he could, and advancing from Candia with this army, pitched his camp two leagues from Balane*, at a point at which our forces would have to enter his kingdom; and, without revealing anything to any of his people, he set to work on a plan he had formed, which ended in the ruin of our army and the triumph of our enemies.

He wrote an *ola*† to the Modeliar in which he advised him that he was now in the field as he had said he would be, and that on the arrival of our army at Balane, he would put his good faith to the test; he begged him above all to do away with the General, since success depended far more on his death than on the capture of his whole force. He laid his plot so well that any person would have thought that the two were acting in complicity with each other, especially as they were of one race and one tongue. Sending for a Chingala in whom he had reliance, he addressed him thus:—

*The lofty mountain which commands the Pass leading within the mountain Kingdom.

†A Tamil word for The Sinhalese *puskola*.

" By the confidence which I have in you and by the proofs of friendship which you have always found in me, I shall entrust a weighty matter to your love ; what I am going to request from you may appear a trifle, yet it is of the greatest importance to me that it should be carried out with perfect secrecy and care ; if you succeed be assured that you will be well rewarded. "

" To serve you, Senhor ", replied the Chingala, " I would not hesitate to risk my life ; and of the rewards which you have given me I do not consider this to be the least, that you should rely on my ability to serve you, not only in this matter, but also in every other which you entrust to me. Therefore tell me what it is you wish me to do, and in carrying out your desires I will prove to you my affection and my zeal."

" This, " replied Dom João, " is what I had expected from you ; and as to what I desire, go to Balane, where as you know the Portuguese army will encamp to-day. Their vanguard will consist of men from their territory. Do not try to avoid them, but as soon as you meet their scouts, let them see you and immediately flee into the forest and there pretend to fall, so that they may seize and take you to their General ; and always appear as if you were anxious to hide this *ola*—and this is the sole object of your errand—so that it may reach their General's hands. This is the mission which I desire you to execute with the secrecy I recommend, and the caution which is essential. "

The Chingala received the *ola* cheerfully, promising that he would not fail in his mission ; and after taking leave of him he succeeded in his enterprise even better than he had purposed. He conducted himelf with such cunning that he was brought with the letter before the Captain-General who immediately ordered it to be read ; on learning its contents he flew into such a burst of passion that without a word he sent for the Modeliar and gave him the *ola* to read ; then without waiting for a reply he ran him through with his dagger.

The unfortunate but innocent man fell down dead, and when our forces descended the next morning from the hill, they found not a solitary man of the troops raised from our territory, men who were essential in this kind of warfare ; not only the twenty thousand men of the Modeliar, but all the rest had deserted to the enemy when they saw the treatment meted to the Captain whom they all loved so well.

Dom João, who had been anxiously waiting for this result, simulated great grief and vowed to avenge the death, uttering a thousand imprecations against us. He hastened to meet us with all these forces and the twenty-five thousand men whom he already had, as we were on the march. A small body was despatched to block the road in our rear by cutting down the trees, and his archers and matchlocks were scattered through the wood, where they could creep near and wound our men without being perceived. Our men attempted to retire on Balane, but found the road blocked and guarded by a large force ; and thus all lost their lives ingloriously, the Captain-General and his two nephews being among the slain.*

The result would have been otherwise had he not placed reliance on an enemy ; everything which comes to us through his hand should be received with great caution ; to ascertain the truth one should look to the reverse of what is on the surface ; but it is God who disposes everything, and his ways are inscrutable.

After this victory the enemy betook himself to plunder, and the Queen herself was no unimportant portion of the same ; for he valued her greatly for the fulfilment of those ambitions which he had at heart, as we shall see.

*The battle was fought on 6th October, 1594. The General was captured alive.

CHAPTER VIII

Which Narrates the Marriage of Dona Catherina and what Followed

When Dom João held the Queen in his power, he carried out on her the design which he had conceived, ravishing her publicly in the sight of all*, and thereby achieving the fulfilment of his ambition regarding the crown ; for he could not have obtained his desire in any other way, as the people would never have given their consent even though it cost all of them their lives, as he was not descended from their Kings. But when they saw that he had treated her with violence and was also the master of their armies, they consented that he should marry her as they could see no other remedy. The Queen bore him one son, to whom they gave the nick-name of Prince of the Roosters.

When the destruction of Pedro Lopez de Sousa and his army was announced at Goa, they conferred the vacant office on Dom Hieronimo de Azevedo, who started for Ceilão with all the forces which the State could afford. He pressed on the war in every possible manner against the usurper, and after various successes he collected all his forces and entered Candia ; but the final result was such that he considered himself fortunate in being able to retire with the loss of three hundred Portuguese and a large number of the Emperor's Lascarins.†

After Dom João had obtained these victories he did not long enjoy the sovereignty over the kingdoms, for he came by his death‡ just as he had lived. The nobles seeing that the Queen was still young, decided that she should marry in order to avert disaster ; they knew that at Adam's Peak there lived a Prince of the Island, his kinsman, Henar Pandar

*This incident appears to be entirely fictitious.

†A word unknown to Ceylon, and introduced by the Portuguese from the Persian. The incident referred to is The Great Retreat of 1603. See Port. Era. I. Ch. XVIII.

‡Dom Joao was known as King Vimala Dharma Suriya. He died in 1604.

by name, a *Changata** or heathen priest who was fulfilling a penance (for necessity makes men religious) ; they brought him from there and married him to the Queen. After some years of soyereignty, seeing that he had also received as his dower a war with the Portuguese from which he could not hope for a successful result, he treated with them for a perpetual peace ; this was granted† on the condition of his declaring himself tributary to his Majesty and paying each year a tribute of two elephants with tusks of a certain length ; and this he continued to do punctually year by year so long as we did not wage war against him.

He was very friendly towards our nation, for he saw in us an excellence, affectionate disposition, good faith and other qualities which make a people esteemed. His whole intercourse was with the Portuguese, and he entrusted to their keeping the two sons whom the Queen bore him, that they might be instructed in reading and writing as well as the Latin tongue, music, and horsemanship, and in all this they were skilled, and well versed in the humanities. As for the son whom Dom João had, he always kept him apart in order that his own sons might inherit the kingdoms, and so the former busied himself with cock fights in Matale where he was brought up.

*The Sinhalese Sanghaya, a Bhikkhu. This King was known as Senerat.
†This was the peace of 1617. See Port. Era. II. p. 18.

CHAPTER IX

In which is shewn how at the Death of the Emperor, He appointed the King of Portugal Heir to his Kingdoms, and the Convention which was held

The Emperor Dom João Paria Pandar conceived such an affection for the Portuguese that he would not leave them, but continued in Colombo till the year 1597, Dom Hieronimo de Azevedo being the Captain-General of the Conquista ; in this year the Lord was pleased to call him to the blessed state. And when he felt that his hour was drawing near, he set about arranging his affairs and distributed his property among those who had served him. In his Will* he declared that he had no son to succeed him in his kingdoms, and therefore he appointed the King of Portugal his universal heir to all of them, and thus he became absolute lord of all the territories situated within the Island, only the kingdoms of Candia and Uva belonging to Dona Catherina, while the kingdom of Jafanapatão had its own native King. He also earnestly entreated His Majesty to send away to Portugal a young nephew whom he had, and to get him ordained as a priest, and never to allow him to return to India for fear of his creating a disturbance in the Island ; he further begged the King of his kindness to assign to him some ecclesiastical revenue from this Kingdom for his support: all this was ordered by the Emperor and it was accordingly carried out. (We also knew this Prince† and used to call him de Telheiras, from his place of residence, where he built an Oratory for the Friars of St. Francisco.)

The death of the Emperor was greatly lamented both by his own subjects and by us, and he was interred with

*More correctly, Deed of Gift, dated 12 August, 1580, and subsequently twice confirmed.

†He was created a Grandee of Spain, with the privilege of remaining covered in the Royal presence. His portrait was preserved at this Oratory, where he was buried, and is reproduced in Port. Era. I. p. 232. The original has since disappeared.

all possible honours in the Convent of St. Francisco at Columbo*, which was now a beautiful city where many noble families lived. After his burial and when his obsequies had been performed with the dignity due to his position, the Captain-General summoned the Captain of Columbo and the other Councillors, to discuss the steps to be taken to induce the people to acknowledge His Majesty as their Lord and King without having recourse to force. After much discussion they agreed to issue a notice to all the provinces (called Corlas) of the kingdoms that they should send to Columbo on a fixed day, two delegates from each Corla authorised to take the oaths on behalf of the rest, to the King of Portugal as their King and Lord. They assembled on the appointed day, on receipt of the notice ; it was then proposed to them, that as they were the vassals of his Majesty it was but reasonable that they should receive his laws as and in the same manner that the Portuguese themselves did, and for the nobility to enjoy the revenues and privileges which they held.

To this they replied that such matters demanded careful deliberation : they had no doubt that they would be able to do everything which was required of them, but they should be allowed the opportunity to discuss them and to urge any reasons of their own : they would always look to what was most to the interest of the King their Lord. Two days were allowed them, and after deliberation they reported that they were Chingalas, brought up from the beginning in the laws which they possessed and observed : that it would be a very grave matter for them to abandon those laws and take in exchange what were now proposed ; the result of so great a change would probably be that neither the one law nor the other would be properly observed, to the great prejudice of His Majesty. They admitted the King of Portugal as their rightful Lord and King just as if he were their Emperor, native born in their country ; as such they would serve him with the laws in which they had been brought up ; but those laws must be preserved by His Majesty and his Ministers without any alteration at any time. They would

*Its site is now occupied by the Gordon Gardens. It was left to the British Government to destroy the tomb.

obey him and render him all the dues to which they were liable, as they had at all times rendered to the Kings who had reigned in the Island before, and they would take an oath to act accordingly. Moreover as the King their Lord had his appointed Ministers there, these too must take an oath on his behalf that their laws and privileges would be guarded and preserved in their entirety.

When we saw that there was nothing else to be done, a Public Instrument was drawn up, confirmed by solemn oaths on either side. Our deputies promised in the name of His Majesty, always to preserve for the kingdoms and vassals of Ceilão all their laws, rights and customs in their entirety without any change or diminution whatever. The natives similarly took another oath promising to serve the King our Lord well and faithfully as if he were their native King, and as such to render to him the same taxes, dues and all other obligations which they had rendered to their Kings in times past. Liberty was secured for the religious orders to preach in public when and where they pleased, the Faith of Our Lord Jesus Christ ; all who wished to receive their doctrine were not to be hindered in any fashion or manner, and there was to be no opposition even as between parents and children ; if any one disregarded this condition he was liable to punishment at the discretion of the person authorised, and for the future no one was to be exposed to violence or to persecution, but whoever voluntarily desired to be a Christian was to be at liberty freely to embrace the Faith.

With this agreement the *Cortes* came to an end ; the documents were copied and each Delegate took away with him a copy to his province, where the people were well content, especially as they saw that they would have so brave a race for their defenders. The Captain-General immediately sent for the Archives of the Emperor, among which was found the Tombo of dues and services not only of each kingdom and province, but also a detailed statement of the payments leviable from each village and household and any further dues to which they were liable. All this was translated into our tongue with the same detail*

*He probably refers to the new Tombo prepared in 1607—1618, and now at Lisbon The Convention was held not at Colombo but at Malvana.

CHAPTER X

THE REVENUES WHICH THE EMPERORS ENJOYED AND SOME DETAILS WHICH WE OUGHT TO KNOW

WE have stated that all the territory from Chilao as far as the Grevayas, being fifty-two leagues of coast, and inland as far as the frontiers of Candia and Uva, was bequeathed by the Emperor to His Majesty. This included twenty-one thousand eight hundred and seventy-three villages, over which our Captain-Generals exercised the same authority as the Emperor with the title of King of Malvana*, which was allowed them by his Majesty for the maintenance of the respect and authority of the office among the Chingalas ; for his jurisdiction extended up to the palm groves of Bengala with the powers of a Viceroy.

No native could address† him except as " His Highness ", and the King of Candia gave to him the same title, from which we can judge of the power which he enjoyed and the respect shewn to him. The Portuguese alone addressed him as " *Merce* ", for in the State of India the title of " *Senhoria* " was only applied to Governors, and that of " *Excellency* " to the Viceroys who were titled.

From all these territories not a coin of tribute or taxes was obtained, because from the earliest times the land was all partitioned among the various ranks and offices appertaining to a State,—as also among the fighting men,—soldiers, Captains and officers ; these had to come with their own arms in case of hostilities, and were bound to bring from their homes food for fifteen days, at the end of which they were entitled to a similar period of leave. Of this kind of fighting men we had in our dominions fifty thousand, and the

*A village on the Kelani Ganga, 12 miles from Colombo, where de Azavedo fixed his head quarters. The details of tenure in the Kirawali Pattuwa of Beligal Korale, taken from the Portuguese Tombo, 1614, are set out in Jr C B R A S Vol. xxxvi. Part iv. pp 141—185

†No nation, not even the Sinhalese, exceeded the Portuguese in punctiliousness in respect of these matters. Solemn instructions were often sent from Lisbon on such subjects.

number could neither be increased nor diminished, because they all held lands which they enjoyed under this condition of service ; and it was the same with the nobility and the handicraftsmen among whom the villages were divided.

Each one had for his maintenance a piece of mud land which he sowed, and a large tract of fruit trees from which he obtained a considerable profit, as well as a garden where he had his house. To this portion they gave the name of *Paravenia**, and all the inhabitants, whether noble or plebeian, had their duties, each serving in his own way the King or the Lord of the village. Thus the soldiers, nobles, handicraftsmen, and the various grades and classes, of which there were many, had all their services to render, and they were free to enjoy their *paravenias* ; nor was there ever lacking a person to occupy them subject to the same conditions as they were liable to. For instance, if a soldier should die in war or otherwise, his son if he have one, or some other member of the same family, will enter into possession of the *paravenia*, and although he is not a soldier, he becomes one now ; and the same is the case with the other services ; and from the *paravenias* the number of men of each rank and grade is ascertained.

And here we should note that the *paravenia* which belonged to a soldier could not pass to a handicraftsman, and that of a worker in iron always belonged to a worker in iron, and everything else was subject to the same rule. By the manner in which the lands were divided among all classes, taking the case of those held on military tenure alone, as the men were always ready with their arms, it could be seen that whenever hostilities broke out the King was not put to the expense of a single *real* upon them : though if a King were to maintain a very small army, a vast treasure would not be sufficient even for a few years.

When the King waged war he used sometimes to promise a sum of money to the first person who reached some post of the enemy which he named, or else cut off a head ; and this promise he fulfilled in its entirety on the spot.

To avoid confusion I now proceed to explain the various classes and the duties of each. The villages consist of Mayorals,

*A Paravenia came very near to a land held in Fee Simple.

who were the same as the *cidadoes* among us ; these were bound to supply three full meals a day to any fighting man who came to their village for the period of his stay there, and similarly to the Lord of the Village whenever he was in residence. This duty the Mayorals who held the village undertook in turns, thus dividing the expenditure among all. They had also to purchase for the Lord at their own expense everything which was to be found in their country, such as chickens, hens, butter, kids, cows and hogs. In all these villages there were *culles** for carrying burdens, and they performed the same work as men who were paid, as this was the tenure on which they held their *paraveni*, and such service was not in any way considered to degrade them : where a man was of an honourable caste he lost nothing, and where of a low caste, as many were, he always remained of the caste he was. These conveyed to the Lords of the villages what the Mayorals bought, and they were obliged to attend as often as they were summoned for this or any similar task.

The workers in iron had to serve in the workshops of the King for fifteen days, during which they had to supply their own provisions just as the fighting men did ; and when this period expired they had a similar period of leave ; and for this service they were not paid a single *real*. Where there were several qualified persons in one house, such as sons and relations, none of them were liable to render service except the head of the household, as it was he who had the enjoyment of the *paravenia*. They were also obliged to make, free of charge, the agricultural implements for all the inhabitants of the village, who had only to supply the material for the same. Besides these there were other workers in iron, and these were they who extracted the metal from a certain kind of stone ; they lived separately in villages which belonged to the King and rendered him each year a fixed quantity, and whatever they extracted in excess of that quantity they were at liberty to sell. The gem-cutters†, jewellers, carpenters, turners, gun-stock and pike-makers, were all obliged to render service in the same fashion on behalf of the King.

*The cooly of to-day. The word is not Sinhalese, but of Dravidian origin.

†These six classes form the divisions of the Smith caste.

Those which follow are lower in caste : the tom-tom beaters went in war time to beat their drums, and they returned with their own company. The wood-cutters lived in separate villages which also belonged to the King ; they felled the trees they were ordered to, and on the field they had to convey the ammunition and surplus arms, a duty of which they were so proud that in case of a defeat they would rather lose their lives than abandon their stores. There were the potters and the washers, the latter of whom washed the clothes, and the former supplied pottery to the whole villge, free of charge. The jagreiros* made a kind of sugar from the liquor which they drew from certain trees, and of this they gave a fixed quantity to the Lords of the Villages.

The shoe-makers, *Pachas*† and barbers were all very low in caste and they too had similar duties, each according to his grade. The *Cornacas* were those who tamed the elephants and acted as drivers ; they lived separately in villages the same as the *Pachas*, the villages of both of whom belonged to the King. It was the same with the villages in which lived the *Chalias*, the people who peeled cinnamon and each of whom had to render the number of *bahars*‡ at which his *paravenia* was assessed ; for all of them were not subject to the same amount of duty, some paying more and some less. These carried at their waist a small knife with which they stripped the bark of the trees, as they enjoyed the privilege that no one could demand from them any other kind of duty ; they would all refuse to perform any service except that to which they were subject, even if they were to be condemned to the fire, for they say that this would establish a precedent. The amount of cinnamon which they procured each year for the King was three thousand and two hundred *bahars*, each bahar being thirteen *arrobas* and seven pounds of our weight, making a total of ten thousand five hundred and seventy five *quintals*.

The Emperors, even when the amount collected in any one year could not all be sold to the ships of Persia, Arabia, Meca, Malavar, China and Bengala, which come for that

*Jagreiro and sugar are both derived from the same Sanskrit word, *sarkara*.

†Paduvo.

‡A Bahar weighed 176.25 kilgr.

commodity owing to their being fewer one year than in another, would not reduce the price, which always remained the same ; whatever was left unsold was ordered to be destroyed by fire, so that the *Chalias* might not acquire the habit of bringing less than was due. Accordingly this was the chief source of the revenues of the Emperor, and for this article they used to bring him all the wealth which the Orient possessed.

They did not attach much value to their gems, and only twenty-five *paraveni* of those whose duty it was to procure them were found in Sofregão. These served fifteen days in the year, under a headman who was known as the Vidana of the *Agras**. The Emperor, when the season drew near, used to fix the number and quality of gems they had to procure, and these he would present to the Kings, his relatives and friends on the coast of India. In the same fashion they continued to procure gems on His Majesty's account, subject to the order that they brought all the stones of one *pardao*† and upwards in value ; and so long as His Majesty was Lord of Ceilão, there were not wanting Portuguese anxious to be the Vidana of the *Agras*. Although the position was not considered one of much authority among our people, it involved the handling of stones of value, which they embezzled ; nor did they lack accomplices and friends ; for the King's Treasury is like an owl from which all the birds pluck a feather, and this is an evil that cannot be remedied. The stones collected each year were taken to the city to be cut, and then they would be put up to auction all together. As a rule they fetched from twenty up to twenty-four thousand *patacas*‡, and until the next year there would be no more talk of them.

Twenty to thirty elephants used to be sold one year and another to the Mogul for a very heavy figure ; and thus the revenues of the Emperors were derived from cinnamon and elephants. In the same fashion the King our Lord was in the enjoyment of this Island, and was able to obtain more from it than Spain did from all the kingdoms which she had in the West, as we shall show in its proper place ; we hope these details are not tedious, for it is desirable to know all this in view of what we are going to relate.

**Agras* is not a Portuguese word, but is the Sinhalese *Akara*.
†Worth at the end of the sixteenth century 4.2 to 4.6 pence.
‡Pataca, a piece of eight.

CHAPTER XI

HOW THE VILLAGES WERE DIVIDED, AND THE OTHER DUES WHICH THE NATIVES HAD TO RENDER

THE villages in which the wood-cutters, the *Chalias*, *Pachas*, *Cornax* and the people who produce the iron resided, the villages of Butale Gama*, and a hundred others in various provinces, were all possessed on behalf of His Majesty ; in all there were four hundred which were always the property of the Emperor. These had their Vidanas to collect the fruits and hand over the proceeds to the Factor, who in turn delivered them to the Clerk of his department to be entered.

The Captain-General had twenty of the best villages in rent for his expenses. The Captain-Major of the Field, the Vedor da Fazenda, the Captains of Columbo, Galle, Negumbo and Caliture, the Sergeant-Major, the Dissavas, the Bandigarrala†, the Captain of the General's Guard, the Factor, the Ouvidor‡, the Juiz da Alfandega, several of the Religious Orders, down to the Captains of the Infantry, had each one or two villages. These were all annexed to the same offices ; all the others were divided among the settlers according to the grants which had been made to their ancestors or as they had obtained them in dower at marriage ; all were granted for three lives, and could be renewed by good services ; and thus everyone had sufficient income on which to live in comfort.

The natives, in addition to the dues already mentioned and which were on the King's service alone, had to render others to the Lords of the Villages, and from these neither the soldier nor any other person was exempt in respect of the *paravenia* which each held. The chief kind consisted of areca, which is highly valued in the whole of India, and the quantity due from each was entered in the Tombo ;

*Bulatgama, which was always an appanage of the Crown.

†Bandigaralla is explained by some writers as being an officer of the Household, but Ribeiro himself in ch. XVIII would make him a high judicial officer. The derivation of the word points to a connection with the Royal Stores.

‡A judge, he who hears. Compare the formula "Oyez, Oyez."

and this might be two, three or four *amanoes** each year, an *amanoe* being a fixed number. There were other contributions besides, such as pepper, rice, &c. ; thus no one objected to pay what was due from him.

In each village there was one *paravenia* which was always the largest and situated in the best position ; this was called the *Motteto*, and on it was constructed a handsome house where the Lord of the Village resided whenever he was in the village ; everything which the *Motteto* produced belonged to him. It was the duty of the Mayorals to plow, sow and reap the field of the *Motteto* ; they had also to collect the areca, pepper and other fruits without payment, and the *Culles* conveyed them to the Lord's house in the City without any expense to him ; and thus whoever owned the village knew how much food he had yearly. All the Sapan† belonged to the Lord, and he alone had the right to collect it within the village limits.

On no foodstuff which was shipped was any export duty levied ; imports other than foodstuffs paid five per cent on the appraised value, which was always favourable. The forests produced a large quantity of *Coca*‡, and also of a resin which the trees distilled and which resembled the French article ; another kind was found in mud lands, very clear and transparent and of the colour of amber ; this the natives used in various medicines, and it commanded a high price throughout India, where they give it the name of *chandarrus*. These articles some of the settlers used to collect and purchase in large quantities, for they were the commodities which the forest yielded and which they sold outside.

Having now explained how the villages were possessed, we shall proceed to relate what Columbo grew into from being a small stockade.

*An Amuna of arecanut consists of 24,000 nuts. See Ch. III.

†Caesalpinia Sapan, still largely exported for its red dye.

‡According to Vieyra, this is " a poisonous narcotic berry." I am doubtful what is meant, unless it be the *Strychnos Nuxvomica*, S. Kaduru. or does this refer to the coconut ?

CHAPTER XII

The Position and Fortification of Columbo, and the other Forts in the Island

Columbo, from being a small stockade of wood, grew to be a gallant city fortified with a dozen bastions ; it is true these were six-sided after the ancient fashion, and of small size, but they were conveniently situated. The ramparts were a single line of *taipa**, a sufficient defence against the natives, with a ditch and moat on either side ending in a lake which skirted a third of the city on the land side. Its artillery consisted of two hundred and thirty-seven pieces of three kinds, from ten up to thirty-eight pounds, all mounted. It is situated on a bay capable of holding a large number of small ships, but exposed on the northern side ; and its line of circumvallation stretched over one thousand three hundred paces.

On the Point of *Recife*, which is to the south, there was a large breastwork named Santa Cruz, provided with the heaviest kind of artillery ; this commanded and defended the whole of the harbour. From here the open city extended to the south through what was known as the *Galvoca*† which on account of the ridge of rocks required no ramparts; at the end of this and right on the sea was a bastion. The ditch commenced at its foot and ran on with a new rampart and another bastion called that of Mapane, where there was a gate with a drawbridge, the two continuing side by side till they reached the lake, being finished off by the bastion of St. Gregorio. From the sea up to this point was the best fortification which the city had, and it was in no way inferior to that of the lake itself, which encircled it for a distance of four hundred paces and was more than two leagues in circumference and abounded with crocodiles.

One hundred paces beyond this bastion was another alongside of a large house and a powder factory ; with the

*As now used in Ceylon, this word means walls of clay. In Brazil it is applied to walls formed of split logs.

†The Sinhalese Gal Bokka, appearing to-day in English as Gallebuck. This is the descriptive name of the high rocky ledge on the side of the Fort facing the Ocean and terminating in the Recife.

help of the water which was drawn from the lake, two *quintals** of powder were made daily. From here there started a brook which traversed the middle of the city, and was provided with two bridges. A low wall ran down side by side with the lake till it reached the bastion of St. Hieronimo, where the lake ended. In the middle of this stretch rose the bastion of the Mother of God; beyond was the Queen's Gate, and close to it the bastion of St. Sebastião, from the foot of which there started a moat which was continued past the base of the bastion of St. Estevão and finished at the gate and bastion of St. João with another drawbridge. This was the most northerly point of the city, and from here a strong stockade of pointed beams ran along the shore as far as the sea. At this point the bay opened and there was a handsome breastwork in front of the College of the Society; beyond lay the bastion of the Custom House, and so the rampart ran till it finished with the breastwork of Santa Cruz.

The portion which the brook cut off from the city, the brook we mean which issued from the powder factory on the south, was the strongest part of the city, owing to there being a hill in the middle, on which stood the Convent of St. Augustinho. Within its enclosure we had an extensive vaulted building where we kept one hundred and twenty large jars of gunpowder, which was wonderfully preserved in them without the necessity for being refilled. We had two other magazines, both vaulted though not of the same size, one in the House of St. Francisco and the other in that of the Capuchins, both full of jars of gun-powder.

There were in the city nine hundred families of noble settlers and more than one thousand five hundred of various handicraftsmen and tradesmen, all within the walls; two parishes, the Mother Parish and that of St. Lourenco; five Convents of the Religious Orders, those of St. Francisco, St. Domingos, St. Augustinho, that of the Capuchins,

*In 1554 a Bahar=3 quintals "of the new weight"
=20 faracolas
Faracola =19 lbs. 3½ oz.

The correct weight of a Bahar, which is an Arabic term, appears to have been 176.25 kilogr.

and the College of the Fathers of the Society, who held classes in Latin and Morality ; the house of Santa Misericordia*, and a Royal Hospital, with seven parishes outside the walls. All the inhabitants were enlisted in companies, the Portuguese in some and the natives in others, and they all mounted guard on the bastions and outposts with their own arms, in the use of which they were well skilled, and they had a large supply of ammunition. When a company of Portuguese, of eighty or ninety men, mounted guard, it would increase to two hundred all under arms, for the servants and domestics accompanied their lords and masters on such occasions.

The fortress of Galle was built on a point of land with the sea on two sides ; on the north was a steep line of rocks, and there it had no other defence. On the south side was the bay, protected by a palisade of pointed beams ; while a line of ramparts with its moat and three bastions cut across the land side from sea to sea, with a gate and drawbridge in the middle ; the position was well protected with this fortification. The inhabitants called it a city, but it was merely a fortress. The only alteration made by the Hollanders after their occupation was to build the bastions in the modern style and enlarge and deepen the moat. There were within two hundred and sixty-two families of Portuguese, six hundred of various handicraftsmen, all Christians ; the Captain of the garrison, the Adjutant, a parish priest, the Convent of St. Francisco, the House of Santa Misericordia, the Hospital, the Customs House, the Factor and his Clerk.

Caliture was a very small fortress built on a hill at the mouth of a river of the same name. The Hollanders greatly strengthened this position and it reverted into our possession with their improvements, as I shall mention in its proper place. It had two small bastions with four iron cannon, a garrison of one company of infantry, a chaplain and magazines of stores and ammunition.

Negumbo had a Captain with some invalid soldiers ; it was a square enclosure of stone and mortar with two redoubts

*The Poor House.

both of which were small and plain, with five iron cannon, a chaplain, and a magazine of stores and ammunition.

Malvana stood on the bank of the river about three leagues from Columbo, and was also small with a square redoubt, not protected on the flank ; here were stationed a Captain, an Ensign, a Sergeant and the soldiers who were sent from the hospital to recruit there, and who returned to their own camps; there were also a church, a chaplain, and a magazine of stores and ammunition.

Batecalou was built on a point of land and protected a bay capable of receiving vessels with high sides. It was a square structure with four bastions of ancient design armed with a dozen iron cannon, and its garrison consisted of a Captain and fifty soldiers with a condestable, twenty settlers, a chaplain, a church and a magazine of stores and ammunition.

Trequimale was a triangular fortress with three bastions carrying ten iron cannon, built on a hill at a point of land adjoining the sea, close to the Bay *Dos Arcos*. A Captain was in charge of it with fifty soldiers, and there were also a condestable, sixteen settlers, a chaplain, a church and a magazine of stores and ammunition.

Jafanapatão, a quadrangular fortress, had four bastions and four half-moons or *cobelos* in the middle of the line of ramparts, all of which were built of pumice stone*. Here was kept the necessary artillery, and it was also the residence of the Governor of that kingdom†. On one side outside the walls stretched the town‡, where resided three hundred families of Portuguese, and seven hundred of handicraftsmen, with the Convents of St. Francisco and St. Domingos, the College of the Society, the Mother Church, the House of Santa Misericordia and the Hospital. Two leagues away, at the

*De pedra pomes. This must refer to the coral stone which is used in such abundance in the northern peninsula.

†Jaffna, which was under a Tamil King and was reduced in 1618, was always regarded as a separate Kingdom, and its Administrator was called Governor. He was largely independent of the Captain-General at Colombo except in matters affecting the work of the Conquest.

‡The Pettah, still called Parangi theru, the Portuguese Quarter.

mouth of the channel, was a fort similar to the one of Bugio*, with good artillery and garrisoned by a company of infantry. The full number of men for the defence of this Kingdom was two hundred Portuguese forming six companies, with some native Lascarins.

Manar, although built on an island which gives it its name, is almost in Ceilão, being separated from it only by a narrow strait. It had ten leagues of territory in the latter island, consisting of the lands of Mantota. It was a very small fortress, four sided, with two small redoubts on the two opposite angles overlooking the strait. It had no garrison of infantry, but stretched alongside of it was a settlement of one hundred and fifty families of Portuguese and two hundred of handicraftsmen ; a Captain also resided here.

Besides these fortresses which we have enumerated with their garrisons, there were others which were not entitled to be called by that name—such as those at Manicavare, Sofregao, and Beligao, and others of the same kind,—for they were all made of a little earth and we kept them up so long only as they were occupied by our garrisons.

*Which protected the approach to Lisbon.

CHAPTER XIII

OUR USUAL GARRISON IN CEILÃO, OUR CAMPS THEREIN, AND THEIR POSITIONS

IN the Four Corlas, five leagues from Balane and eleven from Columbo, there was a position in the midst of the villages, known as Manicavare* ; here was stationed our chief army for opposing the King of Candia and for defending the Seven Corlas. It consisted of twelve companies of three hundred and fifty Portuguese *Soldados*† under the command of the Captain Major of the Field, and there were also a Sergeant-Major, two Adjutants, a Captain of Munitions and a Franciscan monk as chaplain. It was further the residence of the Dissava‡, an officer corresponding to a military Governor of a province over the natives, who always had in hand in time of peace three or four thousand Lascarins with their officers, which number could be greatly increased in the event of war.

In Sofregão there was another camp controlling all the territory as far as the frontiers of Uva; this consisted of four companies of one hundred and fifty Portuguese infantry under the command of the Dissava of the district, with an Adjutant, a Franciscan monk as chaplain, and four or five thousand well-equipped Lascarins with their officers.

These two armies, which comprised the forces for the defence of the Island, were always in time of peace on duty at these stations. There also resided at Mature the Dissava of that district with one company of infantry, a Franciscan monk as chaplain, and three or four thousand Lascarins and their officers. His jurisdiction extended as far as the frontiers of Uva and Batecalou and along the sea-shore up to Columbo.

*Menikkadavara, subsequently the headquarters for the military operations against the Sinhalese.

†A *Soldado* was the unmarried professional soldier, as opposed to the married *casado*, who served only under exceptional circumstances.

‡The four Disavas which existed under the Sinhalese Kings—Matara, Four Korales, Seven Korales, and Sabaragamuva—were continued by the Portuguese. See Portuguese Era. I. Ch. XV.

In the Seven Corlas there resided the Dissava with a company of infantry, three or four thousand Lascarins, their officers and a chaplain of the same order. His jurisdiction extended from the frontiers of Candia and Matale as far as the mountain of Grudumale. On the entrance of the Hollanders another camp was established close to Galle ; this was commonly known as the Mature camp and we shall speak of it later.

These four Dissavas had within their respective jurisdictions, authority to cut open with an axe or impale the natives ; they could also hang a Portuguese on any tree without any process of law or legal formality, and by merely saying " do this ", their orders were immediately executed and they rendered no account to anyone but God*.

In our camps discipline and obedience, as well as punctiliousness and high spirit, were maintained amongst the soldiers. Any one infringing any order which had been proclaimed with the penalty of death was invariably executed even though the offence were very slight, such as travelling by a particular road or going to this point or that. And always when a higher officer gave such an order, there was some reason for it which it might not be convenient to make public ; for it might be, as often was the case, that the enemy were near or something similar. Above all soldiers should not speculate on the actions of their superiors, but only obey orders ; and whoever was guilty of disobedience was immediately placed against the trunk of a tree and executed.

In our camps quarrelling was forbidden under the same penalties ; and though soldiers are so sensitive on points of honour, yet they refrained from quarrelling, for their officers who looked after them secured the honour of all. However a league away from our camps, by the high road, were certain trees called *Das palavras* set apart for this purpose; and out here they could have their fights, brawlings, challenges, or any other quarrel, in which sometimes death occurred. And when this happened the offenders had to withdraw

*In the later times of the Portuguese, the powers of the Disavas in their districts were very little controlled by the central authority. Under the Sinhalese the power of life and death was vested in the King alone.

for a few days, though not where only wounds were inflicted ; at the end of eight days their officer gave them a safe conduct with which they returned to the camp, and nothing more was said about the matter. And just as they had no punishment so there was no setting at liberty, for there were no legal proceedings nor technical documents.

Challenges if made could not be declined, and if anyone did so he was regarded as vile and contemptible by all, it may be by his own brother: The aggressor or the challenged in a quarrel in which he was wounded and worsted, immediately upon his recovery would be accosted in the street by some soldier of position who would ask him the cause of the quarrel ; this would be the same as making the parties friends, and no one would deny them, for such was the custom. If anyone did refuse, he was at once challenged by the soldier who accosted him ; by doing this they would make the two people friends, and no reference would ever be made to the matter again by jibe or jest With such an education they were all very obedient and very proud, treating each other with ceremonious respect.

As we have shown, the garrisons of the fortresses and camps which the Portuguese maintained so long as the Hollanders did not have a footing in the Island, were seven hundred men, which was the usual full number. They were paid two quartels in the year at the rate of ten *pardaos** to each soldier, twenty to each Alferes and Sergeant, hundred to a Captain, with a soldier as page and a drummer, and so on to all the rest according to the office which each held. Payment was at Christmas and at the Feast of St. João, and the money was intended to supply the soldiers with clothing. For his sustenance His Majesty allowed for each soldier, whatever his position, one *pardao* a month for extras and one and a half measures of rice a day, both of these being given

*The Sanscrit *pratap*, originally a gold coin from the native mints of West India, and afterwards applied to a Portuguese silver coin of degenerating value, and averaging about 360 reis. Under the Portuguese pay might consist of *Soldo*, which chiefly depended on birth, *Mantimento* or subsistence allowance, *Ordenado* or pay of an office, and *Percalsos* or profits, which soon took the place of all others.

into the hands of the Captains because they provided the soldiers with cooked food three times a day.

Their arms were not entrusted to the Captains but only to the soldiers themselves, and they took the greatest care of them at every fight ; for it was considered an infamous thing to save one's life with the loss of one's arms. Therefore in any defeat which befell us, everyone who escaped whether wounded or not invariably brought his arms away with him. Whenever we obtained a victory, all the booty was held for the King and given over to the Factor. In case of an engagement with the enemy the Captains would make out sworn statements where anyone had distinguished himself, and the higher officers did the same as regards the Captains ; these certificates would be attested by the Captain-Generals themselves whenever the Captain or the soldier had the opportunity of gong to the City on this business. Often this would not be for six or eight years, but it made no difference whether it was during the term of office of the same General or of his successor.

Everyone lived in the Island as in a military encampment ; no one could go outside without the permission of the General, which was rarely given. The Captains and masters of merchant ships had to give security in three thousand *pardaos* that they would not take away any person without such permission, and anyone arrested in attempting to escape by land was inevitably punished with death. None of the soldiers asked for promotion, though this was what all desired and they served with this object : for since all of them knew the claims of each other, what was common talk was regarded as of greater value. But the majority of the Captain-Generals used to direct the Captain-Major of the Field to keep them informed of any special service rendered by anyone, and this they used to do punctually ; and so when it was least expected there would arrive a letter and a patent from the Captain-General. Such promotion used to be an occasion for general rejoicing, just as if the promotion had been received by each individual himself ; and it used to encourage them in such fashion that when an engagement took place all felt compelled to proclaim any deed of merit.

The soldiers were not obliged to remain in one company more than six months, that is from one pay day to another; on that occasion it was customary for the Captain-General to visit the camp, and issue an order that all should come two days later to receive their pay. When this was done the soldiers were free to join any company they selected. Now as the Captains used to supply the soldiers with their food, and as several of them did not do so in a reasonable fashion, and as at the same time it was considered a disgrace to complain about the food supplied by one's Captain, all of them found their remedy in this opportunity which was allowed them. All the same no Captain was without the same number of soldiers as the rest: for the Captain-General used to revise the lists of the companies, and take the total of all and divide them equally among the companies at the rate of thirty-six or thirty-eight each, making them all equal more or less; but the Captain who had the better reputation obtained the better following, and the others received the worse. Some of these officers the General would speak to and remonstrate with once or twice and if they did not blush for their evil deeds, they would be deprived of office and their companies given over to other persons.

As the Captains supplied their companies with cooked food three times a day, each of them had to assist him in this work, two villages, and the *Culles* from these would come turn and turn about to work for them for fifteen days at a time; and when they were on the march, a sufficient number of *Culles* used to be summoned to convey the food and utensils. The Mayorals provided the companies with cows, hens, chickens, butter, spices and all other necessaries, the money being supplied them for these articles by the Captain: it was for this reason that they held their villages, and to give the soldiers some extras from the *pardao* a month the King allowed them. They attended to those invalids who could be cured without the expense of sending them to the hospital in the city, which latter used to be done only when the illness required treatment which could not be obtained on the spot, for which the surgeon had to give his certificate. Even on such occasions the soldier would take his arms with him, and if he died in hospital the priest* who attended on him would give them over to the Factor and obtain a receipt.

Those who recovered used to go to Malvana to recruit, and when quite restored they would return thence each to his own camp, taking nothing with them except their arms on the journey ; and wherever they happened to be at the hour of dinner or supper, they would enter one of the numerous villages on the road firing their guns, and immediately the Mayorals would come and take them to the house of the Motteto, and bring them any fruits they had, and in a short time supply them with an abundance of food. If they remained there for the night they would give them supper too in the same fashion, and after breakfast accompany them to the road. And while they were thus lodged there would be no treachery or evil feeling ; for if a soldier happened to be killed while enjoying their hospitality, even if it be by an enemy, that village would be destroyed with fire and sword ; and if they knew any danger were near, they would look after the soldier with greater care than if he were their own child. Nor could they refuse such entertainment, as such had been their duty from ancient times ; and all along the road they would proceed in this manner till they reached the camp.

A soldier, Captain or higher officer who married was at liberty to leave the service of the King the same day if he so desired, for this practice had been introduced.

*The Hospital at Colombo, which was an object of great solicitude to the Home authorities, soon grew to be such a scandal for its mismanagement, that one by one the various religious orders declined to have anything to do with it.

CHAPTER XIV

THE RITES, CEREMONIES AND EVIL CUSTOMS OF THE CHINGALAS

IN the last chapter we have depicted the life of the Portuguese in that Island, and it will be but reasonable that in this we should describe the customs, rites, ceremonies and dress of that race. To begin with, these Gentiles in their superstition and worship of idols resemble all the people of India, though differing in some respects. They acknowledge one God as the author of nature and superior to a large number of deities to whom they give the name of *Deo*, attributing to each his own sphere, such as agriculture, the elements, or something similar. Their idols are of various shapes : such as a man, or woman, or monkey ; some like an elephant with numerous arms, and others represented with a bow and arrows ; they are a large number of diverse figures. But there is one whom they reverence above all and whom they call Bodu ; his figure is that of a man, and he is represented as of a very great size, to illustrate his peculiar sanctity. I have seen one at a temple of the height of six *covados**. He was, say they, a great *Deo* who spent a very holy life on the Island, and they count their years, which they call *Auruda*† (beginning from the new noon in March) from the date of his stay.

By calculating we find that this occurred forty years from the coming of our Redeemer‡ and according to many conjectures they refer to the Apostle St. Thome, who all assert lived in this Island and passed thence to the coast of Xoromandel, where is still preserved a good deal of the Christianity which he established ; and this is confirmed by their statement that Bodu was not a native and that he did not die in

*Covado=30 inches. Figures of Buddha of eighteen cubits are to be found at most Vihares.

†Or New Year, now falls in the middle of April and is the greatest social event among the Sinhalese.

‡Two systems are used by the Sinhalese, the Buddhist era commencing 543 years before Christ, and the Saka Era commencing 79 years after Christ. Ribeiio appears to have mixed up the two.

the Island, but departed to the opposite coast. God knows what the truth of this may be ; I can only state what their tradition is.

They venerate all their kings after death as gods*—of salt, of gunpowder, of the chase, of betel, of the sea, or the river, etc. They give them distinctive titles in accordance with their own fancies, and offer them sacrifices with much superstition. When they address them they call them *Deo*, and first of all stretch themselves on the ground three times with the hands clasped together and raised over their heads, and so long as they remain in their presence they maintain this posture ; and this salutation is such that the devil himself could not devise an attitude of adoration better calculated to deceive and attract to himself the living. This superstitious reverence was also employed towards the Captain-General as King of Malvana, and it was acquiesced in as being the custom of the country, and in order to maintain the authority of his position†.

They do not deny the immortality of the soul, but they assert that when a bad man dies his soul enters some animal with the same vices : a good man's, that of a domestic animal, and above all a cow's : and a brave man's, that of a tiger, leopard, etc. But this is only for one birth, and when the animal which the soul had entered, dies, it wings its way to another world where, so they say, it has the same career as in this, the evil one doubling his wickedness, though he is punished by many torments, and the good man doing better actions and being greatly honoured for the same. Some of them assert that the wealth which a man has accumulated in this world is doubled in the next, and for this reason these Gentiles do not inherit a single *real* from their parents, and even married people do not show each other the money which comes into their hands ; what each one acquires he buries‡ where he considers safe, and so no one has anything of his

*Deification is not very different from Canonisation, though it is usually fear which compels worship. Raja Sinha was deified after death.

†Compare the *Kow tow* of the Chinese. The Sinhalese Kings received this method of salutation—and not from their subjects alone—till the very end.

‡The floor of his hut is still very frequently the villager's only safe.

own, and when they die they only find a few cattle or implements of tillage or similar articles.

Any act of valour performed in war is rewarded by the King with the gift of some piece of jewellery or a chain; this is immediately registered and the grantee enjoys the possession of it only during life, and at his death it is restored to the King*, who would inevitably punish his sons and heirs with death for failing to do so. And it is for this reason that no one would ever destroy such a reward; for apart from its being a token of honor, it is considered a grave sin to have to pay for what has been thus misused.

*As in the case of the insignia of the European orders of chivalry

CHAPTER XV

The Understanding which these Gentiles Maintain with the Devil

With the Devil these people have a close understanding of which they avail themselves in the manifold sorceries they employ. Whenever anyone is ill, they apply those medicines which are known to them, for they are great in the knowledge of herbs ; if these prove unsuccessful, they take a board, on the surface of which they fashion out of clay the figure of the invalid in low relief. They then give notice to all their relations and friends of either sex, and celebrate a feast on an appointed day, and about the ninth hour of the night they all assemble near the house in a suitable place. Here after the entertainment is concluded they form a circle leaving a space in the middle, and after lighting many torches they beat their drums and blow their flutes and continue thus for a whole hour. Then one of the girls of the company, who they say must be a virgin, gets up and dances to the sound of the instruments and the singing of the bystanders, and whirls about. In a short time she throws herself on the ground foaming at the mouth and with her eyes blazing like live coals. Immediately one of them addresses her with many entreaties, saying that the invalid was always very friendly towards him, and had always shown that by offering the best fruits ; that he should not allow him to die, but tell them of some remedy against his illness. At this the Devil speaks through the mouth of the girl, and says what they should do for his recovery. Some recover and some get no benefit ; if afterwards they should complain to her about his death, she would say that they did not understand him.

It happened once that while the girl was lying stretched out as I have explained, to give her reply, she exclaimed " There is in this company some one whose enemy I am and whom I hate with a bitter hatred ; I can give no reply while he is here " ; upon their examining those who stood near, they found the son of a Chingala woman and a Portuguese, who was a Christian, but who had been brought up among them and spoke their language well. They accordingly requested him to go away from the scene, and when he had done so the Devil gave a reply.

They also render great honour to him and call him *Jaca** and place for him cooked food at the foot of certain trees which they called *Bodiames*†, and which they deck with many flowers, and none of the passers-by would dare to touch any of the offerings. They dedicate to him a tree which bears most and has the best fruit, and those fruit which escape being eaten by the monkeys fall to the ground. On our march we have frequently seen these trees laden with fruit which was well ripened, and when we ate it, it was none the worse to taste. Once when I was Captain, I questioned a Mayoral of one of my villages who understood our tongue well, if the *Jaca* was their God. He smiled and replied that he was the worst creature in the world. " If that is so ", I answered, " why do you and all the others offer him sacrifices and make offerings of the best you have ? " He answered, " If we do not do so, he will work us great harm, for he is an evil and revengeful creature, and it is to our advantage to have him for our friend."

They are also very great magicians ; by means of a certain charm they call the snakes, of which they have five very venomous kinds in the Island, and these animals will go to their hands and they will play with them, and at the same time they are so obedient that at the word of command they depart. They cured the bites‡ which these animals inflicted on some of our men by means of their charms, but unless relief were given immediately, the patient would die of the poison. They use herbs and roots as medicines against the poison, but few know what they are. They have also charms for crocodiles and they can bring about that they should not interfere with those who ask them if they wish to bathe § ; but they must not go outside the spot which the Chingala

*Yaka, a Devil, a rendering used to cover a multitude of ignorance.

†The Bo, Ficus religiosa, the sacred tree of the Buddhists.

‡Wonderful cures are still performed by the Sinhalese in cases of snake bite.

§ It was not so very long ago that the British Government used to employ a man to charm the sharks which disturbed the divers at the Pearl Fishery.

made secure for them, because if they did so the crocodile would devour them. Often when on the march, as we were always going barefooted through much water and marshes, our people used to suffer from severe pains in the stomach ; a *Culle* would then place his burden on the ground, and laying his hand on the pit of the stomach recited some charm for the space of a *credo*, and immediately the pain ceased. I have often seen them do this to soldiers and Captains, and out of curiosity I have asked them if the pain really left them, and they would assure me that they were as free from it as if they had never felt it. They say that there are many other sorceries but I only recount what I have seen with my own eyes.

There are among them astrologers whom they call *Nangatas** these are without doubt greater sorcerers than the others, for by following this line they are better fitted for everything. These all consult before making a journey about which they have a presentiment of any kind, as to the hour at which they should begin a war, fight a battle, sow a field, build a house, or any other transaction whatever ; everything is done with their advice. These *Nangatas* are men of low caste answering to our drummers.

**Nekatiyas.* Lucky hours and times are still sought for in all the important events of life.

CHAPTER XVI

THE NATURE OF THEIR MARRIAGES, AND THE OTHER CUSTOMS OF THE CHINGALAS

THEIR marriages are a ridiculous matter. A girl makes a contract to marry a man of her own caste (for she cannot marry outside it), and if the relatives are agreeable they give a banquet and unite the betrothed couple. The next day a brother of the husband takes his place, and if there are seven brothers she is the wife of all of them, distributing the nights by turns, without the husband having a greater right than any of his brothers*. If during the day any of them find the chamber unoccupied, he can retire with the woman if he thinks fit, and while he is within no one else can enter. She can refuse herself to none of them ; whichever brother it may be that contracts the marriage, the woman is the wife of all ; only if the youngest marry, none of the other brothers has any right over her, but he can claim access to the wives of all of them whenever he likes. If it chances that there are more brothers than seven, those who exceed that number have no right over her ; but if there are two, up to five, they are satisfied with one woman ; and the woman who is married to a husband with a large number of brothers is considered very fortunate, for all toil and cultivate for her and bring whatever they earn to the house, and she lives much honoured and well supported,and for this reason the children call all of the brothers their fathers.

These people have a custom that their nobles should under no circumstances, not even to drink water, enter the house of a man of low birth ; and also a man of low caste cannot enter the noble's gate, but must stand outside and ask for what he desires or is in want of. If a woman belonging to an honourable caste have intercourse with

*The custom of polyandery is now illegal in Ceylon, though it is still practised in various parts of the world, as it was once in Britain. Its origin in Ceylon may probably be traced to the land tenure by service, which necessitated the absence of the husband from home for long intervals at a time.

a man of a low caste, the inevitable punishment is death, and her accusers are her own parents and brothers, for all their honour depends on this. Those who are barbers, sandalmakers, or of any other low caste from the beginning, if they display special valour by achieving some gallant deed in war, are rewarded by the King with money, jewels, villages of people of their own caste, and by promotion ; but he is not able to improve their social condition nor that of their descendants, and they always remain of the same caste and must be treated as such. Among their fighting men are also men of the low castes : the *Carias* are fishermen, the *Mainatos* washers, and the *Pachas* sandalmakers. All these have brave Corporals and Captains, but all serving in one army: and if in an honoured caste there is wanting a Corporal, even if there is one of those (*i.e.*, of lower caste) who may hold a higher post, he cannot command those of a high caste. It is not possible for them, wherever they are, to conceal their caste, as this is always evident from their clothes ; for they may not wear their cloth below their knees, while those of high caste have it down to the middle of the leg.

The Modeliars, Apuames, Adigars* and other great folk among them wear a shirt and a doublet, which those of a low caste may not do. All of them are of the colour of the quince, some being browner than others ; they wear their hair *a la* Nazarene†, with their beards full in the ancient Portuguese fashion. In features they are well shaped and in no way different from the Spaniards. Their bodies are well proportioned and very strong ; an ugly woman is very rare among them, because all have beautiful eyes. They are very clean and tidy, their cooking is tasty, and they pay much attention to their hair. The dress of their ladies is superior to that of our women in India ; they too wear a jacket and a cloth which reaches down to the point of the foot, in a very dignified and stately fashion.

*These were officers who exercised certain judicial functions over Korales. The title was applied in South India and Jaffna to officials of various castes performing various duties.

†The custom of wearing combs was probably introduced by the Javanese a century later.

They have a language different from the one in common use, just as Latin among us* ; only their chief men learn it, and they are of subtle intellect. Whenever they have any business with an official, before broaching the subject they relate to him two or three pleasant things so that it may not be possible for him to refuse their request. In their own fashion they are good poets, and their singing is very soft, and gives pleasure ; though we did not understand what they said, yet we used to leave off any occupation in which we were engaged, to listen to them, for their verses were sonorous and the syllables well rounded. Their handicraftsmen take a great pride in their work, and use very few implements. They are ambitious and this makes them treacherous and ready to acknowledge Christianity ; but they return to their own sacrifices with the same ease, and whenever our men have to withdraw to the city, they hasten to worship their images.

Towards their Dissavas, who are the Governors of provinces, in case of our sustaining any defeat their soldiers would maintain great fidelity, and get them into safety even if it cost their lives. They are very lazy in cultivation, for their forests yield them food in abundance and the only article they lack is salt†. They live to a great age ; I have known and sometimes talked with two of them, father and son, the former being one hundred and twenty years and the latter ninety years of age ; and these two used to go every Sunday and holy day to Mass though they lived a league away, without a stick or any other support. I have known others of about the same age.

The fighting men alone use arms ; they carry swords of two and half palms which they call *calachurros*‡; the soldiers are Lascarins, some are pikemen and their weapons are eighteen palms long ; others are espingardeiros and are skilled in firing ; though they have no flints and are fired with cord, yet they have a spring as if they had ; others use

*Pali, in which the Buddhist Scriptures were written.

†The control of this was a powerful weapon in the hands of their enemies; see the *Port. Era.*, II. p. 79. *Ceylon and the Hollanders*. p. 139.

‡For description of *Calachurros*, and manner of using it, See *Bocarro*, 409.

bows with which they can shoot very accurately. Some carry muskets* with a barrel of eight palms and weighing forty pounds, from which they shoot a ball of four ounces. They do not fire these from the breast, but there are secured to them, on the *terco* of the butt, two legs of a *covado*† each in length. When they wish to fire, they place it on the ground and sit down with their legs spread out and their feet placed against the legs of the musket, the butt which they make half round coming over the top of the left shoulder, and applying the match they discharge it without any trouble, and they have the same effect as a merlin. This kind of weapon they call foot muskets ; the King of Candia had five thousand such musketeers, and in our territory we had another four thousand who served in our armies.

The King of Candia whenever he proposed to attack us, used to place in the van of his army some war elephants to break our lines, fastening to their trunks large swords or knives of the breadth of a hand ; each animal carried on its back two Cornax‡, so that if we killed one, the other was left ; and he, to prevent our seizing it, used to take it back to his own people. For in the camps we used to be provided with fire lances, and when we knew that they brought elephants, in engagements some were entrusted to powerful soldiers, who would thrust the blazing torch in the elephant's eyes and the animal could not withstand this, but would turn in flight and in his rage do to his own men what he was to have done to us, without the Cornax being able to restrain him. They placed such confidence in these animals that often they turned their backs on us, and our Lascarins would soon appear with their heads fixed on the points of their pikes. On such occasions as a rule the Captain-General or the

*Jingals, such as the Filipinos employed in their warfare with the Americans.

†Three quarters of a yard.

‡The elephant drivers, *Sinh.* Kurunayaka.

Captain-Major would promise one *pataca** for each head to encourage the men, and they are so avaricious that they would cut off the heads of their own fathers to obtain this reward. In the same fashion the Candians treated us whenever they defeated us, sparing the life of none ; for their King would give nothing for a live Portuguese, though he never failed to give the reward which he promised for a head.

CHAPTER XVII

Some Peculiarities of the Elephants

Since we have already spoken of these animals, there is no reason why we should pass them over in silence : at least we will say something about them ; and since others have written on the same subject, we shall speak only of one animal which we possessed with its offspring and their descendants. He was the most handsome animal that one could imagine, and he served us only in some case of extreme urgency, because there were others which we used in every-day work ; but this one we employed only to capture the wild elephants. Its name was Ortela*, and it took part in the famous siege of Columbo, bringing us palm trees night and day for the seven months that it lasted, to repair the ruins caused by the continuous firing ; and out of the fifteen which we had this alone escaped being eaten by us when we ate up the others. The King of Candia tried to obtain it from the Hollanders, who kept it at Betal†, and he would have given any large sum that they required for such a valuable possession ; for every year it used to bring His Majesty more than fifty thousand *patacas* ; and because some might consider this a mere fable, before proceeding further it is right we should explain how he did so.

These animals wander about the forest in herds, and always there is one among them larger in size and more respected than the others, and him they call the guardian of the herd. They destroy the crops of the natives and cause them considerable loss, so that whenever they knew of a herd they would immediately send information of its whereabouts. As soon as the Captain-General received the news, he used to despatch Ortela alone with two Cornax and some *alias*, which are the female elephants. They would proceed to the spot and leave them at the nearest village ; and when the

*In Sinhalese *Huratala*, the Little Pet. It lived to see the British flag float over the walls of Colombo in 1796. See Emerson Tennent's *Natural History*, p. 100.

†*Sinh.* Wattala, at the mouth of the Kelaniya river, and on the further bank. *Pas Betal* was the name applied to the village on the Colombo side.

Cornax found out where the herd was, they would go there taking Ortela with them. As soon as the guardian of the herd noticed him he would come up very proudly while the others remained behind. All this time one of the Cornax was hidden behind Ortela, who was quietly walking up to the wild beast ; as soon as they met Ortela would throw his trunk around its neck and hold it in such a fashion that it could not release itself for all its wrath, as our animal was so large and powerful.

The Cornax who was below had a lasso, which he slipped on one of the fore-legs of the beast securing it to Ortela himself, thus fastening them to each other. The second Cornax who stood watching hastened with another lasso which he secured to one of the hind legs of the wild beast, and made both fast in the same fashion. The animal would now become like a lamb, and immediately they would bring up the two *alias* and secure it to the neck of one of them on the opposite side, and removing Ortela they placed the other on the other side. In this fashion they would bring the animal to the city, frequently returning with their prize in two or three days. It was in this manner they used to capture the twenty or thirty animals which they sold every year to the Grand Mogul*.

The price of these animals is one thousand *pardaos* the *codo* which is from the point of the large finger to the elbow. The largest elephants would be about nine *codos* from the point of the forefoot to the shoulder. It should be noted that this was the usual price, but at the same time they would pay more according to the perfection of the animal, its carriage and its points, just as in the case of a horse. The lowest price of a Ceilão elephant is eight thousand *pardaos*, but some fetch from twelve to fifteen. These animals are found in many parts and are sold to the Moors, but they pay more for one animal from this country than for two or four from any other part. Ten or twelve from various parts were employed in dragging logs at the docks in Goa, but when one of the Ceilão animals was sent to work

*Ceylon elephants were reserved for the use of the Royal Princes at his Court. For the tribute of elephants from the Wanni, see *The Kingdom of Japanapatam*. pp. 22-27.

at the dock where all the others were, as soon as ever he entered, the others made him an obeisance with great humility although they had not seen him for an hour ; and as he passed among them, however small he may be, he would not in any way acknowledge the salutations of the rest. It would thus appear that by some instinct they recognized him and respected him for his superiority. The inhabitants of Goa have observed what I have narrated, whenever elephants from Ceilão were sent there.

They are very chaste, and the sexual act, or even the desire for the same, has not been seen among them. Once out of curiosity I asked the Cornax if they had ever seen this act on the part of Ortela, for we had his progeny among us and the matter would be noticed. They replied that they had never noticed even the manifestation of such a thought.

To avoid being tedious I omit many of the peculiarities of these elephants ; it is sufficient to know that any animal which was brought from the forest becomes so domesticated in eight days that it would not only not try to escape, but would also perform whatever it was ordered, without any instruction . What assists most in taming them is to prevent their sleeping for a moment for the first three days and nights, diverting them by blows should they attempt to do so ; after this period they speak to them kindly and encourage them, and they become tame within the period which I have mentioned. One writer has stated that these animals lie down only to die ; in saying so he is partly in error, for they always lie down at night to sleep, and those which are employed in carrying burdens receive the same lying down ; for otherwise owing to their height it would be impossible to load them. If however they lie down while on the march, it is not possible to induce them to rise again, but they die there ; and this happens when they are exhausted.

CHAPTER XVIII

The Annual Assizes Called Maralias

Since we have preserved to these people the laws and customs of their ancestors as I have stated above, every year there were selected four Portuguese who were designated Maralleiros, officers corresponding to *Corregedores* among us ; they were nominated by the *Bandigaralla*, who answered to our Chief Justice, subject to the approval of the Captain-General. These were allotted among the districts of the four Dissavas, each holding his own assizes and deciding complaints according to the laws of the people. Each Maralleiro was accompanied by two Interpreters skilled in their laws, as well as a *meirinho** and a Clerk, all of whom were natives.

Before starting they would send notice to the people of the province where it was customary to hold the first *Marallas*, of their intention ; and on the day appointed they would come and meet them on the road, accompany them to their lodging, and entertain them with every mark of honour and hospitality, as was the custom. All the neighbouring inhabitants who had a complaint or a petition would come and remain there until their business was transacted, and the same would be done in all the other provinces.

The first matter to be dealt with was that of the estates of deceased people and the inventory of their property ; their heirs would assemble and they would be put to the oath if anything appeared to have been suppressed from the inventory. If anyone were convicted of this offence he would be condemned to pay three fold, the principal going to the estate and the rest to the Royal Treasury. The native kings were expressly the heirs of deceased people †, but our King relieved them of this exaction as it seemed barbarous, contenting himself with the same share as any of the other heirs.

*The Fiscal's officer of to-day.

†A custom also found in the Kingdom of the Great Mogul. The share of the Crown varied according to whether the deceased left children or not and also according to the sex of the children. To encourage conversion great concessions were made by the Portuguese in the case of Christians.

Creditors who had any claim to make would come, and usually their claim was for some cattle or food stuffs ; so would also the thief ; all these are required by the parties to appear before the *Marallas**, where they would be questioned. The debtor if he admitted the debt was ordered to make restitution ; and if it was known that he could not, the Maralleiro would order him to do so within a certain time. If the thief confessed his crime he was condemned to pay the highest value of the article which satisfied the other party, and as a penalty for his offence double its value to the Royal Treasury. If any one denied the theft or debt, the Maralleiro put him to the oath ; to do so they would bring his son or daughter or some other person whom he loved, according to the choice of the other side. The party taking the oath would place three or four small stones picked up from the ground on the head of the son, and say " I did not commit this crime ", or " I do not owe the debt which is claimed from me. And if what I say is false, may God convict me by killing my son in as many days a there are stones on his head ". On taking this oath he was absolved from the claim, and the opposite side had to pay the costs. They assert that such is the force of this oath, that if anyone perjured himself his son would die within the period, and till it expired they would watch to learn the truth from the result.

Murderers who were in sanctuary† also came to free themselves from their crime, for, if they were arrested within sixty days, the General or Dissava would condemn them to death as he thought fit ; but after that he had no power to punish them ; so at the *Marallas* they would come and confess their crime, paying a fixed sum equal to one hundred and twenty *reals* of our money to the Royal Treasury. They would then be given an *ola* of discharge and became free for ever on payment of costs ; nor was any mention made again of their crime. But if a man of a low caste killed one of a high caste, he would not be discharged but was always sentenced to death.

*This word is almost equivalent to Death Duties.

†Sanctuary was recognised both by the Sinhalese and Portuguese ; see *The Portuguese Era*, I. 62 ; II. 90.

The crime which they considered the most serious was where a woman of a high caste had carnal intercourse with a man of a low caste ; she would be denounced not only by her husband if she were married, but also her own father and brothers were among her bitterest accusers ; for this was a matter of the greatest concern as affectihg the honour of their family. And because those who were accused have no proof but what was indirect and conjectural, for if it were established by witnesses they themselves were entitled to kill her without committing any crime, to allow her to prove the negative the Maralleiro put her to the oath. And this was the greatest of all—for out of two it had to be one : she could either plunge her hand into a cauldron of boiling oil, or lift up a red-hot bar of iron* and hold it in her hand for the time required to repeat the oath and say " may this fire kill me if I have committed the offence imputed to me, and may God prove my innocence and the purity of my life. "

After the oath was taken as proposed, she would go to the house of her father or husband and purify herself ; and if within a day she showed no sign of having been burnt, she would be greatly congratulated by her kinsfolk ; but if the result were otherwise they put her to death in the presence of witnesses, for that was the only way to clear the stain. This ordeal might be barbarous, but I have heard one of our own peope who had been Maralleiro several times assert that he had seen many women come out of it unscathed.

They came with various other matters which the Maralleiro decided according to his discretion in conformity with the opinions of the two Assessors on points of law ; and when the sessions was over he returned to the city and rendered an account of his collections at the *Maralla*, which were entrusted to the factor on a receipt.

*The stringency of the ordeal has been exaggerated by the writer. The iron bar and the oil had only to be touched with the tip of a finger. Queen Emma, mother of Edward the Confessor, cleared herself of a charge of guilty intercourse with the Bishop of Winchester by walking barefoot and unharmed over nine red-hot plough shares.

CHAPTER XIX

OF THE GREAT ABUNDANCE OF FOOD STUFFS, THE ANIMALS AND THE DISEASES WHICH ARE FOUND IN THE ISLAND

THE whole Island abounds in food stuffs, cattle, buffaloes, goats, sheep and swine, the best of which are worth two hundred *reis* each. There is much game—wild boar, stag, elk, gazelles, deer, *macareos*, porcupine, and hare in abundance. Of birds there are peacocks, *carvoeiros*, turtle doves, wood pigeons, green pigeons, snipe, ducks, woodcock, and wild fowl ; while the number of small fowl is so great that they cover the fields. Much poultry is also reared and they cost two *reals* the twenty, which is also the price of seven *canadas** of cow butter. There is also found in the forests an animal like a lizard and of a brown colour, three palms in length, called the *talagoia*†. The natives and many of our own men prefer its meat to chicken, and declare that there is nothing to equal it in taste and nourishment ; however that may be, I have never myself tasted this dainty.

The rivers and brooks abound in fish and shrimps ; fruit is plentiful and of various kinds, all very tasty ; nature provides two crops in the year without any assistance from man. The Chingalas never eat the fruit fully ripe but only as they ripen, or green, when they cook them for food : they say that the ripe fruit is harmful. Above all the fruits which the Island has is the king orange‡, and it seems to me that if the earthly Paradise were there, our first ancestor could have been tempted with this alone ; for nowhere else in this world can any fruit be found so excellent. Rice is abundant and I have seen on the same field the plant ready to reap, others in the ear, and others again but a palm high. There are various other kinds of grain which are used for food, and also plenty of vegetables, potatoes and yams ;

*A *canada* is equal to three English pints.

†The *iguana*. Its meat is nearly as delicate as that of the frog.

‡This must be the Mandarin, which, as its Sinhalese name shows, is an importation.

wherefore none need suffer from hunger, for this land is a Paradise from the universal fertility of its soil. The valleys are covered with flowers and trees, with streams of water of the purest crystal ; the air is healthful ; and though the Island is so close to the equator, it is neither hot nor cold.

The sicknesses which were usual among the Portuguese were dysentery and some kinds of fever due to poverty of blood. This latter does not occur often and among the natives it is never found, the reason being that they bathe so frequently in the rivers. I have myself put this to the test, for during my first two years I suffered from two attacks of this illness and I resolved to bathe morning and evening, and for the sixteen following years I never had a pain in hand or foot. The Portuguese in the Island were subject to another disease which the natives call *bere bere* ; when a man was apparently in good health and free from pain, he would suddenly fall to the ground ; and this was the worst disease of all; he would have no sensation from his hips down to his feet, which would seem quite devoid of life ; one might cut off his legs without his feeling it, just as if they formed no portion of his body. This malady can only be cured by eating pork and biscuits, by drinking palm wine* and smoking tobacco ; after three or four months continuous treatment the patient regains perfect health. The Captain-General Dom Antonio Mascarenhas, after consulting the native medical practitioners, issued an order in the army that everyone should use tobacco ; as they were unwilling to do this he himself set the example which all followed and thus the disease was entirely eradicated.

The most dreaded disease among the natives themselves is the small-pox, which they regard as a pestilence ; so much so that if a son, brother, wife, or even one's own mother is attacked by it, the patient is immediately segregated in a separate hut built fifteen paces to leeward of their dwelling. His food is placed on a shovel and brought near his house but no human being would venture close to him, and he is thus left isolated ; this is why a large proportion of them die.

*The liquor extracted from some of the palms of Ceylon is recognised as a specific for certain diseases, including "sprue."

They call this disease *Deane charia*, which in our language means "a matter with God."* Syphilis they call *Parangue rere*†, which means the Portuguese disease ; and with reason, for it was we who introduced it among them. As a rule they are a healthy race ; anyone suffering from fever is not prohibited from drinking as much water as he likes, so long as it is boiled with dried coriander‡. They are great herbalists and in case of wounds, tumors, broken arms and legs they effect a cure in a few days with great ease. As for cancer, which is a loathsome and incurable disease among us, they can cure it in eight days removing all viscosity from the scab without so much as leaving a mark anywhere to show that the disease had been there. I have seen a large number of soldiers and Captains cured during my residence in the country, and the ease with which this was done was marvellous. In truth the land is full of medical herbs and many antidotes to poison, which I have myself tried to learn as a remedy against snake-bites.

*The *Pattini Deviyo*, the Goddess of Chastity, presides over the smallpox.

†*Ribeiro* has mixed up "Parangi" with syphilis, to which it is similar. There is no doubt that parangi, the scourge of the wilder and waterless districts, was introduced by the Portuguese.

‡Still an everyday remedy in the Sinhalese home.

CHAPTER XX

The Wild Animals of the Island

The variety of wild animals found in the Island is remarkable and includes tigers* and leopards, which however do not kill men, as they find an abundance of cattle and game for food ; bears are numerous in some parts of the Island but not in all. The monkeys are countless and of five kinds, some of them being the pretty *sauguins*, and others called *roqueas*. On these the wives of the Portuguese doted and valued them highly for their colours and pretty ways. There is also an abundance of parrots, paroqueets, and other birds called *sayros* all of which talk well, but that which talks best of all and most clearly is the martin. Civet cats are common, but no trouble is taken to rear them.

There is an animal called the mongoose, differing in some respects from the weasel, which has such a hatred of snakes that if it sees one it will not rest till it has killed it ; and as the snakes are very venomous, and bite them when they fight, whenever they are bitten they look for a certain herb which they eat and become free from the poison ; but it is not possible to rear poultry along with them. The soldiers used to bring them up for fear of snakes, but they are dangerous. I knew a man who brought one up from its infancy and used to sleep with it ; but one midnight he commenced shouting lustily, whereon everyone hastened to see what was the matter, and they found that the mongoose was atacking a portion of his body in such fashion as almost qualified him for entering a Seraglio to serve the Sultanas ; and though assistance was given him at once, he was compelled to trust himself to the hands of a surgeon for some time.

There are also four kinds of venomous snakes ; one is always found in warm marshy places, and is about two palms in length, of a brown colour with a wide belly. When they bite anyone, the patient cannot shake off a fearful and deep

*Tigers are not found in Ceylon, their place being taken by the "cheetah" which must not be confounded with the Indian animal.

slumber in which he dies in the course of six hours unless relieved by remedies. There is another kind the bite of which renders the patient mad, but it is possible to save him if assistance is given within twenty-four hours. There is a third kind which is still more terrible ; whenever it bites a man the poor patient's blood pours out from all the openings in his body, and when he reaches this condition he is beyond remedy. There are others again which are called the *cobra de capello* ; although these are very poisonous no Chingala will kill them, or consent to their being killed if he can prevent it. They assert that these are the queens of the others, and that they do not bite anyone unless they are offended ; and also that if any man kill one its mother, father, or sister will take vengeance for the death ; and they are so possessed with this idea that if one were to bite their wife or child once or twice, he would not do it any injury, but only summon it by means of a charm and reprimand it ; the consequence is that they kill the more*.

There is still another class of snakes the description of which would appear like a fable ; I would myself not mention it had not the truth of it been vouched for by a prominent man born in the Island itself, and very well acquainted with everything in it ; for though the report is persistent it is impossible to believe it ; I refer to my comrade Gaspar Figueira de Cerpe†. This snake is of the thickness of a top string, its length is three palms and its colour brown ; it places itself on a branch, and as a bull, buffalo, wild boar, deer, elk, elephant, or any other animal passes below so that it can touch it, the poison is so virulent that wherever the animal is touched, the bones, nerves, and the flesh of the part through which the venom passes rots to the thickness of the snake's body, leaving however the skin on the outside intact and in its usual state ; but the animal remains there and has not the power to move; and once when they opened some of these animals to find out what was the matter, they discovered

*The cobra is still respected. He is the gentleman among snakes, and does not bite unless in self-defence.

†Of whom we shall hear later. He was the son of a Sinhalese mother and Portuguese father, and was the one brilliant figure which resulted from the Portuguese policy of intermarriage.

that such were its effects. The same ill-luck befell a Chingala, and he lived for some years in this fashion without being cured ; but they do say that these snakes are not numerous.

There are others of a green colour, of the same length and thickness as the former ; these too lie on branches, and as a man or animal passes by they pick out their eyes, but I have never seen any man blinded by them. Another kind which they call the mountain snake will swallow a heifer or a stag, and some of these animals I have seen when killed by our Caffres who eat the flesh and say that it is very tasty and nourishing ; each slice had a thickness exceeding one palm ; the meat was very white with scales like the whiting.

In addition to this great variety of wild animals which we have mentioned, the most noxious, harmful and disgusting which are to be found in the Island are the *blood suckers** ; of these the quantity to be found in the forests is so great that the roads are thick with them, and if a person tried to pull one out, two hundred would fasten on him. When on our march we would all frequently have our legs streaming with blood, and often as we were at our meals at night we would pull them out from our very gums, quite surfeited. The smallest are the most painful biters ; the larger are as long as a needle and as thick as packing thread and of the colour of the hazel-nut ; those which we employ are abundant in marshy places, but they take no account of them.

* *Sangesugas*, a much more suitable name than *leech*.

CHAPTER XXI

THE GREAT ABUNDANCE OF PRECIOUS STONES AND OTHER COMMODITIES FOUND IN THE ISLAND

THE stone which is most sought after in Ceilão and is held in the highest esteem for its great value is the catseye ; most people do not know of this stone nor have they seen it, for it is not used among us, but the Moors and the Gentiles value it above all others. I have seen one of the size of a pigeon's egg and bored through, which the Prince of Uva wore on his arm when he fled to us*. In shape they are spherical like musket balls some large and some small, and in weight they exceed every kind of precious stone. They are not cut but only polished ; and they show a colour composed of every colour which God has created. No one colour is seen separately by itself, but they all make a wonderful mixture and appear to be struggling in their anxiety to get first in the race. At a distance the entire stone seems cut across by a straight line such as a cat shows in the middle of its eye at a certain hour of the day. This is styled the *beta*†, and from its appearance they name the stone the catseye. When the stone is moved one *beta* disappears and another takes its place and others still follow, so that the sight is doubtful as to which it saw first ; for by this movement in the midst of its glitter one line appears and the others disappear. The stones of the greatest value and most prized are those which have most lines; they are found with three, five, sometimes seven, and rarely with nine, such as the Prince's was, but never with an even number.

There is an abundance of rubies, the finest in the whole world, all in crystals and very clear, and plenty of sapphires and topazes, both of an immense size and highly prized among the Moors‡. These are the four most valuable kinds

*This is Vijayapala, brother of Raja Sinha. He was really the Prince of Matale. See The Prince Vijayapala: Pieris, 1928.

†Properly, a vein of gold in rock.

‡And it is so to-day. The gem-cutting in Ceylon is exclusively in their hands. Sinhalese stones were cut cabochon fashion, and not with facets.

of stones sought for in this Island ; we have already mentioned the other kinds in the third chapter. A great quantity of crystal of various colours is produced among the mountains ; the white they call the water crystal, some is of the colour of the yolk of egg, some green and some violet. The lapidaries of this country cut from these stones many curious figures such as of Our Lady and the infant Christ, crosses and other quaint images with little trouble*. They only employ two wheels of emery and bitumen, and with these they make what they wish, heating the wheels at the fire to make them smooth, pointed, half round, or any other shape which they desire.

There is also made in this Island oil and wax from cinnamon, and though this industry is sufficient to engage a large number of people owing to their being greatly esteemed and valued all over the world, yet I have only found three families engaged in it. The fruit of the cinnamon is taken and mashed and put into a cauldron full of water, and a strong fire is kept up for three hours when it is taken off. When quite cold they skim off from the top a very white paste like grease and globules like oil are then found floating on the top ; these are picked out with a feather and put into a small bottle which is placed in the sand in the sun till all the moisture is dried up ; the oil is then cleaned and put into a large bottle, and in a short time they collect a quantity which they sell for a high figure. This oil is greatly prized all over the world and is employed as a remedy for various diseases ; the grease which is removed is called the wax and is sent to India. It has various medicinal uses and candles are also made of it, two or four of which are placed on the thrones at festivals and they give forth an odour so sweet that the church appears to be the picture of glory.

None of our people used to distill the water, nor did they understand how to do it ; for with us everything was neglected. This point did not escape the attention of the Hollanders who distilled it with great ease ; for they had the cinnamon ready to hand with all its moisture and essential

*What is probably a specimen of these may be seen in the Wallace Collection in London. See Journal R.A.S. (Ceylon) XXIX. p. 106.

oils, plucked straight from the tree. The article is well spoken of to-day in Europe, where it is taken in large quantities with considerable profit.

As for pepper, even if it is not exported in shiploads as is done in countries like Canara, Cochin, Coulao, Jambe, etc., the reason is that there it is cultivated and treated as the principal commodity. As I have already stated, the local article receives no aid from human effort or cultivation, and it is for this reason that there is not as much of it as there can be, even much more than is found in the countries I have mentioned ; for what the earth yields of its own accord is the best to be found in the whole East. All the same a large quantity is exported to the coast of Xoromandel, Bengala and other parts, in all of which its value is double for it is well matured and powerful. And since the Chingalas have no eyes for this though they have two crops of it in the year, but only gather it for paying the dues of the lords of the villages, they pluck it when it is well seasoned, and usually the greater part ripens on the tree itself. It is picked from the bunches in which it is found and laid out on mats in the sun, when it turns black from being green and the skin wrinkles up ; that which wrinkles most is less powerful and not very ripe ; it is for this reason that the pepper of Ceilão is very good and wrinkles but little.

The merchants who deal in it separate a large quantity which is usually called white pepper ; this is what escapes from the ripe skins, and is sold for a much higher figure as it has medicinal properties. The plants are of the same shape and climb in the same manner as the ivy ; at the base of each leaf there is one bunch. The natives allow only those shoots to grow which climb up the trees by themselves. That which is left over after paying their dues is sold for a low figure, and if they plant it as is done in other countries, they would certainly have an immense quantity.

CHAPTER XXII

The Pearl Fishery in Ceilão

So far we have discussed at length the wealth which the land produces ; now we turn to the treasures of the sea, which in the estimation of people are no whit inferior ; of such is the fishery of pearls, which helps to ennoble the name of the Island no less than the rest. Though it is said that these pearls are found on several parts of the coast of the country, yet the fishery is only held on the shore of Aripo, as this place is conveniently situated and the sea is of a suitable depth for fishing in. Accordingly it is reasonable to relate to those who do not know about it, when the fishery takes place and the manner thereof.

At the beginning of March there assemble from three to five thousand *champanas* all equipped by merchants, Moor and Gentile and also Christian, each providing at his own expense from one to four boats, some more, some less ; sometimes two or three combine and equip one boat where they have not the means to provide more. These boats carry as a rule ten or twelve sailors each with a master, and up to eight divers. When they are all assembled, immediately the ship owners search for the place where the oysters are to be found at a depth of five to seven *bracas*, which is the depth they can dive. Three *champanas* are selected to make the examination, and they inspect the coast for a league up or down, and out of the oysters which they find in their search, each picks out a counted thousand, which are opened with a knife in the presence of the chief ship owners. From the results an estimate is made of its value (for some years the pearls are better than in others), and according to this estimate they decide and settle upon the royalty which they are to pay to His Majesty for the fishery ; and he sends three or four of his rowing boats to accompany them, to prevent their being disturbed by pirates.

After the tribute has been agreed on, each of the owners selects a spot on the shore sufficiently large for storing the *chipe** (for this is the name they give the oysters), which his boats fish up ; this they enclose with thorny branches, leaving one opening through which the *chipe* can be brought in.

On the 11th of March at four o'clock in the morning a signal is given by the firing of a gun by the Captain of the four boats ; all start for the sea and cast anchor at the spot selected for fishing in. Each *champana* carries some square stones of two *arrobas*† in weight, well secured and hanging outside. Immediately on anchoring, one of the divers places one foot on a stone, at the same time clinging to the rope ; he takes another rope fastened to his waist, and a bag or sack made of net tied round it. So they let him go, and he makes his way to the bottom as fast as he can. On reaching this he throws himself from the top of the stone and fills his bag with the *chipe*, which they say is found here one on top of the other.

As soon as his bag is full, he pulls at the rope which he has at his waist. Two sailors stand ready with their hands on this and they draw him up as quickly as possible ; and from the time that he enters the water till he comes up again, would be the space occupied in saying two *credos*. The moment his head emerges from the water another diver plunges to the bottom, and in this same fashion they all go down turn and turn about. And here we should note that as soon as the diver enters the boat he is at liberty (till the other who is at the bottom comes to the top) to open with his knife all the oysters that he can, and whatever he finds inside is his ; and similarly with the rest. In this manner they continue fishing until four o'clock in the afternoon, when at a signal from another gun they sail back, each making for the point of land where he has to unload.

On their arrival the noise which is made every day on the shore during the two hours the unloading lasts, is astonishing. Two planks are run out with a quantity of baskets, and the sailors divide into two parties, one filling them and the other carrying them away. A host of young men and lads from the neighbourhood also come to assist in the work ; they receive no payment but each one steals what he can.

* *Sippi* is the term applied in Sinhalese for all species of sea shells.

† An Arabic word, being a weight of 32 lbs.

After unloading, the boats put back to sea and sail away from the spot to where the Fair is held, leaving the oysters abandoned and unguarded. The place where they are piled is half a league to leeward of where the people assemble, in consequence of the evil smells which hover around the spot ; for the sun causes the shells to open, and an immense quantity of flies which they breed gathers around. The fishery continues in this fashion every day from the 11th of March to the 20th of April when it closes, and they go on piling the oysters one over the other.

Half a league to windward on the same shore all the business men who come there assemble and a free Fair is held, laid out like some gallant city with streets and rows of shops ; where they collect every kind of merchandise which our discoveries trade in with the nations of Europe and the whole of Asia. For this purpose they bring their gold, silver in bars and wrought, all kinds of precious stones, amber, perfumes, carpets, *meleques*, money, with the rarities of all the provinces of the world, in such a fashion that if there is anything anywhere on which one can spend money and time in seeing it, it is this great Fair. From the surrounding country is brought every variety of food, and though the people are numerous and of various races and religions—Christians, Jews, Moors and Gentiles—they can all obtain the food to which they are accustomed. Here everything is bought and sold which each one would like to take to his own country—not only pearls, but everything on which profit can be made. The sailors, divers, lads, and young men—and they are beyond counting—all are busy selling what they steal ; many go about buying and others who have their own shops of merchandise and goods also join in the buying, each one making his own profit. Those who buy in small quantities sort the large from the small pearls and the various grades of the latter ; but it is all sold together to the large merchants at a great profit.

The Fair lasts full fifty days,—for at the end of the forty-one days during which the fishery continues, from the 11th of March until the 20th of April which is the last day, nine more days are allowed for the viscosity which attracts the flies to disappear. On the last day of April the ship owners go with the crews of their *champanas* taking rakes with them, each one to the place where his *chipe* is piled ; the branches of thorns are removed and all the shells gathered on a side. After these are separated they bring small sieves with which they sift the pearls and deposit them on sheets. Then they sort those which have an individual price according to their size and degree of perfection. All the rest they divide into nine qualities ; the first is the best and they call it *aljofar* of the first sifting*, and so on until the ninth ; being of equal size and round its value is known by the agreement which had been entered into with the wholesale merchants for that year : for it may be that in one year it is worth more and in another less, according to the supply of pearls or the number of purchasers who meet there.

By the time the pearls are cleaned, almost all have been disposed of and the earnest money paid according to the agreement which had been made out by the brokers. The baroque pearls are sold for a much smaller price. The minute pearls which fall from the sieves are left on the sand, and in the rainy season the poor in the neighbourhood come to the beach with trays and expose the sand to the air ; when it is dried by the wind they collect what they call the *botica*†. A great quantity of this is sent to this kingdom and also to other parts, and the natives sell it very cheap.

With this the fishery concludes, and so do we with our chapter to continue with the rest of our story ; remarking at the same time that large pieces of amber are found on the shore, and that the fishermen when they draw their nets catch in them branches of black coral, and that the sea throws up a large quantity of this when there are storms. They say that this is better than the red for its appearance and black colour.

*The pearls are sifted through a series of brass sieves pierced with holes of a graduated size. The description of the Fishery as given by our author would apply almost equally well to-day.

†The right to winnow the sand used to be rented out by the Portuguese. See *The Kingdom of Jafanapatam*, p. 42.

CHAPTER XXIII

REGARDING THE FAMOUS MOUNTAIN CALLED ADAM'S PEAK AND ITS PECULIARITIES

THE Peak of Adam as we have said divides at its base the territories of the kingdoms of Candia, Uva and the Two Corlas. This mountain is one of the wonders of the world, for although it is situated twenty leagues inland, on a clear day sailors can see it the same distance out at sea. Its height is two leagues and it is covered with high forest ; owing to its great steepness it is a matter of considerable toil, occupying from early morning till two in the afternoon, to reach the level of a plain or ledge which the mountain forms before one arrives at the Peak. This ledge is entirely covered with trees, and has numerous rivulets which are formed of the water which springs from the Peak, and here there are also some pleasant valleys. At this spot the Gentiles who come on pilgrimage wash their bodies and put on clean clothes which they bring with them for the purpose ; all this they perform with considerable ceremony before arriving at the spot which they consider sacred, and they think that by doing so they are cleansed from all sin.

After going through these superstitious ceremonies they begin to ascend to the summit of the Peak, a distance of more than a quarter of a league, by means of iron chains made like ladders ; and were it not for these it would not be possible to reach the top because of its steepness. At the end of their journey they come to a very round level piece of land with a diameter of two hundred paces, where there is a pool of excellent spring water more deep than wide. From this pool arise all the waters which form the streams where they perform their ceremonies; they run down the slope of the mountain till they reach its foot, and there they form the three largest rivers in the Island.

In the middle of this space there is a large slab of stone placed over some ornamented blocks, and on this is impressed as if it were on wax a footstep two palms in length and eight fingers in width. This footstep is greatly reverenced by all the Gentiles of India, and many of them come on pilgrimage to see it and to fulfil their vows and promises. Twenty paces to the left of this there are some huts of clay and wood where the pilgrims rest ; on the other side is a pagoda, which is the same as a church with them, and near it is the hut of a *changata* or priest who resides there to receive the offerings ; and he is careful to assure these barbarians that they win many rewards and are cleansed from every sin in recompense for their devotion and trouble, and that this is the footprint of the first father of the human race* who left it impressed there as a memorial of himself.

On this round surface of stone there are planted a large number of well-sized trees which make the spot pleasant and healthful ; here they remain performing a kind of Novena and offering up their sacrifices at the pagoda. And what most convinces these Gentiles of the peculiar sanctity of the place is the fact that while this is a mountain so lofty, round, and well proportioned, at its foot there spring up two others on the two sides, the summits of which bow towards the Peak as if performing obeisance. In explanation of this marvel of nature these Gentiles declare that the immovable mountains themselves acknowledge the sanctity of the spot. But what I think is that this foot-step was some invention of the Gentiles, for it is certain that if it were that of a man he must necessarily have been a giant ; and the foot-step was created to attract adoration to the spot.

Of the three rivers which are formed from the waters of the Peak, one† runs from the northern side dividing the territories of the Four Corlas and passing by Ceitavaca and Malvana, falls into the sea at Matual close to Columbo. The other ‡ runs by the southern side past the Two Corlas, through Sofregão, and after dividing the lands of Pasdim and Reigan Corlas falls into the sea at Caliture. The

*This is the Mohammedan belief.

†The Kelani Ganga.

‡The Kalu Ganga.

last* which is the longest passes close to the city of Candia, runs through all their territories dividing the kingdoms of Trequimale and Batecalou, and enters the famous bay *Dos Arcos* alongside of the harbor of Cotiar, from which place it takes its name. In the same way the other two are named from the districts through which they pass. A large number of streams and rivulets fall into these ; the Island is intersected by an innumerable number of the latter, but they are all smaller in size.

*The Mahavili Ganga.

CHAPTER XXIV

THE HABITATION OF THE BEDAS, THEIR CUSTOMS, AND THE NATURAL BEDS OF SALT WHICH THE ISLAND POSSESSES

IT is not the less worthy of notice that though this country is an Island smaller than Borneo or St. Lourenco, countries which in view of their size and distance from the Continent are able to have a monstrosity of this nature, (for we must note as we have already pointed out that the area of Ceilão is little more or less than that of our own kingdom:) none the less it has for several centuries contained a race which for its customs and ways of life would appear to be some romantic tale ; but all who have been in the Island have heard of it. From the lands of the Vani which belong to the kingdom of Jafanapatão, to those of Trequimale, between the two rivers which divide one from the other, there are ten leagues of coast with a breadth of a little more than eight leagues ; this district is thinly inhabited and covered with dense forest, and here there live a caste of people who are known as Bedas*. In color they are similar to us, and some are ruddy and good-looking. Their language is not understood by the Chingalas nor by any other nation of India, and they can only communicate with one another. Similarly they do not show themselves to any people except those of their own race. They wear the skins of animals, for every kind which is the object of the chase is found in great abundance in their forests. Their arms are bows and arrows in the use of which they are very skilful ; they have no fixed habitation or settlement and each family lives for six months only at some spot in the forest which it selects as suitable for cultivation ; as soon as the crop is gathered in, it changes to another place to do the same.

The chief part of their food consists of the produce of the chase—wild boar, deer, elk ; in no *guisado* do they eat cooked meat but almost all of it is soaked in honey which is found in these woods in much abundance, and is produced

*Of the genuine wild Veddahs, a very few still survive, and have been the subject of much study by European scientists.

by the bees which deposit it in the hollows of the trees. To preserve the meat they cut down some trees of a large size, leaving a stump of a *braca* in height ; this they hollow out and fill the cavity with meat and honey, and cutting out plugs of the same trees they cover over this conserve which they will not touch for a whole year, while they live on the other meat which they had stocked.

When they are in want of arrows, axes, or any other implement of iron, they make models out of the leaves of trees to show the article which they require ; with these they go at night, so as not to be perceived by anyone, to the nearest village, and hang the models on the door of the blacksmith's house, along with their payment for the work, which is the half of a wild boar, or deer, or some similar article which they think is a little more or less than the blacksmith deserves. When he arises in the morning he knows by experience what is wanted, and he accordingly does the work ; and three days later when he goes to sleep he leaves the article hung up in the same place ; and often in the morning the smith will find there a quarter of meat, and so they are glad to perform this work for them.

The Chingalas offer an explanation of the origin of this race which appears to me incredible, but anything is possible. It is that many years ago there was in the Island a young King who was addicted to every kind of vice to which he paid no regard, nor had he any respect for either laws or ceremonies; and going beyond all bounds he ate every kind of animal which God created, not even sparing the cow*—and this among these Gentiles is the greatest sin which a man can commit. When he had finished with the animals he bade them kill a child, which he ate as a *guisado*. When his people and nobles heard of this fearful deed they arrested him with all who

*The Sinhalese had inherited the Hindu ideas with regard to the cow. See what Raja Sinha II had to say of the Portuguese. Port. Era, II. Ch. 3.

had helped him and in view of the horror of his act, they sentenced them to death as infamous ; but as they were unwilling to die, they gave them permission to go where they would have no communication with any man. Those who accepted the offer concealed themselves in these woods, where they live in this fashion.

If this explanation of theirs is false, it is not badly conceived ; for the majority of the histories of these Gentiles are fables and fictions which they have concocted. Our own criticism is that if this were as stated by them, in view of the length of time and the fact of their having no war with any nation, as they had taken with them all the women who followed the King, they should have multiplied in such fashion that at the least they would have densely populated that district ; but as a matter of fact they are so few in number that they wander about in these ten leagues through the forests, and hardly hold any intercourse with each other except by accident.

I have come across a young man from India, a Mistico, who had chanced to get wrecked in that country in a boat ; he had made his way to the shore by swimming and there he was found by these people who made him marry their queen, who was a widow. Here the poor fellow was compelled to remain for nine months, and he had such a good kingship of it that he set about discovering some means of escape ; he turned the sandals which he wore so that the toes pointed to the heels, and started on the road. He thus effected his escape and came into our territory, where he gave us a deal of information regarding these people. They have no idols, no religion and no ceremonies ; their families wander about separately in the forest searching for food, and as a rule all of them give the queen provisions, each one on his day by turn —rice, millet, potatoes, meat fresh and steeped in honey— sufficient to maintain six or seven people. Her palace is a straw hut in the forest ; she sees no one except those who bring her food daily, and these do not entrust the food to anyone save to the queen herself, to whom they make a profound reverence which she only acknowledges with a nod. Her bed is made of straw, with a bear skin for a coverlet, and her clothes are also made of other skins. Their meat is soaked in honey and eaten, and it is very savoury ; the fresh meat is wrapped in leaves and buried in a hole, over which they make a fire, and when this is burnt out the meat is found very tender and agreeable ; they eat it without salt, which article they do not possess. They made a flour out of millet and rice and from this they cook cakes. He told us various other facts which it is not possible to relate.

In the old kingdom of Jaula which has ceased to exist for many years, there is close to Balave* a stretch of land three leagues along the coast and two inland, very low-lying and level. In rainy weather the force of the south wind drives in the sea in such abundance that it floods all the plains, and in the hot weather the sun converts this water into salt†, and it is from this that the greater part of the Island is supplied, especially the surrounding country which forms the kingdoms of Candia, Uva, Batecalou, Trequimale and the territories of Villacen, and some of our own, as it costs less to go and obtain it here than to buy it at our forts, where it is brought in large quantities from the other coast.

The King of Candia, when he was at war with us, used to lack this commodity only, but was able to supply himself from these salt beds with ease. He would send from December until April droves of five or six thousand cattle and buffaloes which returned loaded, and some fighting men to protect them. This journey they performed two or three times during

*Named after the Valave Ganga, the chief river on the South Eastern Coast.

†The system of manufacturing salt by solar evaporation, which is followed in Ceylon, was probably introduced from China where it has been practised for unknown ages.

that period. Sometimes we seized them, but we were not able to do so always, because our camp was situated at a distance. We have used this salt many times ; it is excellent for seasoning but it is of no use for salting, because the salinity does not last. It is different from every kind of salt which I have seen, for it is clear as crystal ; those who come to collect it bring pick-axes, as otherwise their trouble would be wasted ; for it is as compact as if it were all one solid slab. The smallest pieces which they take are lumps the size of walnuts ; it is also difficult to melt, as it is not porous.

Four leagues inland from this spot there is a pagoda held in great reverence by the Gentiles. Here are preserved the offerings which had been made for many ages consisting of gold, jewels, and precious stones, and five hundred armed men were always maintained for its defence. We had several times made inquiries about it, in our desire to obtain this wealth and to relieve them of their anxiety regarding it. At the beginning of 1642 I went in the company of one hundred and fifty Portuguese and two thousand Lascarins the majority of whom were Christians, under the command of Gaspar Figueira de Cerpe, who was held in high respect among them, a man of ability and well versed in their language and customs. When we came near the spot where they said the pagoda stood, we captured a native residing close to the spot, and our Commander inquired from him if he knew where the pagoda was. He replied that he did, and that it was close by ; he acted as our guide and led us through a hill covered with forest which was the only one in that district, and this we wandered round and re-crossed many times. It was certain that the pagoda was at the top of it, but I do not know what magic it possessed, for out of the five guides whom we took, the first three were put to death because we thought that they were deceiving us, for they acted as if they were mad and spoke all kinds of nonsense, each one in his turn, without the one knowing of the others. The last two deceived us and did exactly the same, and we were forced to turn back the way we had come without effecting any thing and without even seeing the pagoda, which is called Catergão*.

On our return we captured from the Candians part of a convoy of salt exceeding two thousand head of cattle, the rest escaping into the forest ; with these we returned lighter than we expected to be when we started. For all the things of this world are no more than mere shadows, and the reality is always different from that which shows itself to us. So now we shall leave these minute details which we have related regarding the Island of Ceilão, and proceed with the narrative of the war in that Island, which has been calling to us from the grave of forgetfulness when it ought to be alive in our remembrance.

Kataragama, the temple of the terrible War-god, and one of the most ancient shrines in Ceylon.

BOOK II

THE PROGRESS OF THE WAR WHICH WE CARRIED ON IN CEILÃO WITH THE NATIVES AND THE HOLLANDERS.

CHAPTER I

THE REASONS WHICH LED TO THE COMMENCEMENT OF THE WAR

WE have shown at length and to the best of our ability what Ceilão is, its products, the rites, laws and customs of its people, and everything else which we have seen, experienced, and observed during the eighteen years of our stay there. It will therefore be reasonable to set out the motives which led to the breaking of the peace which was existing with the King of Candia, and the progress of that war at the end of which we were driven out of the best parcel of land which the Creator has placed in this world; and therefore we shall go back to the stage at which we left our narrative in the eighth chapter of the first book, so as to trace our history with greater clearness.

We left Henar Pandar, who had been a *changata* at Adam's Peak, occupying the throne of Candia and married to the Queen Dona Catherina, a tributary to His Majesty as already reported; this continued for some years until Constantino de
Sa e Noronha was re-appointed to the Office of Captain- 1623
General, a position which he had occupied before*; during his administration war was begun again, and we shall give an account of the same and its results, as well as of the career of this brave Captain, with all the brevity possible.

On his arrival in the Island in 1623 he was warmly welcomed by all because of the reputation which he had acquired when he was here before. His first action was to go in person
to build the fortress of Trequimale†. This was greatly 1624
resented by the King of Candia owing to the hindrance which it offered to the commerce of the whole of his kingdom at the port of Cotiar; but as he did not have sufficient forces to begin a war, he veiled his resentment for the time.

*From 1618 to 1619.

†Three temples of the greatest sanctity throughout India occupied the crag of Tirukona Malai, and these were destroyed to supply the materials for the new Fort.

When the Captain-General saw how greatly we would benefit by the establishment of another fort in the harbour of Bateealou*, he went with a sufficient body of troops to carry out his design. As soon as the work was begun the King was alarmed, for he saw that we had deprived him of the harbours of which he was the recognized lord, and he got together his people to prevent the work; but though he made his preparations, he yet hesitated to attack us.

1627 The Captain-General having entirely finished the fortification and placed a garrison there, withdrew to Malvana; but the King in his anger determined to wage war on us, and made some inroads into our territory. The Captain-General with great rapidity set out to meet him, but when the King learnt of his advance, he retired to Candia without waiting for him. The General tranquilized those districts, and as he saw that it was the King who had begun the war and that he was very over-bearing and arrogant, with the object of curbing his pride he started with five hundred Portuguese soldiers and the black people of our territory, all well armed and delighted that war was begun.

He pushed on into the King's own country where he
1628 was opposed by the King's Dissavas, who were however defeated in several engagements; as the King had no other remedy he withdrew to Uva, his most inaccessible district and the remotest from our territory. The General ordered the Capital, which was deserted, as well as the Palace itself, to be set on fire; and after killing the cattle and committing other acts of hostility which war permits, he selected rapidly a few Captains and some lightly armed soldiers, who seemed good to him and they were not many, and leaving the larger portion of his army to plunder the kingdom, with these few he boldly entered Uva, destroying everything with fire and sword, and sought the King who hearing of it did not wait. After achieving this he fell back on the main army, and they all retired to Manicavare without loss and victorious.

1629 The same thing happened the following year, *viz.*, 1629, when he entered Candia and set the city on fire, while the

*On Puliyantivu.

King with his men withdrew to an inaccessible mountain called the Rock*. But while our army was laying waste the whole of that kingdom, the General was advised that the King had sent five thousand chosen men to Jafanapatão under the command of a Modeliar of his Atapata, the Captain of his personal Guard; he knew that that kingdom and fortress were feebly garrisoned, and that Felippe de Oliveira†, who had brought it under the dominion of the Portuguese, was dead. One could write many volumes regarding this Captain, who was no less courageous and no less modest than a Christian ; indeed it was said of him that he never mentioned his parents, and at his registration he gave the grass as his ancestors—a characteristic so different from what is usual among this people, where everyone claims to be descended from the stars‡.

The King had attempted to create a diversion so as to prevent our disturbing him at Candia this year ; but neither benefited him since he could neither prevent his city being burnt nor the fortress relieved. When the General received notice at Candia, he selected four companies and three thousand Lascarins under the command of a brave and experienced Captain called Foão de Pina ; three other companies and the same number of Lascarins were placed under a second Captain called Luiz Teixeira de Carvalho, who on account of his small size was known as Carvalhinho. These two were despatched with orders to march as rapidly as possible by separate routes, and to effect a junction on an appointed day close to Jafanapatão ; this manoeuvre was executed with all the care which he had recommended, while the General with the rest of the army retired to Manicavare without the enemy disturbing them.

The reliefs met at the spot and on the day appointed, and without any delay fell on the enemy who were besieging

**Penelo* : This is Meda Maha Nuwara, the city of refuge for the Sinhalese Kings.

†He died on the 22nd March, 1627, leaving behind a great reputation as the conqueror of Jaffna and the destroyer of five hundred temples. See *The Portuguese Era.* II pp. 118-166.

‡"Riches are not here valued, nor make any the more Honourable. But it is the Birth and Parentage that inobleth," so wrote Captain John Knox in 1681 after a captivity of nineteen years among the Sinhalese.

the place; nor did he fail to offer a fierce resistance in which we lost some of our brave blacks, but he was finally routed and we cut off the heads of more than three thousand. Those who escaped retired as best they could, leaving the fortress free and seven thousand prisoners in our hands. These were natives of our territory who rendered either obedience or assistance to the enemy, and as they were subjects of this Crown it was not posssible to keep them as slaves ; but they were distributed among the officers and soldiers and had to purchase their liberty at a small price, a custom which was then introduced, for in this campaign they had no other plunder. There were however cases where the same degree of kindness was not shown them, for some were impaled and others hacked open with an axe*.

In a few days our victorious troops returned by way of the Seven Corlas to Manicavare, for the main army was stationed here. The General passed on to Malvana, here the King earnestly begged for peace on any conditions we desired. The General was not unwilling to agree to this, both because of the conditions that were offered and also as the soldiers were worn out by two years of continuous marching and exertion, during which he had lost some of his men in battle and a large number had been killed by disease. Further he had but little money, and both men and money are essential in the conduct of war.

But at this time there came an order from the Viceroy, the Conde de Linhares, in which he gave him definite instructions to reduce this kingdom once and for all, at the same time accusing him of a certain degree of negligence. The Conde was influenced in doing this by some people who were ill-disposed towards the General ; for there is no man who can escape envy, and the greater the services of a man, the more they appear to be the medium with which to purchase this poison. And here we should note that this very matter had already been discussed several times in the Council of

*I quote from what I have written elsewhere regarding the doings of Teixeira in 1619, on his way to Jaffna. "Diabolical atrocities marked the route of Teixeira. By his orders men were hacked in two with axes like trees, the breasts of women were torn off, the wombs of mothers were slit open."

State in the time of the Count-Admiral*, and that the General had expressed his mature opinion on the subject as one well versed in the affairs of the Island and of the disposition of the natives. It had been resolved that it was to the advantage of His Majesty that this King should be driven out of the Island, but that to acheive this object they lacked both men and money ; for our usual garrison of six hundred Portuguese was only sufficient for guarding the fortresses, while the invasion and conquest of the two kingdoms of Candia and Uva with a race of people so warlike and with territories so inaccessible, could not be effected without increasing the army as suggested. But none of this carried weight, and the Viceroy was persuaded to make his order without accompanying it with the assistance which was demanded.

Immediately these instructions were received, the Captain-General gave up all thought of peace and prepared to carry them into effect the following year of 1630. Some members of the religious bodies and Captains of experience advised him not to undertake this expedition, since his men were few and he was well aware of the trouble he had encountered in his previous attempts when he had far greater numbers, while these kingdoms still had the same force. In spite of the fact that we had killed a large number of men, they still had an abundance, and at the same time they risked a fight only when it suited their plans, and when it did not they changed from one mountain to another, a fact of which we had experience; the difficulties of subduing them completely would be much greater. To all this the Captain-General replied that he was quite aware this undertaking would cost him his life ; he only regretted the ruin of the fortresses and of the Island which belonged to the King his Lord ; he had received his orders and had no alternative but to obey, since he had already offered his opinion on the subject and that opinion had not been accepted.

There were serving in our armies four Modeliars, natives and all Christians born in Columbo, members of the noblest families in the Island and related to the chief Portuguese

*Don Francisco da Gama, Conde de Vidigueira, Viceroy 1622—1627.

settlers*, all men of wealth who had received high distinctions, whom the General greatly respected and kept by his side, and in many matters followed their advice. They were in command of the fighting men of our territory, and were named Dom Aleixo, Dom Cosme, Dom Balthezar, and Dom Theodozio†. Though they were under such a debt of gratitude to the General, and though as we have said they had been brought up among us, yet they conspired with the King of Candia in such a manner that they were the cause of our total ruin, as we shall see ; for in the end the blacks are all our enemies.

*De Sa set himself to encourage intermarriage, but the defection of these four Mudaliyars gave the death blow to the policy.

†These Portuguese names were what were conferred at Baptism, but the use of their Sinhalese patronymics and honorifics continued side by side. The title of *Don* was jealously confined to the nobles among the Sinhalese.

CHAPTER II

The Expedition, and the Treachery of the Modeliars, by which the General Constantino de Sa and all His Army were Destroyed

With the preliminaries which we have described the eldest Prince of Candia, named Raja Cinga*, invaded our territory 1630
so as to rouse the Captain-General, in accordance with the arrangement made with the Modeliars. After ravaging two of our provinces, in which he behaved very ferociously, he retired to Uva and entered his capital, and immediately placed it in a state of defence, erecting such fortifications as he had time for. The four traitors hastened to the General and urged on him that it was due to the credit of the King their Lord and of the Portuguese nation that he should punish the rashness of this Prince, whereupon the General resolved to invade Uva.

The Portuguese soldiers available did not number four hundred, and he accordingly picked out some inhabitants of Columbo who were fit to accompany him, making in all a force of five hundred men with about twenty thousand Lascarins. With this force he started, and when he reached their kingdom it was noticed that the Prince waited for him in the city itself with much pride ; but as the General prepared to ascend the mountain on which the city was built, the Prince retired on the other side. Seeing this the Captain-General ordered the place to be set on fire, and halted with his army on a hill within sight of it, and in order to refresh his men after the exertions of the forced march which they had made, he remained there two days ; at the end of which the enemy appeared in such numbers as to cover the hills and plains.

He was now warned of the treason which the four Modeliars had hatched, and how they had also won over some of the chief people to join the plot ; it was however too late to take

*As a matter of fact he was the youngest of the three Princes.

precautions against the danger. That afternoon the enemy did nothing but shout at our men as was their custom, saying : " This is the last hour you have to live ", and adding insulting words ; and so night came on. When the General saw their disposition and recognized the careless confidence with which they opposed him, he had no longer any doubt as to the plot, and therefore he harangued our men so as to encourage them ; after this all prepared to lose their lives. He ordered all the baggage to be collected in a heap and set on fire, reserving sufficient provisions to last for three days, so as not to hamper the soldiers and to relieve them of their burden ; for otherwise it would all have gone to benefit the enemy. That night all confessed before the priests who were in the army, encouraging each other, while the cheerfulness and resolution of the General animated all.

In the morning our men moved up to attack the enemy, with our Lascarins under the command of the four traitors in the van, as was the custom. The enemy on their side were seen advancing to meet us, and the first to declare his treason was Dom Cosme, who slew a Portuguese soldier and placed his head on the point of a spear, this being the signal which he had arranged with the enemy. The rest of the conspirators turned their arms against our men. The main body of our Lascarins were astounded at this unexpected event, but as they were all of one race and these were their officers they followed them almost to a man, and there only remained with us a little more than one hundred and fifty, who bravely resolved to follow our fortunes. Simultaneously the rebels fell on us, being the first to start the fire among those of Candia and Uva ; but they found our men offering a stout resistance, fighting as men do who would sell their lives dearly and killing a large number of the enemy all that day. They did not give our men a chance of any rest even at night, as they worried them on all sides with arrows and javelins and much shouting.

The General was everywhere, encouraging them and bidding them attend to the wounded and see to the burial of the dead. The night was now far advanced and the pressure of the enemy somewhat relaxed ; our men were anxious to obtain some rest from the terrible exertions of the day, to prepare for what awaited them on the next ; but God in his wisdom was pleased to ordain that a great thunderstorm should come on, and such a flood of rain as to deluge the plains ; the powder and matchcord could not be protected and were soon rendered useless, and the arquebuzes were the chief weapons which we used against the enemy in the Island.

When all saw that this was the act of God, they submitted themselves to His will, the priests urging and exhorting them to obtain the reward of glory. The few Chingalas who remained with us, and who did not exceed one hundred and fifty in number, and the Portuguese, were greatly encouraged; it was a source of much consolation to the General to see how all were resigned to the dispensation of Providence. That night he was urged to escape with a few men, and this he could easily have effected ; but the General would not agree to this advice, for his generous soul and affection for his people would not allow him to leave his companions in their terrible affliction.

In the morning they started on their march in the same order ; they had not advanced many paces when all at once from every side they were attacked by this multitude. They tried to make use of their firearms, but could not do so owing to the condition of the fuses and the powder, which was as we have described. At this the enemy pressed on them the more freely ; they would not however come within the reach of our swords, the only weapons our men could use, but shot their matchlocks at them and showered their arrows in such number that they seemed like clouds. In a short time almost all our men were dead, and the few who remained were in confusion.

When the Captain-General, who was at every spot encouraging his men, saw this, he took his sword, which was a broad-sword, and wielding it with one hand, for his right was crippled, threw himself among these barbarians and raised a mountain of corpses in their midst. And that the devil might not be deprived of his fair share, no one ventured near but was sent to join his company. At last wounded by bullets and arrows he yielded up his soul to his Creator. He has earned on the roll of fame a place no lower than the greatest heroes of the world, not only for his valor, but all those qualities which compel affection. After this tragedy until the last hour when we were driven out of the Island, his memory was kept alive among us ; and while a Portuguese remains in the State, the life and courage and wisdom of Constantino de Sa e Noronha will be lamented*.

Such was the end of this undertaking from which followed terrible disasters to our fortresses for the space of one year ; for the King laid siege to Columbo with all the people of the Island and assaulted it repeatedly, and once he succeeded in effecting an entrance within the city, but was driven back by the courage of the inhabitants and forced to retire with loss. None the less the city and all the other fortresses in the Island suffered much through want of provisions and other necessaries ; for though the King raised the siege, yet he remained within our territories which were all in revolt.

The news of this tragical loss and of the siege spread over the whole of the East, and the death of Constantino de Sa was bemoaned by every one. With all the speed possible some galliots of provisions were sent over from Cochin to Columbo and Galle, together with every soldier they could spare, who were one hundred and thirty in number. From Malaca there
1631 were sent two hundred veterans, the best in that fortress. From Goa the Viceroy despatched three hundred more with Dom Jorge de Almeida, a Fidalgo, as Captain-General ; but the violence of the storms which were encountered in the Gulf drove them from their course, and it was by good luck that the General reached Columbo at the end of October, 1631. As soon as he landed he advanced to meet the enemy, who had fortified himself with stockades two and three leagues from Columbo ; he did not fail to find a stout resistance, but the enemy was defeated in various encounters. After

*The defeat was on the 20th of September, 1630. De Sa was later deified by the Sinhalese.

all the territory had been reduced to the allegiance of His Majesty he compelled the King to sue for peace, which was 1633
granted to him* under the same condition of his delivering two tusked elephants a year.

After this the Island remained quiet until there arrived as Governor of the State Pedro da Silva Molle, who appointed Diogo de Mello as Captain-General of Ceilão in succession to Dom Jorge de Almeida.

*On the 15th of April 1633. See *The Portuguese Era* II, 198.

CHAPTER III

The Reasons which led to the Renewal of the War with the King

The King of Candia Henar Pandar, who survived his wife Dona Catherina, died* and left the kingdom of Candia to his eldest son Raja Cinga, and that of Uva† to his second son, the one who came over to us in the year 1641 and died a Christian at Goa ; of him we shall speak later. He left nothing to the son whom Dona Catherina bore to Dom João, but the Prince of Uva always protected him so long as he was in the Island. As already stated in the eighth chapter of the first book, the Princes of Candia were brought up with the education of Portuguese, whom they always treated with courtesy as brothers, making minute inquiries as to our customs and adopting those which seemed good to them and of which they approved. They learned all the arts which we taught them, as stated before, and with this education they appointed officers in their palaces just as our own Princes do ; and they used to declare that of the nations of the world we were the most worthy of honour, and if only we did not eat beef, we would be as good as they were.

While this state of friendship existed, a Portuguese who was staying for some time in Candia went to visit the King, and in return for the favours which he had received at his hands he took him a present ; for all these Kings consider it an act of discourtesy when they do not, and they would not receive such a visit nor listen to such a person‡. As our Portuguese had nothing with him but was unwilling to be wanting in the custom of the place in showing his gratitude, he took with him a box full of vials of rose water, which they value greatly, some white sandal wood, and a beautiful horse

*In 1636. He had abdicated the throne some years before.

†As a matter of fact Uva was left to another son, Kumarasinha. On his death Raja Sinha took Uva for himself, and this led to estrangement with the second Prince, Vijayapala, who had received Matale. It was this last who fled to the Portuguese.

‡An Oriental custom which has served as the cover for much corruption.

for the King's personal use. The King set great store on this, being much pleased with the gifts and the display of gratitude on the part of the Portuguese. He kept him as his guest for some months, and when he wished him farewell before starting, was not willing to be less liberal and presented him with some valuable jewels and a handsome tusked elephant, with which he took his leave with due thanks and started by way of Columbo, so as more conveniently to embark the elephant and sell it on the other coast.

The General seeing the Portuguese with such a handsome beast, laid hands on it, declaring that the King was in arrears for the tribute of the previous year, and that as he would not make payment he must take the animal on account. All the entreaties and prayers of the poor fellow for its return were in vain, and as he saw that he had no other remedy he returned to Candia and related to the King what had taken place.

The latter was greatly annoyed and said : "I owe no tribute to the King of Portugal in spite of what the King of Malvana says ; though if I did and had not the necessary animals, it is no difficult matter for me to send and capture them. However what surprises me is not that this act of injustice is done to me, but rather that it is done to you ; for even if it be as he says, it is unreasonable that he should take from you what is yours. Apart from your being a Portuguese as he is, he ought not for the credit of the race to have allowed himself to be so blinded by avarice. But tell me, if he treats you with such injustice, what can I expect, who am a black and not of your people, and who do not follow your religion? I have noted with care that all your people are very tractable, pleasant, courteous, generous, dignified, and above all, courageous—qualties which should be as highly valued as I value them ; for I love all your people, and of the great number of them whom I have met, I have not found one who is not an illustration of what I say. But I also find that there are some among you who so long as they hold no office, are very virtuous ; but as soon as they receive an appointment, they appear immediately to renounce all their good qualities, and replace them by vices twice as many, in proportion to the virtues they previously cultivated. Power turns them into devils.

"I cannot understand the principle of this, and as it was said that it might be the result of your system of religion I examined it and found it altogether a holy one. If a man had been proud or overbearing, I could see this was the effect of nature; but I have known many Portuguese and seen in some the high qualities which I have mentioned; and when I learn that such are appointed to a government, I am delighted and consider the people fortunate. Yet in a short time I do not fail to hear innumerable complaints against almost all of them, and to learn of the acts of injustice they commit, as if they had changed into other beings from what they were before. While I look to see the Viceroy punish them as they deserve for their crimes, I find on the contrary that they receive promotion. And so I am lost in wonder and cannot understand all this, unless it be that there is some hidden rule or law among you, which you will not reveal except to each other.

"The wrong which the King of Malvana has done to both of us only annoys me so far as you are concerned; it is a pity you do not spare each other: but that fact induces me to overlook it so far as it affects me; however, since he has taken what I have given you, you have here what will replace your loss"; at the same time giving him double the value in precious stones, and adding, "I do not wish that this should happen to you a second time; so go back by way of Chilao," He ordered him to be supplied with guides, and the Portuguese bade him farewell with much gratitude.

CHAPTER IV

Of the Rest of this Incident, and the Destruction of Our Army in Candia

The King took no notice of this outrage, and when the usual time arrived for the payment of the tribute, he sent the two elephants for the year; but the General, when he saw what a heavy price the King had given for one horse, procured two very handsome animals which he despatched on their arrival to Candia to be sold for elephants, without thinking of the fact that the Portuguese had not sold his animal nor trafficked with the King, but had only given him a present as a token of friendship and respect, as we have related. As soon as the King saw the two horses in the city and learned the object for which they had been sent, he told the man who was in charge of the business: "Tell the King of Malvana that he has taken from me an elephant of greater value than these horses; when he sends it back to me I shall return him his horses, and in the meantime I shall take care that they are well looked after." 1638

On receiving this message the General was enraged at the King's daring to offer him such an affront, and also because his hopes of making a profit were foiled; for it was impossible for him to escape heavy loss through the failure of his speculation; even if the horses on which he had spent a large sum of money were restored to him, he did not know what to do with them. He desired to take the road to Candia at once, to exact satisfaction for this act of insolence. While he made his preparations he sent the King word that he was coming to Candia to look for him and to punish him as he deserved, and he demanded that his horses should be sent back without delay or reply. The King did not waver, but only told the messenger that he took this step merely to obtain the restitution of his elephant; so long as it was not sent back to him, it was useless asking for the horses; if His Highness were anxious to punish him for seeking to recover his own, God was the judge of all men and he would determine everything as was right; if he came to Candia he would not retire to the other coast; for apart from the great love which he had for his country, it was given him by God to defend, and it was his duty to do so.

On obtaining this reply the General started with all the fighting men of our territory whom he could get together in that short space of time ; these were twenty eight thousand Lascarins and seven hundred Portuguese, the choicest men we ever had in the Island. The King, receiving notice of these preparations, warned his brother the Prince of Uva to come with his own forces and join him in Candia as quickly as possible ; this the Prince did with all zeal, bringing with him ten thousand men, the best in the Island, from his own kingdom. As soon as the General arrived with his army at the mountain of Balane the King, either to avoid extremities or through fear, sent for a priest who was at Candia and entrusted to him a confidential message and gave him a crucifix, begging him to go with it to our army and tell the General, in the name of the Lord who we believed came into the world to die for the salvation of man, not to invade his territories, since he was a vassal of the King of Portugal ; he had given no cause for the General to do so, except that he desired to recover his own : the quarrels of the King of Malvana were his private affair, and he should remember that it was not right that the innocent should pay what was their debt alone ; he should restrain himself and give all the satisfaction that was just, but if he did not desire to do so the King made his protest before the same Lord, whom he took for his judge in the quarrel.

The reply which the General gave the envoy was that he should tell the King that he was come there only to see him whipped for his insolence, and he immediately ordered his army to advance. They descended the mountain and halted alongside the river, leaving some men on the slopes to prevent the enemy cutting down the trees and blocking the road. These soon deserted to the King and so did many of those who accompanied the General for they were all men of one tongue.

While they were thus close to the river, some of our men were wounded and several killed without our seeing who did it. The enemy had cut down on the further bank a large number of trees, and these served them as a stockade not only to guard the approach to the city, but also to stop our men from taking one drop of water, and thus they were not only harassed by the continuous discharge of matchlocks and foot-muskets which the enemy kept up all night long, killing and wounding the bulk of them, but they were also oppressed with thirst and passed that night in great distress without any relief.

At dawn the General learnt that the Balane road was occupied and that it was impossible to withdraw. He realised his position and sent a message to the King by a young fidalgo, Fernão de Mendoca, asking for a cessation of hostilities, and offering to retire to Columbo, and re-establish peace on the existing conditions. The King vouchsafed no reply, and leaving the messenger, whom the Prince of Uva took into his charge, to wait, ordered the attack. The enemy soon appeared on our flanks under cover of the forest, and opened such a heavy fire, that few escaped being killed. Then, seeing the havoc they had caused, they boldly closed on those who were still defending themselves. Their number was overwhelming and our men were soon utterly defeated and put to the sword.

The rout was complete, whereupon the King and the Prince of Uva issued orders not to kill the Portuguese who still remained alive. The King's men took fifteen prisoners, and the Prince's eighteen, for he had no small share in the victory*. The King was very moderate in following up his triumph, for he did not lay siege to our fortresses, but only reduced all our territory under his dominion. This however did not fail to create a famine in Columbo, for the season did not permit of assistance being sent from India with the rapidity which the urgency of the case demanded. Such was the end of this ill-fated expedition, in the course of which not only did our General come by his death, but in spite of every effort even his dead body could not be traced.

*The battle of Gannoruwa, as it is called, was fought on 23 and 24 March, 1638.

CHAPTER V

THE ALLIANCE WHICH THE KING FORMED WITH THE HOLLANDERS

THE King having arrived at the conclusion that his affairs could never be safe so long as he had to deal with the Portuguese, resolved to enter into an alliance with the Hollanders, and with this object he sent two of his noblemen to Batavia to arrange matters. They were well received, and after their proposal had been discussed, the members of the Council resolved to send to Candia two Hollanders* with full instructions and authority to do what was necessary. They arrived in the Island in March, 1638, and were welcomed and entertained by the King. Before entering into the question of an alliance, the King made numerous complaints against the Portuguese and their Captain-Generals who were harassing him only with the object of seizing his kingdom ; not satisfied with the payment of tribute, they invaded Candia every time the caprice seized them, burning his capital and even his palace, waging every kind of hostility which they could against his territory, and ignoring the several victories he had obtained over them ; so long as they maintained fortresses in the Island, he was bound to be exposed to the same oppression at their hands ; and to protect himself he had determined to send ambassadors to Batavia to arrange a treaty which would be to their mutual advantage.

The Hollanders replied that the Company and the States General were very well aware of the extravagant behaviour of the Portuguese all over the State ; for this reason and because they were subjects of the King of Spain †,

*They actually arrived and were received by the King in November, 1637.

†With the death of Dom Henrique on 31st January, 1581, the Portuguese Royal family became extinct, and the Crown fell to Philip II of Spain who was proclaimed as Philip I of Portugal. This was the commencement of the Sixty Years' Captivity, as it was called, which terminated in 1640.

their chief enemy, they were waging all the war they could against them. They well knew the many acts of oppression which the King had suffered at the hands of the Portuguese ; apart from what his ambassadors had related to the Council of Batavia, they could see for themselves what was well-known to all. In order to obviate all this they had come to his Court, and their Commanders were prepared to serve him with all their forces till the King himself and the whole of the Island were freed from their tyranny ; it was therefore desirable that the King and the Honourable Company should enter into a temporary agreement, so that the enterprise might be executed with all zeal. Their desire was to assist him against the oppression which was being practised not only in Ceilão but in the whole of the East, and to relieve everyone from the suffering which the Company was determined to wipe out of India. They had sufficient forces to capture the fortresses which the Portuguese maintained in the Island, but they had no desire to seize the property of others; for they were well aware that Ceilão had only been usurped by the Portuguese, while it belonged by right to the native King. The intention of their Commanders was to relieve him without seeking anything for themselves : (this they said to please him the more).

They therefore proposed that they should enter into an alliance on the following conditions : that all the forts and territories which they took from us in the Island should belong to the King, and that the Hollanders should take nothing except the booty, which was the property of the soldiers : the King should assist with his own army and men of service so long as the war lasted ; he should reimburse them their expenses and pay them for every ship that they lost in the enterprise, a certain figure to be calculated by the tonnage of each and a further figure for each artillery shot in accordance with the calibre, which was to be settled by their account books : similarly with each person who should be killed in the war—one sum for a private, and for the rest in proportion to their rank ; similarly for those who had a leg or an arm injured, with a difference between the right and the left ; and so with a foot or a hand, an eye or any other limb, according to its usefulness or the degree of damage that had been sustained. All this was set down in writing when the terms were agreed on, and the ambassadors left for Batavia, all parties well satisfied with the arrangement ; there they speedily took steps to carry out the undertaking, according to their agreement with the King.

CHAPTER VI

The Capture of our two fortresses of Batecalou and Trequimale

By way of a beginning and in fulfilment of their undertaking, as well as to show themselves zealous in the service of the King, early in the year 1639 six ships of the Hollanders came from Batavia with a large force of infantry and all necessaries. In order to prove that they had no private interests of their own, and that they were only prompted by their desire to serve him, the commander of the flotilla was under orders to proceed to Batecalou and Trequimale, fortresses which we held in the Island but which were of little strength, and as soon as they were surrendered, to raze them to the ground ; for they were aware that this was a small matter and that all we obtained from them was expense, while their position rendered them of no advantage, but at the same time their capture would be agreeable to the King and leave him free on that side.

The flotilla arrived at Batecalou in February of the aforesaid year and landed the troops without any obstruction ; for the fortress did not contain more than forty soldiers capable of carrying arms. They also took on land some artillery, but did not require much, as the bastions were small and the walls single. In a few days they razed one side of the ramparts and two bastions ; whereupon the besieged who were few in number and defenceless, had no alternative but to surrender*. The enemy at once destroyed the fortress, without leaving a trace to show where it had stood. All this occupied twelve
days, when they went on board and in a few days arrived at 1639
Trequimale where they disembarked in the same fashion and laid siege to it, erecting batteries against the fortress. In two days they reduced it into a ruin, as the bastions were only filled with earth and there were but little powder and other necessaries. They killed twenty-three out of the garrison of fifty which the place contained and it was compelled

*As a matter of fact Batticaloa fell on 18th May, 1638.

to surrender in seven days, receiving the same treatment as Batecalou*.

All this was a source of great grief to us, more for the effect it had on our reputation than for the practical advantage which it gave them, as these were the first fortresses which the Hollanders took from us in the State. The flotilla returned to Batavia leaving the King of Candia well satisfied, and promising him that the rest of our fortresses in the Island would be captured with the same facility.

*Trincomali surrendered on 1st May, 1639.

CHAPTER VII

THE ENCOUNTER WHICH TOOK PLACE AT CAIMEL BETWEEN OUR ARMY AND THE HOLLANDERS, AND THE LOSS OF THE FORTRESSES OF NEGUMBO AND GALLE

IN the middle of January, 1640, there appeared within sight **1640**
of the city of Columbo a fleet of twelve of the Hollanders' ships; they however did not land any troops, as they feared our army, and that the residents of the city would join with it and be able to defeat them. Here the Captain-General was Dom Antonio Mascarenhas*, who had been appointed to the post after the destruction of our army in Candia; he immediately sent word to Francisco de Mendoca, Captain-Major of the Field, who was with the army at Manicavare, and who started as quickly as possible.

Finding the Hollanders disembarked a league to the north of Negumbo at a village called Caimel, our men, whose one method of marching and fighting in the Island was at full speed, charged them in this fashion with as much confidence as when attacking the natives. Their advance was disorderly, and our men were soon killed or wounded, for the enemy were three thousand five hundred strong in six squadrons, and very much afraid of our army. But after they had tried their hand on our men in this fashion, and killed or wounded the greater number of them, they cast aside all fear, and within sight of our army marched on by the sea shore as far as Negumbo, which they attacked at once without paying any attention to our men. They placed a mortar against the gate, and effected an entrance without any resistance†, for the garrison only consisted of one company of the aged, sick and disabled who were all killed in the assault. Those who escaped from Caimel retired with some of the wounded to Columbo, which was terror-struck at these unexpected guests.

*He arrived on the first of June, 1638.

†On 9th February, 1640.

The Hollanders were engaged for some days fortifying Negumbo and building outside the enclosure, which consisted of four single walls and two small redoubts, a very strong palisade of palm trees, earth, and fascines, sufficient to protect the garrison of three hundred soldiers whom they left there with three pieces of artillery, well armed and provided with ammunition. They then went on board and sailed towards Columbo, whence they made their way along the coast.

Our General judging that they would disembark at Galle, re-organized his forces as best he could within the short space of time, with the men from Caimel, appointing fresh Captains in the place of these who were slain. He thus formed a body of two hundred and eighty men under his own Captain-Major of the Field, and despatched them by land to the help of that fortress; but though they made what speed they could, they found the enemy disembarked at the distance of a cannon shot from it. Here they were immediately attacked by our men with great courage and resolution; but as their numbers were so great our men were unable to break their ranks, and the enemy handled them in such fashion that few escaped with life. They did not however purchase their victory cheap, for they lost more than four hundred men, while they destroyed all the forces which we had for the defence of this Island. In the middle of the fight the Captain-Major of the Field with some of his Captains and soldiers, cut his way within the ranks of the enemy, where all bravely sold their lives for a high price.

Forty-eight men escaped from this defeat and retired within the fortress, which was now laid under siege, and on the following day batteries of heavy artillery were erected against its three bastions. Lourenço Ferreira de Brito was in command of the garrison and was present at the repairing of the ruins, encouraging the inhabitants and the soldiers who laboured with the same zeal at the posts to which they were appointed. But the fire of the enemy pressed them so hard, that in eighteen days the bastions were laid low. One morning at daybreak they assaulted the place, and though the garrision offered a stout resistance, the majority of the defenders were slain and the bastions entered, while some of those who effected their escape retired within the church.

Here occurred an incident which I ought not to pass over in silence. Lourenço Ferreira de Brito, the Captain of the fortress, was a *casado* and had his wife there, and when he visited the outposts at night, she would not consent to his going without her. To please her he would sometimes agree, though he was alarmed at the danger to which she exposed herself, and though the presence of women causes embarrassment in military duties. One of these nights, which were very frequent, chanced to be the one on which the place was assaulted ; she there displayed great courage by the side of her husband, who carried himself on this occasion as he had done on others, and received five wounds and a musket shot which broke his leg and felled him to the ground. The enemy rushed on him to kill him ; but his wife seeing this, threw herself over him crying out that they might kill her but that they must not touch her beloved husband, who was so badly wounded that he was now at his last gasp.

The Hollanders, who heard her cries, saw a sight which they had not seen before in the thick of the fight, while some were struggling to seize the fortress and others to defend it. A Captain of the enemy faced round and kept the others back, telling her that she could be assured that he would defend her, for her courage deserved even more. The matter spread abroad and was so much praised by all that the General of the Hollanders ordered them not to kill any one, and so they spared those who were captured in the houses, which they only sacked, and those who had fled to the church*.

The General sent his surgeon to do all he could for Lourenço Ferreira, and provided his house with every article that was necessary. In a few days the surgeon declared him out of danger and that he could go on board ; the General therefore ordered all the Portuguese with their wives and children to be distributed among the ships, reserving one which was very roomy. He sent for the Captain of this, and directed him to give up his own cabin to the Commandant of the fort who was proceeding in her with his family ; he was to be treated

*Galle was captured on 13th March.

on the voyage as if he were the General himself. He also ordered them to send on board every provision that was necessary for the voyage, and accompanied them in person to the boats, and they reached Batavia well looked after.

Some days before a despatch-boat had arrived there with news of the capture of the two fortresses, and mention had also been made of this matter ; and this was a subject of rejoicing to all. As soon as the Hollanders' General was informed of their arrival, he sent people to meet them and boats in which to land. They were received with all honour, and escorted to some houses which had been prepared for them with every necessary ; and for the fourteen months they remained there, they never lacked for anything. At the end of that period they were sent back to Columbo, where I spoke to the aforesaid Lourenço Ferreira de Brito, who was subsequently Captain-Major of the Field.

CHAPTER VIII

How on the arrival of João da Silva Tello, Count de Aveiras, as Viceroy of India, he sent Dom Filippe Mascarenhas as Captain-General of Ceilão and recaptured Negumbo

On the eighteenth of September, 1640 the Count de Aveiras, João da Silva Tello, arrived in India as Viceroy, succeeding Pedro da Silva Molle whom he found dead, the Government being administered by Antonio Telles de Menzes who was subsequently appointed Count de Villapouca. It was with this Viceroy that I came on service.

He found Ceilão suffering from the disasters which I have related, and to remedy this state of things he summoned a Council of State. Money, the chief essential for equipping a relief force, was lacking ; the previous winter the Hollanders had burnt at Mormugão* the three galleons which we kept for purposes of defence : consequently everything was in a perilous state. It was agreed that the loss of two such important fortresses as Galle and Negumbo should be remedied as soon as possible, and steps taken to avert the disasters which threatened us. And because the Captain-General Dom Antonio Mascarenhas, during whose administration these misfortunes had overtaken us, was the one to whom they would cause the deepest grief, and as he was a fidalgo who had served the State and given great satisfaction, it was desirable to appoint someone who would be acceptable to Dom Antonio and who would not be in want of money† : for the State treasury was quite empty, and it was not possible to raise a loan owing to the poverty of the nobles of Goa, consequent on the blockade which the Hollanders had maintained with their ships for some years ; each summer they used to be stationed at the mouth of the harbour, capturing the merchant ships.

*One of the three harbours of Goa.

†Officers appointed in the King's service were expected to use their private funds when needed.

In view of all this, the Council resolved that the proper person to appoint as Captain-General of the Island was his brother Dom Filippe Mascarenhas, for in him they found all the qualifications they desired. They did not ignore the fact that he had seen very little service, but they recognized in him great talents and they thought he would render a good account of himself in everything. In a word the necessities of the case and the reasons given above, added to the fact of his being a man of great wealth, induced the Council to advise the Viceroy to entrust the command of the expedition to him. This he accepted with generous courage; nor were they deceived in their expectations, for he excelled in his good qualities and virtues, all the fidalgos whom I have met in the State during my nineteen years.

Sixteen galliots and fustas, with four hundred soldiers and some brave Captains, were selected, and he started as quickly as possible in the beginning of October, arriving in eleven days at Columbo, where his brother Dom Antonio came to meet him with the cheerfulness which his affection demanded, and the respect paid to a father. He handed over the Government to him, and took a pike and continued serving as a soldier on every opportunity that presented itself, till he was slain in battle by the Hollanders. His death was greatly lamented by all, for apart from his being a brave soldier, Dom Antonio was a very learned man.

Antonio da Mota Galvão was at the time in Columbo; he had marched there overland from Jafanapatão with a relief force of two hundred and fifty men out of the fleet which had conveyed Dom Braz de Castro, and he had also been appointed Captain-Major of the Field. The Captain-General set out with these men, some others who had been wounded at Caimel, and the four hundred of us who had accompanied him, and laid siege to Negumbo, as that was the nearest, and it would leave him free to follow up with the siege of Galle. Immediately on his arrival we erected batteries, and pressed them so hard that in twelve days they asked for a parley. But the conference led to no settlement, and therefore we continued our attack that night so vigorously that the following day* they agreed to surrender on the terms we had offered.

*8th November, 1640.

One of these was that they should be supplied with ships in which they could proceed wherever they wished, so long as they did not land at any port in the Island : and this undertaking was badly carried out by them, for they landed at Galle. But in truth the ships we gave them were old and so badly equipped that I do not know how they reached even that port, though it was not distant more than twenty-five leagues along the coast. Those however who subsequently fell into our hands paid dearly for this breach of faith. The men who surrendered, whether wounded or otherwise, were two hundred in number, as the rest had been killed in the siege.

While the siege lasted one of the four traitors who had taken part in the rebellion against Constantino de Sa, Dom Balthezar by name, appeared on our rear, for he had been ordered by the King of Candia to support the fortress with twenty thousand men ; and immediately after the surrender we attacked him with six companies and two thousand Lascarins. We fell on them and routed them with great loss of life ; and there was no little rejoicing because the slain included the traitor, who left his head to pay the price of his treachery. With this success the surrounding country soon submitted, and our affairs were in a better state than before.

Dom Filippe was anxious to recapture Galle at once, but there were several difficulties, the chief being the want of a fleet, as without this his trouble and expense would have been thrown away ; for the fortifications of that fortress were sufficiently strong to withstand a protracted siege, and so long as the defenders had the sea open, double the number for which they had applied to India could come to reinforce them. But in order to prevent their collecting any cinnamon in the meantime or obtaining any provisions from their lands, he despatched Antonio da Amaral de Menezes with ten companies of infantry, consisting of three hundred and fifty soldados, and the Dissava of Mature with one thousand and eight hundred Lascarins. With this force in the Galle Corla, the enemy could not obtain anything from their lands ; indeed the population was driven away from the Corla itself, so that they might get nothing in the future. A hundred and twenty-eight of them were killed and forty-three taken

1641 prisoners in an ambush we laid for them close to the fortress* ; this loss taught them such a lesson that they never fell into our hands again.

And since the lands of Sofregão had submitted to the King of Candia, and their reduction required a person of experience, Antonio da Mota Galvão, the Captain-Major of the Field, started to subdue them with five companies of one hundred and ninety soldados, and the Dissava of those territories with four thousand Lascarins. He did not fail to find considerable difficulty and had several encounters with the native enemy ; but in spite of all he reduced the whole district under the dominion of His Majesty.

Dom Antonio Mascarenhas volunteered to proceed to the Four and Seven Corlas. He took with him nine companies of three hundred soldados, and the two Dissavas of those districts, who were followed by seven thousand Lascarins. This fidalgo encountered very great difficulty in reducing the district. As soon as he had reduced one and routed the enemy, he found a strong force opposing him in the other, and when we went to attack them, if it did not suit them to wait for us, they changed their ground to the district we had already reduced, so that they were in a perpetual state of insurrection. The wretched inhabitants did not fail to pay for what was only the fault of the enemy, and many were put to death on the charge of complicity. This expedition occupied a continuous period of one year, at the end of which God was pleased to let us find the enemy off his guard in the Seven Corlas ; we defeated him with such great loss that he was compelled to retire to Candia and we were left masters of all those territories, for the people of Candia no longer dared to disturb us, and the Hollanders could not venture outside their fortress.

*The Hollanders threw down their arms and fled, and for their cowardice a number selected by lot were shot.

CHAPTER IX

How seventeen Portuguese who were Prisoners in Uva were put to Death

Before continuing our narrative it is necessary for a clearer understanding that we should turn aside to relate the course of events up till now. I have already stated that when that disaster befell our army in Candia, the Prince of Uva contributed most to the victory by the assistance which he gave his brother; and since his education among the Portuguese had made him kindly disposed towards them, when he found himself victorious and our army destroyed, he ordered all the Portuguese who were taken alive to be brought to him; there were eighteen of them, including a priest and also Fernão de Mendoca, whom he had detained when he came on his message to the King. With this fidalgo the Prince formed a great friendship as he was a young man of birth and parts, and he loved the rest of his prisoners as if they were his brothers, and treated them with extreme kindness.

After their captivity had lasted four years, one day he addressed them as follows: "My friends, you can easily understand how great a regard I have for you; for the time you have spent here must have proved to you my affection. As you know you came here prisoners, and in my power; but in truth, since I have mixed among you, I am far more the prisoner of your good behaviour. You have always been very grateful for any little service I have rendered you, and so you have not only compelled me to desire every solace for you, but also to entertain a great feeling of affection for all. When men arrive at such a stage, they should prove their words by deeds; and that you may all realize the truth of my words, I have decided to set you free; you can therefore make your preparations, for you can start whenever you think fit."

Hearing this, the men did not know how to give expression to their gratitude for such astonishing kindness; they all threw themselves at his feet, but he raised them and embraced them with tears in his eyes. They declared that they no longer cared for liberty, nor did their love for their country weigh with them ; they only felt the grief of parting from their honoured Prince. Some days passed without their taking any steps, on which the Prince inquired why they were not arranging for their journey They replied that they could not leave His Highness ; that their sole desire was to please him, and that he could do with them as he thought fit. The Prince thereupon summoned a Modeliar, the Captain of his Guard, and gave him secret orders to be ready with a few men to accompany the Portuguese to our territory the next day.

At five o'clock the next morning they all waited on the Prince, who embraced them with many expressions of affection and wished them farewell. Our men started on their road with deep regret, filled with wonder at the high qualities of the Prince. They however chanced to fall in with the guards maintained by the King of Candia on his frontiers, who detained them while they sent a message to the King for his orders. Though he was aware that it was the Prince who had set them at liberty, he dissimulated and ordered them to be sent back to Uva, with a message from himself that those Portuguese prisoners appeared to have been given so much liberty that they had dared to attempt flight ; they had been arrested by his guards on the frontiers and he was sending them back ; but he begged him to have greater care taken of them. The Prince sent word in reply that the custody of the Portuguese was his own concern, because they were his prisoners : as for their attempting flight, that ought to cause no surprise ; they were in a foreign land and without any necessaries and all men desire liberty, the dearest possession in life. At this reply the King was convinced that he had set them free, and given them his own Modeliar as guard and guide ; however as he was astute and sagacious, he pretended ignorance.

The Prince consoled them all and promised that he would shortly manage to send them among us, in spite of his brother ; his friendship for Fernão de Mendoça was specially great, and he was distressed that that fidalgo should lose so much by not being with us. With this thought he sent for him and told him that he was well aware that he was one of the chief fidalgos of Portugal, and that such noblemen went to India to serve their King and acquire wealth: that he was suffering great loss, and he also remembered what happened: he did not think it prudent to send away all the Portuguese, but he would seize the earliest opportunity possible to do so. As for de Mendoça himself he desired him to start at once: though the road was not as short, it was the more secure. He could not do the same with the rest, for fear of his brother's anger; but de Mendoça was only one man, and his going away might pass unnoticed. He accordingly ordered four Lascarins who knew the road well to show him the way, and sent him on his journey accompanied by the priest. After eight days travelling by way of the Grevaias they reached Mature safely, and there they met our people.

None of this escaped the King of Candia, for he had a man in Uva who kept him informed of everything; but concealing his knowledge he sent one to speak to the Modeliar who commanded the Prince's guard (for he knew that the Prince relied on him in everything) with a message that he was well aware that the Prince was anxious to send the men back to the Portuguese, and that he could not do so except by his agency. He would be greatly pleased if the Modeliar would kill them all when the opportunity arose, since his brother was so madly enamoured of their enemies; after effecting this, he should retire to Candia, where he would receive high honours. To further assist him, he would order the guards to be withdrawn from that part of the frontier.

The Modeliar pledged himself to do what the King desired; the Chingalas were jealous of the Prince's great predilection for the Portuguese, their bitter enemies, and this gave rise to complaints among some. The Modeliar noted those who had this feeling, so as to utilise them in carrying out his promise when the opportunity arose.

The Prince was anxiously looking for the means and opportunity to fulfil his word, and not fail in what he had begun in setting the Portuguese at liberty. On receiving news that there were no guards stationed on some of the roads, especially those leading to the Two Corlas, he sent the Modeliar to ascertain the truth of this report, (and indeed the latter knew more about it than the people he sent to make the inquiry). He got his informants together and took them before his master, that he might learn from their own lips that the roads were free. Pretending to be very pleased, he exclaimed : "Your Highness now has the chance you have wished for, of doing what you desired for those poor Portuguese, without any interference from the King". The Prince, as he was a man of great courage and considered him a faithful servant, replied : "Our opportunity has come and we must not neglect it. Be ready to-morrow morning with a hundred of my guards—men who you are confident will give a good account of themselves in the task they have to perform. If they meet my brother's troops, they must not only protect the Portuguese from any injury, but also save them from falling into his hands ; for he will not send them back to me a second time, and they will be robbed of their liberty for ever. This would be a great disappointment to me, for it is a long time since I have made my promise to them, and I am eager, as you know, to fulfil it. The journey will occupy but a few days : as soon as you bring them to their own territory, they will be safe, as their army is in Sofregão."

The Modeliar promised to do everything as he was ordered, and added that he could assure His Highness that even if it cost him his life the Portuguese would not fall into this brother's hands. Accordingly he directed them to start the next morning, and distributed some presents among those whom he knew to be poor, and wished everyone farewell. They started the next morning at the appointed hour, well content. The Modeliar according to his orders had sent word to the people whom he intended to take with him, selecting above all three Araches* in whom he had confidence, and who were ill-affected towards the Prince for favouring the Portuguese so much.

After travelling three days, when they were close to our territory, the Modeliar called the Araches aside and told them of the agreement he had entered into with the King, and how he had the King's promise that he would reward the people who helped him in the work : that he had pledged his word and was anxious to keep it, apart from the fact that the Prince so recklessly showed such unreasoning favour to

*Usually an Arachchi at this time was a military officer in command of a company or *Ranchu* of twenty-five men.

their enemies as to desire to set them at liberty, so increasing their forces. These three required little encouragement; they were well satisfied with the proposal and applauded the resolution as a wise one; each undertook to speak to his own men, and all were found to be of the same mind.

In the morning they started on their march, all very cheerful and talking with our men. They crossed into our territory, where the Portuguese drew fresh breath, thinking that they had regained their former freedom. After marching three leagues they halted at Dinavaca, the Modeliar telling them that as they were now secure from the King's men, they desired to bid them adieu. His men were drawn up in two lines, amidst every mark of rejoicing, with the points of their spears resting on the ground just as if they were saluting. Our men marched through the midst of them, bidding each other farewell with great contentment. When thc seventeen stood between the two lines, at a given signal, in an instant they ran everyone of them through, and then quickly retired to Candia and informed the King of what they had done. He was very well pleased, and showed himself so to those who had performed this foul deed.

CHAPTER X

The War which arose between the King and the Prince and how the latter came to us for help

When the Prince was informed of what had taken place, he would not show himself to any man for three days, at the end of which he sent a messenger to the King requesting him carefully to send back the Modeliar and the Araches, to punish them as their audacity and treachery deserved. The King replied that he did not know those men were traitors, but rather considered them very loyal for obviating the mischief which both kingdoms would have receivd at the hand of the Prince by the thoughtless favour he showed the common enemy and by his increasing their forces : he fully realised the great purpose for which God had granted him the victory where those enemies had been conquered, and so far from having done anything worthy of punishment they rather had won those rewards which the King intended to confer on them.

The Prince was furious at this reply, and ordered them to tell his brother that he was well aware that His Highness was entirely responsible for the death of those poor prisoners, to whom it was his duty rather to show favour than to put them treacherously to death. If he did give them their liberty, it was not through any desire to increase the enemy's power, for they in their anxiety for those seventeen would not fail to continue the war. If they showed themselves ungrateful, God, who had once placed them in his power, would do the same again. Those Portuguese had been his prisoners so long that he could not avoid having intercourse with them ; and the various grounds for esteem which he found in them was the reason which induced him to set them at liberty. Therefore His Highness must either send back those murderers, for they were traitors, or if he retained them it was against his will.

The King was incensed at this message, and without giving any reply he turned his back saying "I shall punish this folly". On hearing of this the Prince collected his troops, while the King ordered his Dissavas to get together with the utmost speed all the forces they could. Twenty thousand men assembled and were despatched to Uva with orders to arrest the Prince and bring him in good custody. As soon as they entered Uva the Prince advanced to meet them, and coming on them as they were encamped in some valleys among the mountains, he seized the roads and held them there for seven days without the possibility of moving just as if they were besieged : they gave themselves up for lost, and the Prince conceived that he had them safer than if they were in chains. But as he was full of pity, he spoke to his men and said "Our enemies are in our power, and we can punish them as we think fit ; but the men who are here cannot be blamed for the excesses of the King ; for they only carry out his orders, and where there is no fault, it is unjust to punish. Moreover, if we kill them, and make our country a waste, to whom can we look to defend it? They clearly realise the position they are in, and that their lives are in our hands. But I have made up my mind to spare them, as I do not wish to appear like the King in killing the innocent ; we shall therefore give them an opportunity of retiring." He gave his orders accordingly, and commanded them to retire to Candia under threat of not showing them the same mercy again. His own outposts were withdrawn and the King's men marched out without any loss.

The King received immediate information of the situation in which his men were, and ordered the rest of his forces to be collected at once, as he would relieve them in person ; but when he learnt that they had retired and were on the road to Candia, he was indignant with his officers and upbraided them in an *ola* which he wrote to them for their subservience to the enemy, when he himself was coming to their relief and was already on the road. He ordered them to halt wherever the letter reached them, as he would shortly be with them.

The letter was received three leagues outside the limits of Uva, where the troops had halted for the night ; they waited for eight days, when the King himself arrived with twenty thousand fresh men. Advancing with the whole body, he entered Uva from two points and marched straight to the city. The Prince, who did not expect this sudden attack, hastily retired with a few followers, and left his palace to be occupied by the King's troops. The Prince's men were in such consternation and dismay that he had no other remedy than to make his way to the boundaries of the Two Corlas, close to our territories ; and as he saw that it was impossible for him to face his brother, he wrote to the Captain-Major of the Field, Antonio da Mota Galvão, who was with the army in Sofregão, requesting a safe conduct to enable him to come and discuss with him matters which were of importance to the interests of the King our Lord.

The Captain-Major replied that His Highness could come in perfect safety, and that he would find their desire to serve as prompt as the fulfilment thereof. On receiving this reply the Prince started with six of his nobles who followed him, sending a message to the Captain-Major while on the road to inform him of the fact. The latter learning from the messenger the road taken by the Prince, sent the Dissava with two companies and some men at arms to wait for him at Opanaike. The Prince arrived there the same day, and was received by our men with three volleys of musketry, at which he was highly pleased, saluting all with great courtesy and treating all, from the highest to the lowest soldier, in a friendly manner.

The next day they started, but he could not be persuaded to enter an *andor**, so he walked on foot conversing with the Dissava and Captains, purposely mixing with the soldiers with whom he talked, asking each one where his country was, and praising the special products of each—such as the melons of Charmusca, the pears of Alcobaca, the olives of Elvas, etc. The soldiers were astonished to hear him, and he showed himself as kindly to all as if they were his brothers. This knowledge was the result of his education and constant intercourse with the Portuguese, and he had in his room a map of our country, in which were set out fully its cities, towns, villages, rivers, and other features, and also a manuscript book with minute details of everything.

*A species of palanquin

In three days he reached Cadangão where the Captain-Major Antonio da Mota and the Prince after exchanging visits discussed the reason of his coming. He declared that his quarrel with his brother was in regard to the Portuguese, and he had come to them trusting to find in them the same sympathy and affection. It was notorious that the King's action was due to his insisting on releasing the poor men who had been murdered by those traitors in Dinavaca, and his determination to seize and punish the latter as they deserved; it was equally notorious that the murder had been planned by the King; the matter therefore affected the Portuguese more than himself. He asked for no other help in his attempt than that we should give him one hundred and twenty soldiers in three companies, and those who joined him would never repent it. He had plenty of money for the expenses, and all would be well satisfied and everyone would find in him a brother; not only would he fight the King, but he would also assist us with all his forces to drive the Hollanders out of the Island. If the Captain Major granted him this favour he would be the happiest man on earth: he was resolved to punish not only the rebels, but also the one who had plotted the mischief which compelled him to abandon his state.

The Captain-Major had purposely come to this spot to wait for the Prince as it was four leagues nearer to Columbo than Sofregão, and once there the Prince could do nothing but what we bade him. To his request for assistance the Captain-Major replied that everyone was aware of the truth of His Highness' statement, and the Portuguese were greatly in his debt; but there were several difficulties about giving him the men he wanted, for it was necessary not only to speak with the King of Malvana, but also to refer the matter to Goa for the decision of the Council of State.

On hearing this the Prince, who had expected us not only to grant him his request but also to be zealous in assisting him through gratitude, showed in his face the disappointment he felt in his heart. This was noted by one of the nobles who accompanied him, a man advanced in years, who spoke out and said "This war which the King is waging against the Prince my master is due to his love for the Portuguese; it is for them to carry it on, though they appear so averse to doing so. I feel sure, and every one knows it, if we had gone for assistance to the Hollanders, they would have helped us with all their forces."

At these words the Captain-Major abused him as a traitor and ordered him to be arrested and his head immediately cut off. The Prince was terribly distressed and for the two days he remained there he would not see the Captain-Major, nor did he have another hour of happiness, and gave himself up entirely for lost, but he would always talk with the soldiers who formed his guard, for he was affable by nature.

Two days after this occurrence the Captain-Major sent word that His Highness should go and meet the King of Malvana, and discuss his affairs with him. He replied that when he came to us he was prepared to do everything he was told to: and moreover he was very glad to do so, so he hoped by God's grace to meet with a very good reception from the King of Malvana. They started with two companies of infantry and some of our men at arms, and thus they reached Malvana where the Captain-General, Dom Filippe Mascarenhas, was waiting for him.

They exchanged many courtesies and compliments in a house where there was erected a dais on which were placed two chairs covered with crimson velvet with fringes of gold. The Captain-General would not allow the Prince to sit except on his right, which he had to accept, thanking him for his courtesy. They talked of various matters for more than an hour, without the Prince mentioning the object of his visit; seeing this the Captain-General remarked that the great affection which he had always shown to our nation was well known, and also that his quarrel with his brother arose from the same cause: His Highness would therefore find that all the Portuguese would give their lives to serve him.

He replied that if he received no other benefit from his coming there than the great honours which His Highness rendered him, he considered his time well spent: his grief was that for such a trivial matter they should have killed a man whom he respected like a father. The General expressed his grief and attempted to console him: His Highness should remember what great reason they had to hate the

Hollanders : how much more when his vassal rashly anticipated him, showing himself wanting in the respect and decorum which was due to His Highness, and had rebuked him in his presence : it was for this reason, and for no other, that the Captain-Major had punished him.

" Senhor ", replied the Prince, " that old man brought me up and he loved me as if I were his child. When he saw the justice of the request with which I had come, and how the answer I received was different from what I had expected, he ventured to speak as he did, and not because he did not approve of my coming here. I only blame the Captain-Major for the hastiness of the execution ; even if it were reasonable to punish him, the punishment should not have been so severe". " I am sure", answered the Captain-General, " that had the Captain-Major known that he was a man whom you held in such high esteem, and had the reasons which Your Highness have urged, not even so would he have acted as if he did not understand ; how much more as the words the Captain Major addressed your Highness did not merit that he should go so far ; we should always look for the best method of serving Your Highness, for everything should be built on a firm basis. And so I hope in God that everything will be done as is right. Your Highness should therefore rest yourself, as here you will learn from experience how much we all love and desire to serve you."

The Prince retired to a house which had been prepared for him, and was accompanied by some officers and the principal residents of the city who had come to pay their respects to the General. The latter visited him in the morning, and after some conversation he said that His Highness would find it best to accompany him to Columbo, where he could rest better after his painful journey, and also settle about his affairs in the city. The Prince was anxious for the opportunity to visit it, as it was so near ; he accordingly replied : " My desires, Senhor, are only governed by Your Highness ; I see that everything is being done to please me, so that I may always remember the greatness of the Portuguese gentlemen, which from all I have heard has no limit. I am grateful to Your Highness for all your kindness to me."

After breakfast a handsomely decorated palanquin was sent to him, but he would not enter it on any condition, declaring that when so many gentlemen walked on foot he would only accompany them in the same fashion. The General could not persuade him in spite of all his efforts, and so both traversed those three leagues on foot. Towards evening they drew near the field of S. João, close to the city, where all the companies were waiting for him. The General remained a considerable distance behind so as to allow the Prince to make his entry, and he also requested all who followed him to accompany the Prince.

The companies were drawn up in good order on either side, all saluting him with three rounds of musketry, and wherever he went he courteously returned the greeting of all. In this manner he advanced between our lines till he reached the gates, when he was repeatedly saluted with three salvos of artillery at which he was delighted, as he had not seen a similar thing before. The *Camara* with the Captain of the city, the Bandigarrala, and some of the principal residents, received him on his arrival, and the common people greeted him with many *vivas*. The Prince could not express the pleasure which this reception gave him, and he afterwards declared that he considered the troubles and vexations of his brother a very happy matter, as they were the cause of their seeing the affection which he always had for the Portuguese : he was also satisfied that God gave them an opportunity to repay him for all.

He was lodged in one of the best houses in the city—the majority of them were stately buildings—and he was provided with a guard of one company of soldiers, which was replaced by another at the usual hour ; and all the soldiers who mounted guard did so with great splendour. The Captain-General at his own expense ordered him to be liberally provided with all he required, and he would not sit down to table without having the Captain of the guard as his guest.

Sometimes he went out to visit the General,and he also visited the five religious houses. He was dignified, modest, courteous, of a stately bearing, and appeared about thirty-four years old, slim of body and very erect. His long hair was curled at the ends, and his beard was worn in the Portuguese fashion, with a moustache which was not very full ; his colour was like that of the quince, and he was always very cheerful and friendly with the Portuguese ; but when he spoke with the natives, his bearing was royal, austere, and very stately.

CHAPTER XI

How the Prince's request for assistance was discussed and the question referred to India

After the Prince had been in the city ten days the Captain-General, Dom Filippe Mascarenhas, had some conferences regarding the assistance which he requested, and when the question had been discussed by a Council of all the experienced veterans who had a full knowledge of the country, they agreed that they should give him, and that as quickly as possible, not only a hundred and twenty Portuguese, but as many as we could spare, and they stated their reasons. They argued that before the arrival of the Hollanders we required five hundred men in two camps to prevent the lands which were subject to us from going over to the King of Candia, and even thus we could not check the frequent assaults and invasions of the enemy, which caused us such great loss. If we gave a part of these men to the Prince, we would carry the war within their gates and keep our territory free from invasion, and at the same time we could engage the Hollanders with the rest of our companies and men at arms, and thus we could easily wipe them, as well as the King, from off the Island. Apart from the Prince being a courageous man, this war with his brother was entirely the result of his great devotion to us. He was much beloved by the natives for his kindness, and the men of Uva were the bravest in the Island. With the assistance and encouragement of the Portuguese, they must necessarily destroy the King, or drive him out of the Island.

Even if matters did not turn out so, he would have all he could do to defend himself from the Prince, and thus he would be prevented not only from waging war on us, but also from assisting the Hollanders. We would also have the Prince on our side to assist us when the necessity arose, and at the same time it would not be necessary to incur any expenditure over the Portuguese who followed him, for he was well supplied with treasure to meet the cost. Should we give him this assistance, was it not more for the interests of His Majesty and the advantage of the Island, than a favour we were conferring on the Prince?

Two members of the Council however dissented : the Prince was the King's brother, and they could easily become reconciled again. The King could always make his terms with such advantages that the Portuguese could not fail to be in a worse case than before ; for it was notorious that he had entered into his alliance with the Hollanders with the sole object of expelling them from the Island : they therefore did not consider it desirable to lend the assistance which had been asked for.

The rest of the Council thought otherwise, and urged that even granting everything which had been suggested, it was not many months ago that the King and Prince were in such a state of alliance : did we therefore fail to defend ourselves, or was it we who created this difference between them? And if he did join his brother, what greater evil threatened us? If God had given us this opportunity, it was only wise not to neglect it, apart from the many overwhelming reasons which join in compelling everyone to lay down his life for a man, who in his own country and without any claim on our part, had placed himself on our behalf in opposition to his own blood.

The whole East would be astonished if we did not show our gratitude, for it was incumbent on everyone to render good for good, and we should not obstinately neglect an opportunity which had only come by the will of God. If the Prince proved ungrateful our conduct would be that of Christians and Portuguese, and his that of a Gentile and a black, and it mattered little if we had one more such our enemy. If we acted otherwise, that very course would prove our ruin: for if the King with the people of Candia alone could wage such a fierce war against us, what would he do when he was also master of Uva? "In truth if we refuse the Prince this assistance, the King cannot find more trustworthy friends than the Portuguese, for we make him the undisputed lord of the whole Island. This is our opinion, and therefore his lordship the Captain-General should look into the matter, and take whatever steps he considers most prudent in the interests of His Majesty."

All agreed in these arguments, and the rest of the Council were of the same opinion : so much so that even the two dissentients withdrew their opposition in the face of such cogent and well founded reasons. There was present at the Council the Factor and Alcaide Mor of Colombo. He advanced no opinion on the subject, excusing himself on the ground of his lack of experience of the Island ; but when he saw that affairs had reached the stage of our voting the assistance he asked for permission to speak. All declared that they were anxious to listen to him for they knew his abilities, and with the General's consent he spoke as follows :

"I have been waiting till now to see the conclusion you arrived at, and I have seen the wisdom of those weighty arguments for rendering help to the Prince, whatever the consequences, because the state of affairs so imperatively demands it. But it is my duty, and I may not omit to remind you of an order which I find registered in the Factor's books, whereby their Most Serene Majesties the Kings of Portugal have given express commands to all the cities, fortresses and districts over which we hold dominion in this State, that if by any means or chance any King or Prince, Gentile or Moor, fall into our power, he should not be allowed to return to his territories to continue in their rites and ceremonies. This rule has special reference to the Princes of this Island ; all such are to be well treated and advised in a friendly way voluntarily to receive the water of Holy Baptism. If I conceal what I now tell you, I am liable to punishment ; I therefore bring it to your notice, that the Captain-General may decide with your worships what is the best course to pursue."

All were in consternation at this speech and adjourned the further consideration of the question, the Captain-General requesting them to give the matter their most careful deliberation, so as to arrive at a settlement. Two days later the Council met to discuss the same subject ; the opinions of all were unaltered, for they were satisfied that it was thus in His Majesty's interests ; they declared that their Most Serene Majesties in passing this order had a noble object, at a time when it was not possible to find anything better than the state in which the Island was. At the date of the order we had no such powerful opponents as the Hollanders ; and even if we maintained a state of continuous warfare with the Kings of the Orient, our forces were sufficient to resist their greatest efforts ; but the order should not be followed in our present state of difficulty and his lordship the Captain-General should above all do what he considered best in the King's service.

The General replied : " It is not right, gentlemen, that a matter of such importance should be decided by my single opinion. It is very difficult for one man to show judgment in every matter, for success and failure are in the hand of God. The man who follows only his own opinion is bound to fall into error ; so much so that I do not desire to assume the responsibility in the eyes of the public, who judge rashly, each one according to his own opinion. To obtain the advantage of the advice of all who are present, I invited you to assist me, and when the subject was discussed, I was glad to listen to the numerous weighty reasons which were urged for our rendering the most effective aid to one who on our account finds himself driven from his State and country, and who looks for refuge among the very men for whom he is suffering. In other ways too it is of great importance to us to assist him; if we do not, it is we who are weakened.

" But I wish to know how we can avoid incurring the displeasure of our Lord the King for infringing his orders ? I had the book containing the entry produced, and made a careful inquiry into the circumstances; I find we can follow no other course but what is laid down for us. We must therefore refer the matter to Goa, with a detailed statement of our opinion on the subject for the guidance of the Viceroy, and request him to send a suitable force, if he can see his way to do so. If he cannot, he will submit the matter to His Majesty, and I feel sure that when it is before him, he will order the despatch of sufficient forces to replace the Prince in the possession of his State. "

No one objected, in spite of their disappointment ; for all saw that no other course was open to the Captain-General as he alone would be held responsible.

When the Prince heard of this resolution he did not show his grief in any way ; he only remarked that he greatly regretted the Portuguese should thus increase the forces of the enemy, and that it was not in his power to repay them for the kindness he had received at the hands of all. The Captain General ordered him to be kept well supplied with everything out of his own funds, and that he should be informed of anything he needed for his personal use. He had the best of eight galliots amply fitted out to convey him to Goa, and accompanied him on board ship, where the Prince wished him and every one else who was present farewell with manifestations of gratitude. He showed no grief at leaving, but as much cheerfulness as one could hope for had his request been granted.

He started from Columbo in the middle of December 1641, arriving in a few days at Goa, where he was well received by João da Silva Tello, Conde de Aveiras. He was assigned a sufficient income for the maintenance of himsef and of the two noblemen and the servants who accompanied him ; as for the rest, he had before starting requested the Captain-General to send them back to Uva, which was carefully done.

To finish with the career of this Prince. He lived in Goa and was treated with consideration, spending most of his time in conversation with the priests. In March, 1645, Dom Filippe Mascarenhas arrived from Ceilão as Viceroy of the State, and he earnestly urged him to be converted ; the Prince consenting, the matter was reported to His Most Serene Majesty King Dom João IV with a request that he might act as godfather. His Majesty in a letter which he sent him, warmly congratulated him on the choice he had made, and authorised Dom Filippe Mascarenhas to act on his behalf.

As soon as His Majesty's letter arrived, the Prince was anxious to carry out the solemnity at once. On the appointed day all the prelates, the lords of the Tribunal of the Holy Office*, the Fidalgos, and the rest of the nobility, headed by the Viceroy, met together. First of all before this assembly the Prince delivered an able and polished address : as he realised that no rational being could secure salvation save he be washed in the water of Holy Baptism so as to obtain a

*The Inquisition was established in Goa in 1560, but never exercised much influence over Ceylon.

portion in the blood which Jesus Christ had shed for the human race, therefore he would have all know that no other cause had inspired him save the mercy of the Most High, to whom he rendered humble thanks for vouchsafing him that mercy and for illuminating him with the divine grace, rescuing him out of the darkness in which he was living. He eschewed for ever all the transactions which he had had with the evil one, and only sought to be the son of Jesus Christ through this such health-giving lavation, which he longed to receive in all devotion and humility. He requested them to take down all that he said, and he signed the record. Immediately afterwards he received the Holy Baptism, and he was followed by all who were with him. That was the day of greatest rejoicing and solemnity which the State had seen ; he lived there till the year 1654, when he departed this life with all the signs of a devoted Catholic*.

When the King of Candia learnt that we had sent his brother to India, he was very well pleased, for he was in a state of great fear lest we should assist him, in which case he gave himself up for lost. As soon as he left Uva he ordered the Prince's officials who collected the rents, that when he came they should give them to him ; and he sent to demand them telling them that they should not give anything without his order, for they would have to render an account of everything. When he learnt that he had sailed away he took over the kingdom as his own, but did not press the war, so as not to compel us to bring the Prince back to Ceilão; but on hearing of his death, he immediately began all the mischief he could against us.

*†For details see Pieris : The Prince Vijayapala of Ceylon.

CHAPTER XII

How the Hollanders came with thirteen ships to lay siege to Columbo, but failed to effect anything

1642 In January, 1642, thirteen of the Hollanders' ships with three thousand five hundred soldiers appeared off Columbo, thereby compelling us to abandon our territories and leave our three camps as rapidly as possible so as to check their design. Learning, however, that we had more than eight hundred soldiers, and the residents who were no fewer in number, they were afraid to disembark anywhere though they did not fail to keep us in a state of anxiety, marching up and down the sea shore for thirty-five days as they tacked hither and thither. After this when they saw that they could not achieve their object, they anchored at Galle.

When the Captain-General knew that they did not land in the Island, and that the army we had maintained the previous year in the Galle Corla was not sufficiently strong to oppose the force which the enemy would throw into that fort, he abandoned his plan for reducing the district of Sofregão, and divided the five companies we had there among two camps. One was sent to his brother Dom Antonio, as ten were sufficient for holding the King of Candia in check and defending the Four and Seven Corlas. The other four were attached to the Mature camp, which was thus increased to fourteen companies of the choicest troops we had in the Island. The Captain-Major of the Field, Antonio da Mota Galvão, was also with the latter camp, and accordingly the Dissava of Sofregão, with the men at arms of his Province, took up his station at Ceitavaca, a convenient and strong position with a stone fortress which had been erected by Madune, father of Raju ; from there he controlled the district as far as Cadangão.

Dom Antonio Mascarenhas led his army to Manicavare, where he waited to repel the attack which the King ordered his Dissavas to make on the Four and Seven Corlas ; but the fight was carried on with little energy and merely to satisfy the Hollanders, for when we advanced his men withdrew to Candia without waiting for us, and accordingly we had no engagements with them, and those provinces continued obedient to us.

The Captain-Major Antonio da Mota advanced to Mature ; his command consisted of fourteen companies of five hundred soldiers, all in excellent condition, while the Dissava of that district had a large body of our men at arms. We stopped close to Galle, but as the enemy would not come out to meet us, we pushed on to Mature and reduced all the districts of Corna Corla, the Grevaias and Ballave, after which we took our station at Beligão, from where we constantly laid ambuscades against the Hollanders, who however did not venture outside their stronghold. Our enemy of Candia made some incursions on those districts, giving us more trouble and annoyance owing to the rough roads than achieving anything, for they rarely waited for us.

We went on till June in this fashion, and as our chief object was to prevent the Hollanders venturing outside their fortress to collect cinnamon, we moved up the whole of our force close to it. We also hoped, if our Armada came from Goa, to raise batteries against it. We were posted half a league from the fortress in a village called Acomivina, and our blockade was so close that they could not get a green leaf from outside.

This lasted till the end of February, 1643, without the arrival 1643
of the expected fleet ; but a Commissary of the Hollanders, Pedro Burel by name, came with four ships to Columbo to announce a treaty which had been entered into between His Most Serene Majesty King Dom João IV* and the States, to continue for ten years in India. When, however, they insisted on our giving up the Galle Corla, declaring that it was an appurtenant of the fort, the Captain-General argued that for seven months our army had been the master of it right up to the moat of the fortress, while they did not have possession of a palm of land outside its walls ; all that he could do was to give up to them as much as was covered by their guns. Pedro Burel would not agree to this and set sail for Goa

*In 1640 the Portuguese successfully freed themselves from the Spanish yoke and placed Dom Joao IV on the throne. This was soon followed by a Treaty with the Dutch States, with whom Portugal had no quarrel. The Commissioner was Pieter Boreel.

to settle the point with the Viceroy, the Conde de Aveiras, we on our side advising him of our reasons against giving up those lands.

An armistice was agreed upon pending the discussion of this question, and in the meantime we moved our army, and dividing it into two bodies, went to conquer the District of Sofregão and all the other lands in that direction which belonged to the Crown of Portugal,. The expedition was more irksome than dangerous owing to the length and difficulty of the roads. All night long the Chingalas used to worry us by their calls to arms, shouting at us as usual from the tops of the mountains and saying that we were knaves, with only two hours of life remaining. Some of them were caught by our soldiers in the very midst of their abuse, which they had to pay for in ready cash, for some were impaled and others cut open with an axe and left there to serve as an example to the rest.

CHAPTER XIII

How the treaty was not ratified at Goa, and the battle of Acuraça

After reducing the whole of Sofregão, the Captain-Major of the Field retired with ten of the companies to Mature, leaving with the Dissava the remaining four, which were sufficient for the defence of the district. Our army was encamped three leagues from Mature at a village called Acumana, and in a few days we received information there that the war with the Hollanders was to be continued as before, as the Viceroy had refused to give up the Galle Corla. Pedro Burel also landed at that fort all the infantry from his four ships, and they decided to place an army in the field ; and so they did as quickly as possible, choosing out five hundred soldiers and some Lascarins who were with them in the fortress.

As they were aware that we had left four companies in Sofregão and that the majority of our men were sick in consequence of the long marches, they took up their quarters in Beligão, a naturally strong position. Learning of all their movements, we were compelled to march as rapidly as possible to Mature to prevent the enemy seizing the provisions and ammunition whch we had at that port ; after securing these we advanced three leagues inland, halting at a village named Acuraça, which was the same distance from Beligão.

The Captain-Major sent orders to the Dissava of Sofregão to advance with his four companies and men at arms as fast as he could ; but the Hollanders found out our lack of men and that any delay on their part would increase our numbers ; they accordingly moved on to meet us, so as not to lose the opportunity which presented itself. About eight o'clock on the morning of the day following our arrival at Acuraça, some of our Lascarins appeared with the news that they had encountered the enemy on the march, and that they were rapidly approaching us, and in fact were at the time only a quarter of a league distant. The Captain-Major Antònio da Mota immediately sent on the Captain of the vanguard to meet them, and ordered another company to follow and hold them in check.

These two companies met the enemy a cannon shot from our camp, where we received their charge and fought for half an hour, when we were reinforced by two more companies. With their assistance we attacked them with our pikes and clubbed guns ; two others followed after an interval, and so on with the rest. The fight lasted from nine in the morning till three in the afternoon, when almost all the five hundred were either dead or taken prisoners, though the officer who commanded them, João Uvanderlat* by name, the best soldier they had in the Island, escaped wounded with a few of his men. Of our force twenty-five were killed and sixty-seven wounded, the whole number who took part in the fight being two hundred and forty-three, for the rest were very ill. This encounter took place on the 4th of May, 1643.

Our wounded and the prisoners were despatched to Columbo, and on their arrival the Captain-General ordered that none of them should go to hospital, but he begged the chief residents to receive them in their own houses, one or two each as they had accommodation for, so that they might be better looked after. He visited them all in person, encouraging them to greater efforts, and according to the report of each man's behaviour at the fight he thanked him in complimentary terms, slipping under his pillow a paper with twelve, fifteen or twenty S. Thome† according to the birth, position or claims of each, and saying " Your worship has a brother here, for that is what I am to you, and I am not lacking in funds with which to help you ; before this sum is exhausted let me know, so that you may not be in want of anything. " In consequence of the kindness and praise and cheering words of the Captain-General, all the soldiers were eager for an opportunity of showing their valour.

In a few days the Dissava of Sofregão arrived with his four companies and men at arms : the Captain-General also sent eighty soldiers from Columbo, who were distributed among the companies which were short of men. This brought up the numbers in the army to the same figure as before, and

*Van der Laan. He was subsequently sent to Batavia to be tried for mismanaging this affair.

†These gold coins were struck in Goa in 1548 and were of the value of £1.2.4.

so we started from Acuraça, the Captain of the advanced guard being sent by another route to attack the Dissava of Candia, who was in Corna Corla with a large force. The journey gave us greater trouble than the opposition which the enemy offered ; for we found his quarters empty though not of stores, which latter we took for ourselves ; and wheeling round we joined the army close to Acomivina, occupying the same position as we did when the question of peace was being discussed. Here we remained from the end of May till the octave of Christmas, maintaining a strict blockade on the fortress without allowing them to cross the moat ; we had no further encounter with them, as they did not venture to come and meet us.

On the seventeenth of December there arrived at Galle sixteen ships with four thousand five hundred men who were soon landed. They did not venture to attack us, as we were encamped in a strong position surrounded by marshes ; but they seized the two roads which we utilized for maintaining communications and for the convoy of provisions from Columbo. We were few in number while they appeared sufficient not only to defeat that army but also to capture our fortresses. On the night of the twenty-sixth we broke camp and retired four leagues inland, halting at a village called Mapolegama ; here information was brought to us the following day by our spies, that immediately on our departure the enemy had gone on board. We struck camp at once and hurried towards the sea shore over rough roads, reaching Belitote worn out with the march. We began to erect huts in which to spend the night ; but after finishing our work, towards evening we sighted their ships going in the direction of Columbo ; we could therefore do nothing else than advance along the sea shore, always keeping them in sight.

On reaching the Panature river they sent all their *lanchas* armed with musketry and some falcons, to prevent our crossing ; but they failed in their object, for the Captain of the vanguard occupied the mouth of the river with his men, while the soldiers dug pits in the sand from which they kept up the fight the whole of that day, during which the army succeeded in crossing without any danger. The enemy seeing this, and as it was night, withdrew to their ships. The following day both they and we appeared before Columbo.

The Captain-General had warned his brother Dom Antonio Mascarenhas of the enemy's numbers, and the latter had with all care marched with the army of Manicavare and was halted at Negumbo as he had been ordered. Immediately on our arrival at the city the Captain-General despatched the Captain-Major of the Field. Antonio da Mota, to Negumbo with six companies, and left the Captain of the vanguard, Pedro de Sousa, in the city in command of the rest, to assist wherever necessity arose.

CHAPTER XIV

The battle of Negumbo where Dom Antonio Mascarenhas and Antonio da Mota Galvão, the Captain-Major of the Field, were slain

On the 3rd of January 1644 the enemy's ships reached Negumbo where Dom Antonio Mascarenhas was stationed with his army of ten companies containing three hundred soldiers and some invalids who were on their way to Columbo ; the six companies brought by Antonio da Mota Galvão the Captain-Major consisted of a little more than two hundred men. On the morning of the fourth the enemy landed unopposed half a league to the north of the fortress ; whereupon our two detachments got ready to receive them, informing the General of their plan as the enemy were already on land. He ordered Pedro de Sousa to start with eight companies of three hundred soldiers and some native troops who accompanied them. 1644

The enemy advanced in seven squadrons of six hundred each, all in one line and thirty paces from each other. In consequence of the jungle no more than two were visible in front of our men, and thus they advanced beating down the field. Dom Antonio Mascarenhas and Antonio da Mota Galvão, the Captain-Major of the Field, decided that each should attack the squadron which was in front of him. They came on our men, who were drawn up on a square patch of ground, at their usual rate of march, and after exchanging the first volleys they were attacked by us sword in hand, and the greater part of their two squadrons destroyed. But as our men were careless, we found ourselves outflanked by the five squadrons which advanced to charge us at a quicker pace. We were in disorder, running here and there killing those who had escaped from the two broken squadrons, being thus disorganised and without any formation for receiving their attack. The enemy after two volleys fell on us so vigorously that everyone who was not hit by the balls trusted to the speed of his legs. Dom Antonio Mascarenhas and the Captain-Major of the Field, seeing that everything was lost, threw themselves among the enemy with a few followers and sold their lives dearly.

The enemy continuing on their course with the same rapidity, reached the fortress which they at once entered*; for the only garrison it had for its defence consisted of a few invalids. The Captain who defended the gate was so handled that he could not be recognised for his wounds, and in less than three hours, from ten in the morning till one in the afternoon, not a Portuguese was left alive either in the armies or the fortress.

The eight companies of us were making our way at full speed by that difficult shore, which consisted of five leagues of loose sand, where one went as much backwards as forwards. Half way on the road, at a place called "The Little Well,"† we met the fugitives with the tragic news of this unhappy disaster. We advanced another half a league to try and collect any of our men, but as we learnt from some Lascarins that the defeat was complete, we halted till our commander received orders from the Captain-General to retire at once ; which we did, reaching the city three hours after nightfall.

In this encounter there fell several Captains and Officers and the Captain-Major of the Field, who was a *casado* of Columbo. The whole city was plunged in grief, and when the Captain-General saw this, early in the morning he put on his richest festal robes and paraded through the city ; stopping wherever he heard lamentation, he would send a message by the Captain of his guard to tell the one who was weeping that there was no reason for tears, but rather for much rejoicing that such honoured cavaliers had so happily sacrificed their lives fighting with the enemies of our faith for their King and country. The action of the General and his messages had such an effect that there was no more public display of grief, nor did any one put on mourning, and it was an excellent means for preventing their attention being distracted when the victorious enemy were so near.

*9th January, 1644.
†Pocinho. I have been unable to identify this spot.

The Captain-General at once set about reorganising what remained of the army of his brother Dom Antonio and the detachment of the Captain-Major Antonio da Mota, out of which he formed eight companies of two hundred and eighty men, our losses in the fight being a similar number ; with these we had a total of sixteen companies of five hundred and eighty men. The Captain-General appointed João Alvres Beltrão as Captain-Major of the Field, a position which he had sometimes filled, till an appointment was made by the Viceroy; he stationed the army at the Salt Tank* close to the city, and placed three companies with the Lascarins who remained with us, at the passage of Betal. He thanked all these natives with marks of great affection and compliments and his own money that they continued with us ; for as a rule they deserted whenever we sustained a defeat.

*Tanque Salgado, now the site of the Colombo Dockyard.

CHAPTER XV

THE ATTEMPT OF THE ENEMY TO REACH COLUMBO, THE EMBASSY WE SENT TO THE KING OF CANDIA, AND THE SIEGE WE LAID TO NEGUMBO

AFTER capturing Negumbo, the Hollanders spent twelve days in fortifying the position and converting it into a regular fort, leaving only the houses of the old position, and destroying the stockade which they themselves had erected when they took the place in 1640. They built four bastions at the angles of the square, placing in each eight pieces of artillery of eight, ten and twelve pounds, the bastions and walls being of earth. Having finished the work they came in search of us, proceeding by the sea-shore till they reached the passage of Matual, intending to cross the river at the tpoint where they found us defending it.

They anchored their ships and *lanchas* at the mouth of the river; and with the baskets with which they had come provided they erected a battery of eight demi-cannon, with which they hoped to dislodge us from our position. The Captain-General as quickly as possible sent from the city some artillery, which we placed on platforms on the higher ground. The enemy kept up the fight for ten days, receiving heavy loss, for they stood exposed on the shore where every shot of ours had its effect: and since the Captain-General took a personal share in the defence, many of the chief residents joined us, and the bastions of the city were manned by a large number of people from within. When the enemy saw the loss they received without any benefit, at dawn on the morning of the 27th January they reshipped the guns and started back for Negumbo, disembarking six hundred men there to serve as garrison; the fleet then returned to Batavia. The General issued pay to our army and ordered it to proceed to the Four Corlas; and as we did not find our Candian enemy there, we went into camp at Manicavare, where we remained till the middle of April, in the interval making our preparations to lay siege to that fortress.

The first step the Captain-General took was to send an embassy to the King of Candia, the reception of which was more satisfactory than the successs it achieved; although the General did attain the object he hoped for, which was that he should not disturb us in the siege we intended to lay to Negumbo. He further begged him to enter into a perpetual peace, though he was well aware that the King could not do so in consequence of his alliance with the Hollanders; but he made the attempt so as to get what he would give us.

He sent the King a handsome present, which was accepted; but to the proposal for peace he replied that it would not suit either the Portuguese or himself, for he could not show himself wanting in what he had agreed with the Hollanders. Our evil disposition and greed had compelled him to look for some one to help him against the oppression he received at our hands. Owing to his affection towards us he had been sorry for our troubles, for he had always had more to do with the Portuguese than with his own natives; he had grown up among us from his infancy, and there was nothing he knew except what we had taught him. But there was no remedy now. He remembered the peace which the King of Portugal had entered into for ten years and that as in the previous year we would not give up the Galle Corla, the peace had not been declared and the war was continued as before: in consequence we had lost Negumbo and so many good lives. The settlement of the question must be made in Portugal, and would undoubtedly reach us at the end of the year. He also was well aware that the King of Malvana neglected no point, and it was of advantage to him to retake that fortress. As far as it was possible for him, he would assist us by not disturbing our territories, so that we might be able to supply ourselves with provisions and men of war and service for carrying on our undertaking. As for anything else which related to his personal affairs, the King of Malvana could look to him for help, and he would find in him the greatest willingness.

He presented the ambassador with some jewels and sent him away with this reply, which left the General very well satisfied as this was all he wished for.

At the end of March there arrived in Columbo Fernão de Mendoça who had been a prisoner in Uva; he was now appointed Captain-Major of the Field, and by the middle of April his command consisted of four hundred soldiers, including some fidalgos. The Captain-General moved from Columbo with this force, while the army of Manicavare did the same ; we met on the 18th of April at the passage *dos Lagartos*,* and reached Negumbo the following day. The enemy greeted us with a salvo of cannon balls, and we began to prepare our quarters The natives brought fascines, and our men exerting themselves, we finished the work in three days. Three more were spent on the approaches to the fort where we raised two batteries, one of eight and one of four demi-cannon, among which were two borers.

On the 25th we opened fire with nine hundred and fifty shot and a hundred and twenty fire-bombs, or rather what looked like them than were so in reality ; for the ingenuity of our Captain-General had led him to have a mortar cast, and in place of bombs he had a large number of coconuts filled with powder, and well covered with tow, resin and other stuffs, which made them look what they were not ; and though the enemy made fun of these bombs, they caused them a deal of anxiety. For the church and houses in the old fort barely accommodated two hundred, and four hundred were lodged in thatched huts, and had always to go about with buckets in their hands to protect them from these fire-balls, which however effected hardly anything else.

The enemy had built on a little island in the middle of the river,a fort which was occupied by a Captain with fifty men and two pieces of artillery. With these they caused us much loss ; for they could fire into our trenches from the flanks, and compelled us to protect ourselves as much from the citadel as this fort. The Captain-General ordered the Captain of the vanguard to seize it one night, and gave him two additional companies for the purpose. We crossed over to the islet in the morning watch and carried it by assault, killing the whole garrison except five who crossed the river by swimming.

We continued the bombardment and set up two more batteries and also made some progress with our trenches,

*The Passage of the Crocodiles, being a translation of the Sinhalese name, Kiṁbulàpitiya.

for we were at a great distance from the fortress. At the same time we changed the guns, for the continuous firing had made it possible to introduce one's arm through the touch-holes. Owing to our distance the walls did not appear to be at all damaged. Our men had little experience of sieges; the Captain-Major considered his valour sufficient for the greatest tasks—an opinion begotten of inexperience in siege work—and so, apart from his great courage—a quality which was not lacking in the rest of us too—he was also vain. Everyone began to despair of ever taking the place, whereupon the Captain-General summoned a Council of his corporals and Captains. A certain German, who had been a servant of Senhor Dom Duarte and who had crossed to India by land to serve this Crown, chanced to be present at the Council; and when he saw that everyone's talk showed more courage than military knowledge, he addressed them as follows :—

"Gentlemen, I am a German, and my affection for the Portuguese has brought me from my country to these distant parts only to serve you; for I was brought up by one of your Princes, and I therefore sought for an opportunity and the first which offered after my arrival in Goa was this, in which I endeavoured to take part following His Lordship the Captain-Major who is here. While serving my lord and master in my own country I have been present at several fights and sieges, where they followed tactics different from the present. I do not say this because I find a lack of valour in the Portuguese gentlemen; rather I venture to say it is because they have too much. In my opinion we should push on with our trenches and draw closer to the fortress. At present we are a considerable distance from it, and the lay of the land does not permit us to reach the enemy rapidly. When there we have the choice of three plans, not only for capturing the place, but for entirely wiping them off. The first is this; the General should send by the river some beams and make with them a wooden castle. If we do so, as the position is small and affords no shelter, they cannot avoid the destruction our musket fire is bound to cause among them; for we will be covering them, and as they have their artillery dismounted, it is of great help to us. If this is not to your taste, we have twenty thousand men at arms, and a similar number of camp followers. When we get to the foot of the fortress, which is a small square of fascines and earth, we should with these men take with us as much brushwood and firewood as is available close at hand, and pile them up against the bastions and walls and set them on fire. This will compel the enemy to escape to the shore and since Your Worships' courage will not permit you to finish the business except by arms, we can stand at the foot of the ramparts, as we select the most convenient hour and time as somebody who is over them for falling on them. But standing as we do at this distance they do not feel themselves forced to surrender, nor have we any means of compelling them ; because after all with their six hundred men they have three garrisons."

I know little, but in my opinion the stranger was not far from the track when he spoke about getting near the ramparts by means of our trenches ; for our last trench left us at a distance of two horse-gallops from the fort.

The answer given to the German was that Portuguese needed no castles in the air nor to beat about the bush ; the assault would take place the next day by daylight, so as to give everyone an opportunity of showing his courage. Orders to that effect were issued immediately and everyone directed to get ready, which they did, confessing and receiving the Communion. They enemy had fixed on the side of the moat, which was not more than four palms in depth, some stakes two palms long and sharpened to a point, to serve them as caltrops. Every night a Chingala whom they paid highly for the service, used to go out and collect a large quantity of these ; from him the enemy also learnt of our movements for all the plans of our officers were known to the public. Accordingly they were ready to meet our assault, since not even that night did they fail to send him on his task.

At dawn on the 25th of July, being the feast of St. Jago, we were all in the trenches ready for the assault, and there we remained scorched by the sun till ten o'clock ; about eleven o'clock we received orders to charge. We advanced at a run, each to the position which had been assigned to him. On reaching the moat we had no difficulty in crossing it, nor were the scaling ladders we had brought with us required, for the bastions had been so demolished by our fire that we were able to scale them easily. We found the garrison drawn up in good order on the esplanade, the ramparts held by pikemen, and the bastions by musketry. Some carried hooks with which they dragged several of us within, and cut them in pieces ; many were killed at the traverses and flanks, and in spite of heroic efforts we failed to effect an entrance. No one could show his head without being killed or badly wounded for their parapets and walls had the escarpment facing the interior of the fort, so that the enemy never exposed himself.

We kept up the fight from eleven in the morning till two in the afternoon when we retired, being three hundred and ninety-two out of the nine hundred and fifty who had started ; for the rest, including the Captain-Major of the Field Fernão de Mendoça, Francisco de Mendoça, brother of the Conde de Val dos Reis, with several fidalgos and Captains of repute lay at the foot of the wall. Three days later those of us who remained alive, removed our artillery and other stores and retired to Verganpetim, a village between Negumbo and Columbo ; here we laid some ambushes for them and remained at them till December of the same year.

CHAPTER XVI

The declaration of peace and the departure of Dom Filippe Mascarenhas as Viceroy of India, with the arrival of Manoel Mascarenhas Homem as General of Ceilão

At the end of December aforesaid, six of the Hollanders' ships arrived at Columbo conveying the General João Mansucar* who brought the orders of His Most Serene Majesty Dom João IV that we should give up all the territories which belonged exclusively to the fortresses of which they were masters at the time of the presentation of the order, which should be done within a year of its date; at the time only nine months had expired. He also brought patents and orders from His Majesty by which he was pleased to appoint Dom Filippe Mascarenhas to be Viceroy of the Dominion of India in succession to João da Silva Tello, Conde de Aveiras, and Manoel Mascarenhas Homem to be Captain-General of Ceilão. A similar message was received in a short time from the Viceroy at Goa, who added that with the monsoon, a fleet would come to escort the new Viceroy and convey at the same time the Captain-General. The peace was proclaimed
1645 in Columbo for eight years, for two years had already passed since Pedro Burel's arrival with the arrangement which had proved abortive.

The day of the declaration of peace was celebrated with much rejoicing on sea and land. In the distribution there fell to the Hollanders not only the Galle Corla, but all the district from the river Alicam to the Grevaias, extending over twenty-six leagues of coast and stretching ten inland, thus embracing the whole of the district of Corna Corla, adjoining the district of Bebiliagama, which belonged to the jurisdiction of Sofregão'; whereas the Galle Corla, which we had refused to give them on the first occasion, was not a fifth of these districts in extent. The territories of Negumbo were divided at Verganpetin, which is half the distance from Columbo,

*Jan Maetsuycker.

up to Madampe, a distance of eight leagues along the coast, and six leagues inland within the Seven Corlas : all this was thick cinnamon jungle.

One of the conditions of the settlement was that friends and enemies were equally included ; and so before the peace was declared the King of Candia was invited by the Hollanders to join in it, according to His Majesty's treaty with them. The King replied that he would join it, but that he had no desire for any intercourse with us ; he would stay in his lands and we in ours, and if any wrong were committed on either side by rebels, it would be the duty of the side where it was committed to punish the guilty and to afford all compensation and satisfaction the case called for. With this condition the treaty was accepted by all parties ; and the King did not fail to fulfil the promise he had made to our ambassador when we laid siege to Negumbo, nor was he found wanting the whole time that the peace lasted, so far as it concerned our being annoyed by his men. Those who had been residents of Galle returned to their villages which were situated in the districts which fell to the Hollanders, and they did not in any way prevent their enjoyment of them. By this means they staved off the hunger from which they had suffered for five years since the loss of that fort ; in the same way all the others who had villages in those parts continued in their enjoyment, for the Hollanders only took what belonged to this Crown.

The Viceroy Dom Filippe straightway sent and obtained the bones of his brother Dom Antonio Mascarenhas, who had been buried by the Hollanders with due respect. He directed them to be conveyed by sea in a *manchua* draped with black and when it reached the Bay, the Viceroy went with his attendants in the same fashion to receive them. The funeral was conducted with all pomp, the bones being interned in the Convent of the Mother of God belonging to the Capuchins, where the obsequies were celebrated with the honours due to the career of this fidalgo. In the same mourning he started for Goa, which he reached in March 1645, in the fleet which brought the General Manoel Mascarenhas Homem.

After some time the Hollanders seeing that the districts under Negumbo would not obey them owing to the King of Candia being estranged from them about some money

1646 they demanded from him, resolved to send an army outside the fort to reduce them into obedience. The force consisted of three hundred and fifty soldiers and some Lascarins from the same districts who followed them ; they encamped on their extreme boundary, which adjoined the limits of our territories in the Seven Corlas. The King learning where they were, determined to compel them to retire to their fortress, since according to all appearances he could not defeat them ; and as our territory lay between, he sent a submissive request to the Captain-General Manoel Mascarenhas for permission to pass over them without obstruction, to destroy our common enemy.

The Captain-General in his simplicity, and under the belief that he was effecting a great stroke of policy, sent him a very polite reply and allowed him all he asked for : His Highness he said had full liberty to pass that way and everything was at his orders, for we were anxious to serve him and please him in everything. With this permission the King promptly advanced with twenty-five thousand men through our lands, receiving great honours according to the orders issued to the inhabitants. He found the Hollanders strongly encamped and protected so that he could not attack them as he had hoped ; he accordingly besieged them and forced them through lack of food to surrender at the end of twelve days; he took the men prisoners to Candia, and distributed them among the villages.

The Governor of Galle on being informed of this incident sent a complaint to Candia that not only did the King not pay his debts, but he was also making war against them and taking their men prisoners ; his duty was to show them favour, as it was for his sake they had come to the Island, where they had both received and inflicted great loss at the hands of and on the Portuguese, and incurred heavy expenses ; but now he had unreasonably turned on the very men who had served him so well and placed a bridle on his enemies, and made him unquestioned lord of the whole of his kingdom at the cost of their own blood ; he had also formed an alliance with their enemies, while he should rather bear in mind that all the benefits had been received from the Hollanders, and that it was to them he should be grateful.

On receiving this complaint the King did what his own convenience dictated, and did not pay any part of the sum that was demanded from him ; he replied to the messenger that he freely restored all the prisoners he had in his power, a thing which neither he nor his predecessors had ever done to the Portuguese : the Governor should know that he undertook the expedition more to test our hearts than to wage war on them, and with that object he asked for our permission to cross our territory, a privilege which we had willingly and eagerly conceded him. He had accepted it to show them whom they had to deal with in us—a race of men who never kept faith or honour with any nation on earth ; and now it was seen clearly how we dealt with people who were of almost the same religion and country as ourselves ; for this reason they should not trust us, for in every possible way we were sure to employ towards them our customary falsehoods.

The Hollanders were astonished at learning this, and were grateful to the King for restoring all their men; hearing what the King said of us, they took steps to drive the Portuguese out of their territories, applying many insulting terms to them, and would not allow anyone to possess his village, although the agreement was that they should only receive what belonged to this Crown. This step was felt most severely by the residents who had belonged to Galle ; when that fortress fell they wandered round begging, and at the making of peace they resumed enjoyment of their villages ; and now these unfortunates, loaded with their children could only lament and take to begging till they were entirely wiped off.

CHAPTER XVII

THE DECLARATION OF WAR, WHICH LED TO A MUTINY IN THE COURSE OF WHICH THE GENERAL MANOEL MASCARENHAS HOMEM WAS DEPOSED AND IMPRISONED

NOTHING occurred during the continuance of the treaty, except the incident of April 1646 between the Hollanders and the King of Candia which we have related. The garrisons which we kept up during the period were stationed at the following posts. At Manicavare there were twelve companies of four hundred and fifty Portuguese soldados with the Captain-Major of the Field in command, a Sergeant-Major, and the Dissava of the Four Corlas who had a good force of Lascarins. At Sofregão, another camp of five companies with one hundred and ninety Portuguese commanded by the Dissava of that district. The Dissava of the Seven Corlas lived in his Province at a village called Lahoa with two companies of *topazes** Christians born at Columbo and good soldiers though blacks, and some Lascarins from his district. The Dissava of Mature was encamped at Alicam with ten or twelve Portuguese companions from among the poor residents who had come from Galle, and who remained with him to draw the allowance of soldiers—a notable case of wretchedness in the Island—and some native soldiers. In Caliture there was a garrison of a Captain of infantry with his company; there was another such at a stockade which had been made of timber at Canasture, where we had a store of provisions and ammunition which were taken by river for the use of the army of Manicavare. In Columbo the Captain-General desired to have some companies as a garrison and he created three, each of eighty soldiers, which were stationed in that city. At Malvana, in place of those who used to go there in time of war to convalesce, he formed one company of the old soldiers and invalids who would hamper the march.

*They were of mixed descent, as their name implies. Topaz has the same origin as Dubash, viz dwei, bashai, two languages.

Subsequent to the making of the treaty the garrisons we maintained in the Island were distributed in this fashion among these stations, and so we remained till the middle of October 1652, when two Hollanders arrived at Columbo from Galle 1652
to announce the commencement of hostilities. And as peace is often harmful, on their arrival our great vexation showed itself both in our language and in our hospitality, for both were different from what was due to our reputation. Suffice it to say that the house where they were lodged for the night was so badly provided with everything, that they were not even supplied with a light. This led the whole city to lay the blame on the Captain-General for letting his exterior show the feeling of his heart, and hence arose a public complaint against him which gave rise to disgraceful suspicions unbecoming a fidalgo such as he was by birth, and the rules of service which he followed.

There was living in Columbo a fidalgo of position named Ruy Lopes Coutinho, a man beloved by all for his good qualities and accomplishments. He met some of the other leading residents and they discussed the matter I have referred to, and also the orders which had been issued to the armies to retire on the city as soon as they heard seven guns fired. Seven foot-muskets had also been placed on a mountain to convey the signal to the army which was beyond hearing of the cannon. It was well known to them that the armies had been supplied with provisions for a long time from their own districts, and that in place of these being ordered to be sent to the city as quickly as possible, since there was a deficiency there, in view of the orders which had been passed their own scanty stock was being sent to the armies. In consequence everything was in a ferment in Columbo, and they began to entertain dark suspicions regarding the Captain-General.

All this and everything else which any one who was present spoke of plainly, were discussed. Ruy Lopes Coutinho, desiring to make light of the most serious charge, remarked : "I do not think, gentlemen, that our General has the faults you mention : but he appears to me to be too slow a setter for these hares." This saying did not escape being repeated, and on the same day he was set upon by some of the soldiers who had come from Goa, and so badly wounded that they left him for dead.

This incident confirmed the suspicions of the chief residents, and they concluded that the continuance of such a Government must lead to their inevitable destruction. They hastily sent a letter to the army at Manicavare on which depended the chief strength and defence of the Island, for it contained all the best troops and the veterans in the country. In this they represented everything which I have related as being the truth, adding whatever they wished to infer or invent regarding the Captain-General, so as to exasperate the soldiers and thus help on their design. One charge was that subsequent to the declaration of war a large quantity of corn had been sold to the Hollanders by his orders ; if this were so, it would have been a shameful crime ; what I can affirm is that the General could be better accused of negligence than of disloyalty.

The soldiers did not require much encouragement to induce them to believe everything the letter contained, for in September the Viceroy had warned them that the treaty was over and the war begun again. Immediately on receipt of this information the Captain-General had sent an order to the camp that no one there was to speak of war or military matters; any officer hearing such talk was to kill the offender, and any one showing himself negligent in doing so, even though he were a Captain, would be punished as a traitor for not carrying out his orders. This was probably intended to prevent the Hollanders learning that we were aware of what was going on.

He also sent as Captain-Major of the Field his own son-in-law, a fidalgo named Lopo Barriga, with instructions to visit the quarters in which the companies were lodged, every night. This he did at irregular intervals, counting all who were within ; which trouble might well have been spared ; for the soldiers in camp, as they were among Chingalas and Gentiles, did not stray from their companies and only trusted each other. No such inquisition had ever been practised in Ceilão before, nor any order of such strictness against the discussion of military matters issued ; all the soldiers were worried, and therefore they easily accepted as correct and placed reliance on everything the residents of Columbo wrote to them.

The letter was addressd to two brothers, also natives of Columbo, that its contents might be communicated to the chief men in the army. In it they besought the army to have pity on the misery which threatened the city and not to allow its temples to be profaned by heretics, and above all to remember that that Island was the heritage of the King our Lord, who had earnestly recommended its defence to them, and there was not a palm of it which had not been watered with the blood of the Portuguese : on speed or delay, whichever they chose, depended now their salvation or destruction. In this state of affairs, as the soldiers were waiting with their baggage ready for the seven shots which were to give them the signal for retiring to the city ; as they also saw that double the quantity of provisions which was needed was sent to the camp from the city, while they had plenty from the district as I have already stated: they were all in a state of despair. Each one so far as he was concerned, was the opponent of the Government ; not only the residents and soldiers but also the clergy and friars, great and small, were all of the same opinion.

The two brothers to whom the letter was sent were named Gaspar and Antonio da Costa, young men of repute and good behaviour, subject to the duties of people born in the country, and fitted to conduct the business with all care. They communicated the matter to some friends, experienced soldiers who appeared to them capable of keeping the secret and of undertaking a matter of this nature. These in turn communicated with others in whom they had confidence, and in all there were fifty private soldiers, who maintained profound secrecy.

Two days later at dawn they sallied out with their arms, carrying a crucifix in front of them, and calling out : "Long live the Faith of Christ, and death to bad Government !" All the others who were in their quarters hastened out at hearing the shouts, and joined them with their arms. Owing to the facts I have stated, all were of one mind and no one asked what was the reason or cause of this revolution : for those known to them appeared quite sufficient ground for opposing the Government. Whenever anyone went to his quarters to fetch his arms, his two neighbours stood ready with theirs, and so they followed each other. In a moment there was not left a soldier in that Camp who did not join the movement ; had anyone wished to keep away he could not have done so, save at the cost of his life.

They reached the house of the Captain-Major Lopo Barriga, where they were met by his nephew, a cavalier who was beloved by all for his high qualities, and a veteran and greatly honoured soldier of the Island named Luiz Alvarez de Azavedo. The former requested that they should do no damage to his uncle's house, and for this he was killed. The Captain-Major came out of his house ; he was at once arrested and taken as he stood to the Columbo road, surrounded by some sixty men ; they did him no harm, and gave him sufficient native troops to escort him to the city. A brave Captain named Jacinto de Madureira, who was devoted to the General, was killed in trying to oppose them ; another named Bernardo da Cunha Cavallo, who came out of his house to see the disturbance, received a blow with a sword which laid open his skull from the brow to the left ear. The following day they made a list of the effects of the Captain-Major Lopo Barriga, and gave them over to an Arache, who conveyed them to the city with his men.

Their first act was to select a private from each company, such a man as the leaders of the movement knew would suit them ; these twelve formed the Government and decided all complaints. And to prevent it being said that any one was the chief among them, they erected an altar in the house where the Captain-Major gave audience, placing thereon a tall crucifix ; anyone who had a request to make drew up a petition which he placed at its foot, and he found the reply in the same place. Some Captains applied for permission to proceed to Columbo, and it was granted to them ; the rest continued at their posts, and were treated with the same respect as if the Captain-General or Captain-Major were there. If the Board of Government issued any order with a penalty attached, any infringement of the order was promptly punished with great severity.

Eight days after this outbreak the Captain-General sent to the Camp a leading citizen, a man who was held in respect, to announce that he would give the mutineers a guarantee that none of them would at any time be punished for what they had done. They refused to receive this message by word of mouth, and requested him to communicate it in writing. Their reply was that he should tell Manoel Mascarenhas Homem to resign the Government, unless he wished to be turned out of it by force, for thus it was in the interest of the service of God and of His Majesty. If he would not do so as they desired, he was not to send any one else with his message to the Camp, under pain of being well punished for his boldness in doing so.

On receiving this resolution the Captain-General sent urgent orders to the army at Sofregão to abandon that district and to retire to the city, so as to prevent their joining or having any communication with the mutineers. The army obeyed at once, abandoning a quantity of provisions and cinnamon which they had collected. He also ordered two hundred soldiers who had arrived from Goa and formed a garrison of six companies at Caliture, as well as the usual garrison of that place, to abandon the fortress and withdraw to Columbo. The same orders were sent to the company at Malvana, and with the three which formed the garrison of Columbo, he had eight hundred soldiers. At the same time he sent a message and begged the King of Candia to be graciously pleased to fall on our lands with all his forces as quickly as he could and not to leave one of those rebels alive. The King wished for nothing better ; he started at once and came near the camp, where he tried to win the men over to his service with many promises.

They replied that His Highness should not interfere in such a matter ; if he did not wish for something unpleasant, he should leave the territories of the Crown of Portugal. Seeing the resolution with which they spoke and that they might easily carry out their threats, the King broke up his camp and went into quarters to Arandure, from where he made fresh attempts to win them over. The mutiny had now lasted twenty days, during which the residents of Columbo had not failed to urge them with repeated letters each day to abandon the districts under any circumstances and come to the city. They accordingly started, and as the King was encamped a little more than a league from them and saw his hopes slipping away, he attacked the rearguard and kept up the fight a distance of half a league up to Duravaca ; but in consequence of the heavy loss he received he would not descend the mountain. After a march of three days the army reached the passage of Nacolegam, having two men wounded in the fight ; here some of the residents of the city met them, and welcomed them on their arrival.

At this time they had with them in the army a native of Columbo, brother-in-law to Gaspar and Antonio da Costa, a wise, clever and very brave man who had grown up in the midst of war and had there given proofs of high soldiership. He had rendered a very good account of himself in the most difficult enterprises which the Generals had entrusted to him, but was living in retirement in consequence of the treaty ; his name was Gaspar Figueira de Cerpe and he did not fail to take an important share in this matter. At the beginning of the insurrection he was living in his village three leagues from the camp, and here after eight days a company and some Lascarins were sent to bring him as a prisoner—a clear subterfuge, since they allowed him in the camp all the liberty and comfort which was possible. As soon as they reached Nacolegam, they entrusted the army to him, promising to obey his orders to the death in the matter of the deposition of the Captain-General. He accepted the command on those terms, and immediately took steps to appoint such men as appeared to him satisfactory, to be Captains over the companies which had none.

The following day he passed the river to the Columbo side and encamped in a palm grove called Tanque Salgado, a cannon shot from the city. At the end of three days, about two o'clock in the afternoon, he formed all his men into a squadron and advanced on the city. On his reaching St. Thome, which was distant two hundred paces from it, the Captain-General who was on the bastion of St. João which lay in front, seeing the squadron advancing, ordered nine cannon loaded with ball to be fired. These were discharged, but did no harm to anyone. All were waiting for them, for when they commenced their march Gaspar Figueira, to encourage the soldiers, had said : "Some shots will be fired at us, but after that we shall have the city at our orders."

And so it happened ; for at the first shot all the infantry who garrisoned the bastions and other posts abandoned them, declaring to their corporals that they would not fight with their brothers. They joined the residents, priests and friars, and went to the Parish Church where were assembled all the people. From here they proceeded with the Host to where the General stood and from there to the Queen's Gate ; this they threw open, and gave a signal which Figueira well understood. For at the very time this movement took place within the city, he ordered his squadron to march to that spot ; and when they reached the gate, the populace allowed no one to enter till Gaspar Figueira had taken an oath in the name of all that no harm would be done to anyone who was within. After this the whole squadron entered and occupied the bastions with all quietness and moderation, while the rest of the infantry who were within took their orders from Gaspar Figueira.

By this time the Captain-General with his son Estevão Homem, his son-in-law Lopo Barriga, and Luiz de Miranda Henriques, had withdrawn to the Church of S. Domingo, where Figueira sent them a message by a priest that it was desirable for the security of their persons to send them to a place where he could set guards to keep them from any danger ; for without such there might chance what could not be remedied. They replied that they were quite ready to carry out his orders if it would secure them their lives. The four were lodged in a tower called the Tower of Homage, which the same General had built on the bastion of Santo Estevão, and Figueira placed over them as guard a company of fifty picked soldiers under the command of his own brother-in-law Gaspar da Costa.

The following day there met in the Council Chamber an assembly of the Councillors. Among them were Gaspar Figueira de Cerpe, the Captain of the City, Alcaide Mor and some of the principal residents ; their object was to elect a Governor till such time as the new Captain-General appointed by the Viceroy should come from Goa. At the election each one tried to get the chief place for himself, but at the suggestion of Figueira they decided to entrust the power to a Committee of three, who were to take joint action in every matter. The three chosen were Gaspar de Araujo Pereira, who had held the offices of Captain-Major of the Field and Captain of the City : the second was Dom Francisco Rolim, and the third Francisco de Barros ; but these were only Governors in name, and Gaspar Figueira had the power ; they only approved of what he decided on, and he it was who saw to the execution of everything.

As he saw that the city was suffering from lack of food, he started with twelve companies leaving the rest behind in garrison, since the Hollanders were lying off the Bay with nine ships to intercept any relief. He advanced with this force to the Seven Corlas, where the King of Candia had fortified himself with a strong stockade on the mountain of Vedava, and had collected there all the supplies from that district. He was warned by his men of Gaspar Figueira's advance to the mountain, but remained there relying on the strength of the position, which seemed impregnable. However the city's need and his own anxiety to show that the Portuguese had inherited the courage of those ancestors, from whom the enemy had often not been safe in their own mountains, not only spurred on Gaspar Figueira, but he was very pleased with the intention of the King to wait for him. After four days, about ten o'clock in the morning, he reached the foot of the mountain and without taking any notice of the enemy, halted his army to refresh his soldiers after their forced march. This greatly increased the King's confidence, for he thought that our men had not made up their minds to attack him, and that we hoped to force him to retire by threats alone.

As soon as it was night, Figueira ordered the Dissava João Botado de Seixas to advance with six companies and five hundred Lascarins by one of the two defiles in the mountain. His instructions were to get alongside the enemy's fortification by break of day in perfect silence, and that the beat of drums and tambourines would give him the signal to charge on that side, while Gaspar Figueira remained with the rest of the force who were an equal number. Both detachments climbed the mountain with difficulty each by its own path, and at break of day the charge was sounded.

They advanced with great courage from both sides, but found the enemy very strong in their defence, as they had seen our men. Their resistance was such as to compel Gaspar Figueira to be the first to approach and enter the stockade, serving as guide and example to the rest. After effecting an entrance a fierce struggle followed, which lasted till the King retired by a hidden passage, which he kept prepared for that purpose. On his side the Dissava found a vigorous opposition, but after Figueira had effected an entrance he was abe to make his way in and assist in putting the enemy to flight. In this encounter our men cut off the heads of more than three thousand, the rest escaping through the thick forest or each as he could. Our losses included the Captain Rodrigo Delafeta, and Antonio de Freitas Babilão, an Alferes and five soldiers; these all lost their lives bravely; and of the blacks two Araches and three Lascarins.

After this victory the natives of those districts returned to their allegiance; their *cules* and baggage animals transported to the city all the provisions, of which there was such a large stock that for a long time the lack of it was not felt, and it was sold at the usual price. After breaking down the stockade our men proceeded by way of Negumbo, cutting off the heads of some Hollanders in the suburbs, and seizing a large quantity of cinnamon which was found collected in those districts, they then returned to Columbo to rest for some days; and there he was highly praised by both great and small, because within sixteen days of Figueira's departure he had so easily destroyed the enemy, and supplied the city with such an abundance of provisions.

While the army was resting, news was brought that the Hollanders had erected a strong stockade of wood at Angoratota, and garrisoned it with a hundred and forty men, one company of Bandanese, and four hundred Lascarins from the district of Galle, and that these were ravaging the provinces of Reigan Corla and Salpiti Corla. Gaspar Figueira was at once on the move, with fifteen companies of infantry and some black folk who followed the Dissavas of Mature and Sofregão, the former being Francisco Antunes, and the latter Antonio Mendis Aranha. He took this force as the enemy were two leagues from Caliture, which they had fortified and garrisoned with five hundred men. On reaching Angoratota he found them strongly entrenched with the necessary defences, redoubts, flanks, and a moat which protected the fortification; he therefore did not assault them as he had intended, and as he could not accomplish his design he laid siege to the place.

On the third day, in view of the loss we had sustained and as the enemy had stores of all kinds to last for a long time, he ordered two cannon of eight pounds to be brought from the city. On their arrival the first shots compelled them to call a parley and they surrendered on terms, being allowed to march out with their arms, drums beating, banners flying and their matches alight, till they reached the Captain-Major's quarters where they were to surrender their arms and remain in Columbo till the first favourable season for going to Goa, when they would be transported in our ships to Portugal. The Lascarins who helped them were not included in this capitulation, but they were all sent to the city to work in the powder-factory. As for the Araches, seven were ordered to be impaled and six to be cut open, on the plea that they were our subjects, although they were residents and natives of the District of Galle. Gaspar Figueira ordered the punishment of these thirteen Araches under the pretext that they were traitors to the Crown of Portugal; but his real intention was to intimidate the natives who followed the Hollanders. He returned victorious with his prisoners to Columbo, and was received with great applause by all.

While we lay before Angoratota, the King of Candia sent a Dissava of his with a large force to invade our territory and to attack our Dissavas, so as to divert us from the siege we were laying to the entrenchment of the Hollanders. Lazaro de Faria, the Dissava of the Seven Corlas, was at Catagore, a naturally strong position six leagues from Columbo; with him were three companies of infantry, and two thousand Lascarins from his district. The Candian Dissava did not venture to attack him owing to the strength of his position, but he advanced to meet the Dissava of the Four Corlas, João Botado de Seixas, who was in a village named Thiara, also six leagues from Columbo, with forty privates, all volunteers and men of respectability, and one thousand five hundred Lascarins.

The Candian Dissava had a force of eighteen thousand and came on with great confidence to the attack. Our men, who were on marshy ground without any entrenchments, faced the charge and fought fiercely for two hours, but were in great straits as the whole fight was at the point of the spear and the sword. But God so ordained that in the thickest of the fight their Dissava fell dead : otherwise none of our men would have escaped. The enemy retired with some heads they had cut off from our men, leaving about six hundred on the field ; nor was the victory a cheap one for us, for out of the forty they killed nineteen of us, taking away the heads of some, while the rest were severely wounded and some died later. Our black folk bore themselves in this encounter with such intrepidity that they rivalled the Portuguese in courage ; of them we lost four Araches and one hundred and twenty-eight Lascarins, while a large number were wounded.

As soon as Gaspar de Figueira de Cerpe reached Columbo with his prisoners, he was informed that the King had invaded our territory, and was encamped at Metapetim, a strong position in the Four Corlas, with a large force ; from there he threatened all our territories, and several had gone over to his side. Although distressed with the incident at Thiara, he delayed only two days to rest his troops and to collect ammunition and other stores. After preparing everything, he started with thirteen companies of infantry and the same Dissava João Botado who commanded the Lascarins of all the territories subject to us. In four days he arrived where the King was waiting for him ; who would have acted wiser had he not done so, as he was obliged to retire in confusion to Candia with the loss of a large portion of his troops. A great quantity of food was found in his camp, and this supplied the army for many days, the rest being despatched to Columbo.

And learning that a Candian Dissava was overawing the whole of the district of Anapanduma with a large force, he went in search of the enemy who did not wait for him, and as he retired our Lascarins cut off the heads of some of his men. The consequence was that all these districts returned to their allegiance to this Crown, together with the district of Bulategama which had been ours for many years, but of which the King had assumed possession since the making of the treaty. I cannot say how we ignored or acquiesced in this ; what I can assert is, that these villages were really the property of the Royal Crown.

These victories left both our enemies demoralised and disheartened, the city amply supplied with food, and all the districts once more in allegiance to His Majesty. Gaspar
1653 Figueira encamped with his army at the strong fort of Arandure, where he remained till May 1653.

CHAPTER XVIII

THE ARRIVAL OF FRANCISCO DE MELLO DE CASTRO AS CAPTAIN-GENERAL, WITH AN ACCOUNT OF SEVERAL ENCOUNTERS AND OF THE BATTLE OF TEBUNA

AT the end of May aforesaid Francisco de Mello de Castro arrived as Captain-General, having been appointed thereto by the Viceroy, the Conde de Obidos ; he was a fidalgo of advanced years and had occupied the position of Governor of the State. He brought with him two hundred soldiers and a fidalgo born in Bacaim, Dom Alvaro de Ataide by name, as his Captain-Major of the Field ; this latter had filled the same post on the death of Fernão de Mendoça who was killed by the Hollanders in the assault on Negumbo. The Captain-General brought an amnesty issued by the Viceroy regarding the deposition and imprisonment of the Captain-General Manoel Mascarenhas Homem, who was still a prisoner with the others in the Tower of Homage. This he sent on land before disembarking. It announced that in the name of His Majesty he pardoned for ever all the offences which had been committed in the matter of the deposition of the Captain-General Manoel Mascarenhas and the subsequent proceedings, whether done by the soldiers or by the residents of whatever degree or condition.

This amnesty was read in public, but everyone in the city declared that they would not accept it : for a pardon is what is given to criminals, and not to people who with such zeal and trouble had saved the Island from falling into the hands of the enemy, as would inevitably have happened if they had not nipped in the bud those evils which their experience pointed out to them. They had all expected honours and rewards at the hands of His Majesty for what they had done, and they begged the Viceroy to hold an inquiry into the matter and those who were guilty were ready to receive punishment as if they were traitors. This reply was committed to a public instrument and sent to the Captain-General, with a further message that his lordship should come on land and take over the Government of the Island, for every one there looked to him for protection as to a father. The Captain-General landed, and immediately ordered them to take Manoel Mascarenhas Homem and his three companions out of prison, and they and all their friends and servants, none of whom had been injured, embarked for India in the same ships.

The Captain-General made no change in the position held by anyone, as he found that they had borne themselves with such distinction in the fighting against both the Europeans and the natives. And because there was a lack of food in Columbo, owing to the supplies which usually come from the Coast during the favourable season not having arrived, he ordered Andre de Seixas da Silva, Dissava of Sofregão, to enter those districts and collect everything he could, which was to be despatched with all care and speed to the city. He gave him six companies of two hundred and twenty soldiers to accompany him, and as his Lascarins were so few as not to exceed two hundred, the Dissava of Mature, Francisco Antunes, joined him with three hundred of his men. After two and a half days march they reached Cadangão about ten o'clock in the morning, when without any warning they suddenly fell in with the King of Candia, who was terrorising the district with twenty-five thousand men with whom he immediately attacked our rearguard.

The Captain Manoel Fernandes de Oliveiros was in charge there with his company, and he faced the enemy with great courage. When the Dissava Andre de Seixas saw that he could not retire, nor resist such over-whelming forces unless he went by the mountain of Openava—a very difficult matter to achieve owing to its being at a distance of two leagues—he was compelled by the necessity of the case and the danger in which he was, to advance with the vanguard in an attempt to seize the mountain. All along the road the enemy pressed the rearguard hard, attacking them boldly and continuously; but at every point their hopes were frustrated and they left many of their men dead, because those who were there fought as if their sole desire were to sell their lives dearly; for if they cut off one head from our men, it was as good as the destruction of the whole army owing to the fury with which they repeated their attempts. But God so ordered that by four o'clock in the afternoon we reached the mountain without any loss save that of a surgeon whom they killed with a ball. Owing to the surrounding circumstances this was one of the most honourable incidents which took place in the Island, but I will not give details, so as to avoid being tedious.

By nine o'clock at night our men encamped in a village, passing the rest of the night with their arms in their hands, and the following morning by eleven o'clock they reached Ruanella. The Captain-Major, Gaspar Figueira de Cerpe, was with his army at Arandure, where news was brought to him by some natives of the fight and retreat. He set out to meet the men and thanked every one in general in complimentary terms, for their gallant behaviour, singling out a few for their special merit. After spending two days there, when he was about to start for the camp, he issued an order that five out of the six companies should accompany the Dissava Andre de Seixas to occupy Grubebe, a very convenient position for checking any incursion of the King on that side ; the remaining company, which was that of Manoel Fernandes de Oliveiros, was sent to Nossa Senhora da Vida. The Hollanders used often to attack this position, which was situated in the suburbs of the city, and its occupation was of much advantage, as not only did it prevent the frequent attacks of the enemy, but at the same time that company with some Lascarins cleared the district of Salpiti Corla where they had some skirmishes : for as the Hollanders were at Caliture they would frequently send bodies of men to disturb these districts.

They had sent a Captain with sixty Carbineers and three hundred Lascarins from Galle to the other bank of the Panature river ; and as that river could be crossed on foot, they easily made incursions as far as the *Morro* killing and robbing the natives who lived among those palm groves, thus inflicting much loss on the city. For the residents had their plantations depopulated, and they had therefore no one to cultivate them. In view of this the Captain-General ordered the Dissava of Mature, Francisco Antunes, to go as secretly as possible and dislodge this body from its position, and to take with him for the purpose all the companies he considered necessary. The Dissava, who had been brought up in this kind of warfare and was very expert thereat, only wished for the company of

Oliveiros and his own Lascarins, who did not amount to three hundred in number. He started and made his way with great trouble, as the paths were interested by marshes. One morning, before the enemy were aware of our men being there, he had the opportunity of cutting off the heads of the greater number of them ; the rest escaped and fled into the jungle, but they were so demoralised that they did not again attempt to send people to disturb the suburbs of Columbo.

The Captain-General realized that so long as the Hollanders remained at Caliture, our territories would not be free from continuous invasion, as they had rebuilt the fortress with good entrenchments and occupied it with a garrison of five hundred men who frequently sent out bands to the Reigan and Salpiti Corlas to ravage them. This not only caused great hardship to the city by depriving it of the food which came from there, but much loss to the Crown by driving away the inhabitants, and thus preventing our obtaining a stick of cinnamon from them, or our men of war and service. To prevent these vexatious inroads he determined to place there an army consisting of twelve companies of four hundred and fifty soldiers, with the Dissava Francisco Antunes who led a few of his Lascarins ; Antonio Mendes Aranha was appointed Captain-Major and provided with everything necessary.

Before starting he was ordered to invade the district of Negumbo, which he did with great energy, causing much destruction among the new crops and the cattle, which he both slaughtered and captured. He also seized a large stock of cinnamon which they had collected. After killing some Hollanders the army turned inland, crossing the Reigan Corla and making for the Caliture river. His plan was to cross it and occupy a position which he had selected on the same side of the river as the fortress stood, for he could thus take up his quarters close to the mouth of the river. This place was called Diagam, and was two leagues distant from the fortress.

We found this held by the enemy, who guarded the passage against us for five days with repeated and continuous volleys from both sides ; but finally they withdrew to the fortress with some killed and wounded. Our army crossed the river, though not without similar loss, and occupied the post. From here we made frequent inroads on the Hollanders' lands, which led to the majority of them being abandoned by their inhabitants, and at the same time we kept up our blockade of the fortress. All this inflicted such loss on them and caused them so much trouble, that they were no longer able to maintain their communications with Galle by land.

Our army continued this blockade from the end of July
1654 1653 till March the following year, without any encounter worth mentioning taking place ; for the Hollanders did not have sufficient forces to meet the numbers they thought our army had, from the vigour with which it made its incursions. In Columbo there was a dearth of food, and as it was from here that the army was supplied, the latter found itself without provisions. This compelled the Captain-Major Antonio Mendes Aranha to go after all to look for it in the enemy's land. To intimidate them he advanced close to the fortress, and for twenty-four hours stood challenging them to battle. As they would not come out, the following day he went and encamped at Macune where that night they met some forty Carbineers led by the Captain of the Galle Corla, who was himself killed with the majority of his men. In the morning we went by way of Alicam, Velipene, and other villages to see if we could obtain provisions ; we made the circuit of the whole of the Pasdun Corla and only found some fruit and cattle which we used for food, but no rice, as the country was depopulated. The army accordingly made its way back to the river, which we reached on the twenty-fifth of the same month, and lodged close to our encampment.

On the morning of the twenty-sixth some Lascarins came and announced that they had met the Hollanders, accompanied by a large number of native soldiers and some Bandanese, marching out to meet us ; they made this movement as they had received information that our army was suffering from lack of food and had a large number of sick, both of which were really the case. The Captain-Major summoned the Dissava and Captains and told them what I have stated, asking them for their opinions as to how matters should be decided. All declared that that same want of provisions prevented their retiring, and they were of opinion that we should march to receive them. We started on this resolution, but had not advanced five hundred paces when we met them in a village called Tebuna. After the first volley they were attacked by our men sword in hand, and after a confused fight of two hours the enemy were routed and put to flight, leaving in our hands not only the victory but also the fortress of Caliture ; for when those who escaped reached it, they quickly got together the few men who had been left as a garrison and immediately started for Galle.

In this battle the Bandanese—they are the people of Banda, an island close to the Malucas—fought with such valour that it was not possible for anyone to excel them, and it was by their swords that we sustained the greatest loss, though they were only a band of fifty. I shall relate one incident in proof of what I say. A nephew of Jane Mendes de Vasconcellos who had the same name served on this occasion as a private soldier, and in the course of the fight he ran one of these men through from chest to back. The fellow finding himself run through bravely caught hold of the pike with his hand, and raising himself by it without allowing Jane Mendes to draw it out, and reaching up to him, stabbed him with his *kris* below the left shoulder penetrating the right lung, and then fell dead at his feet. We lost in the fight forty-five men including the two Captains Manoel de Sousa, who commanded the vanguard, and João de Lafeta, as well as some officers, and had seventy-one wounded ; but though we expected to find some food with which to satisfy our needs, we only found arms and ammunition ; for they were travelling light and without baggage, and their fortress, where they hoped to retire victorious the same day, was only two leagues off.

That night we received information that the enemy had retired at full speed from Caliture, abandoning the fortress. In the morning we went to seize it and found there a store of rice, which served to kill the hunger of so many days, three pieces of artillery, some arms and ammunition, and a strong fortification which they had erected on the skirt of the hill with a stout rampart, moat and drawbridge, and which was capable of sustaining a long siege. After resting three days and satisfying our hunger, the Captain-Major placed Domingos Sarmento de Carvalho, who had succeeded Manoel de Sousa as Captain of the vanguard, in charge of the position, and sent him to Alicam with ten companies, and Francisco

Antunes the Dissava of that District with his Lascarins. He left two companies as a garrison for the fortress, and after making these arrangements returned to Columbo on the plea of ill-health. As soon as the army arrived at Alicam it encamped alongside the river and soon reduced and re-populated the district of Pasdun Corla, making many inroads on the territory of Galle, laying hands both on the people and the cattle, and taking all the large stock of cinnamon they had collected to Columbo, without leaving a stick behind.

In a short time reinforcements reached the enemy from Batavia, whereupon they formed an army with which they took the field, and went and encamped on the other bank of the same river of Alicam in front of our army, at a village called Bentotta. They brought with them four pieces of artillery of eight pounds with which they began to disturb our men, hoping to dislodge them from their position and compelling them speedily to protect themselves behind a stockade of palm trees. The Captain-General Francisco de Mello de Castro was informed of the arrival of the enemy and the blockade they had begun, and he sent to the army two pieces of ten pounds which we placed in suitable positions, and with them inflicted no smaller damage than they caused us.

The enemy had in his camp seven hundred European soldiers and two companies of Bandanese, and more than one thousand Lascarins from his territory under the command of the Captain of the Galle Corla. As our force was much inferior in numbers, we sent among them spies who kept us informed of their movements ; from these we learnt that they intended to cross the river one night and to fall on our army at break of day, for they knew that it did not consist of more than ten companies with three hundred men at the most, and that it was short of the two who formed the garrison of Caliture.

As matters were in this condition the Captain-General thought it best to entrust the command of the army to a person of experience ; and accordingly appointed Gaspar de Araujo Pereira to be Captain-Major over it.

Immediately on his arrival there he learnt from the reports of spies that the enemy intended to cross at night the river at Velipene, as has been stated. To prevent their doing so in safety he ordered to be set there for six successive nights, an ambuscade consisting of five companies under the command of the Dissava. The orders given to him were to wait till three hundred of the enemy had crossed and then to attack them, as he himself was ready with the rest of the companies to come to their aid at the first shot. The enemy had spies among us who informed them of how we were waiting for them ; and when they saw they could not carry out their plans in this fashion, they arranged the following stratagem by which means they achieved their object.

One afternoon from four o'clock till eight they kept up such a continuous bombardment as to make it clear to the whole army that some new movement was in contemplation ; for they used to fire only whenever they saw our men, but now they were doing so without any reason. In the morning not a soul was to be seen, and it looked as if they had retired. As the Captain-Major had held the command for such a short time, he was very well pleased and had no doubt the enemy had retired in fear ; and without any inquiry or verification, he ordered three companies to cross to the other side and all the rest to get ready to follow. To the whole army this order appeared to come from one who had more of confidence in his own opinion than experience ; for he should have considered that the enemy had a force superior to our own, and that he had no imperative reason weighing on him : even if our forces were the superior, he had the protection of a broad and deep river lying between.

The three companies crossed and landed where the enemy had been posted ; they found here no sign that the enemy were still near, and this was the best warning they had for moving cautiously when they advanced to explore the grove of trees at the turn. They had not gone twenty paces when they were attacked by the whole of the enemy's force in front and on the flanks ; but before they could fire we had done so, for our men were moving warily, thinking their retreat a pretence. The enemy did not give us more time than to draw our swords, though they were of little use as we found ourselves attacked on all sides in such fashion that the greater part were killed. Those who survived threw themselves into the river to escape by swimming, and several lost their lives by musket balls in the water. All that I have related took place in the course of one hour, and out of the three companies and a few privates who accompanied them, only six men were saved.

There was profound grief at such a loss happening on such an inconsiderable occasion. On receiving news of it the Captain-General sent for Antonio Mendes Aranha who had been Captain-Major of this Camp and who was living in retirement at Columbo, and begged him to repeat his success at the battle of Tebuna by which Caliture had fallen into our hands ; as he could not but obey, in a few days he came to Alicam bringing with him one hundred and twenty soldiers to replace the deficiency caused by those we had lost. He found the enemy in the same position as before, for the same day they opened a bombardment on us, and so they continued for little more than a month till one night they passed the river to our side and gave us battle, the result of which we shall see in the following chapter.

CHAPTER XIX

The battle which was fought between us and the Hollanders at Caloamodra, and how the King of Candia attacked our army which was in the Four and Seven Corlas

One the night of the 16th of November of the same year 1654 the enemy crossed the river at Velipene, half a league above our encampment, without attracting the attention of our men. At dawn they were close to our army, which as soon as it was aware of the fact rapidly retired by a path in the jungle. The enemy followed at full speed in the direction of the shore, and in little more than half a league came on our men at a village called Caloamodra. It was not possible to avoid battle and both sides fought furiously for an hour and a half, our men making a virtue of necessity; as they could do nothing else they set on them sword in hand and forced them to check the impetuosity with which they had determined to break our ranks, their battalions being stopped with heavy loss. Even though the victory remained with them our advantage was not small, as they had to allow us to retire to Caliture in good order with our sick, wounded and baggage. In this encounter we had nineteen killed including one Captain, and twenty-three wounded; and our two pieces of cannon were left in the enemy hands, as we were short of men for taking them away.

Towards evening our army arrived at the fort and encamped at the distance of a cannon shot in a grove of palms at a spot called the Garaveto*, which is a gate for the wooden palisade which defended that post. On the morning of the twenty-third the enemy arrived there and fought the whole day in the hope of breaking through; but we kept up a stout resistance till nightfall, when they were forced to retire with many dead and wounded. They did not stop at Alicam but crossed

*The gates of thorn which defended the approaches to a town, S. Kadawata.

the river and encamped at Bentota, from where they maintained their hold over their own lands and left ours free.

Dom Alvaro de Ataide, whom the Captain-General Francisco de Mello de Castro had brought as his Captain-Major of the Field, was not anxious to exercise his office with either army, but was allowed to remain at Columbo ; for he thought that as the Captain-General was a fidalgo of advanced years, he would himself succeed to the post. As age had rendered the Captain-General experienced and he was also good-natured, he pretended not to understand, and sent in his place his own nephew Antonio de Mello de Castro, whom he had brought with him ; he had come from India and was nearly destroyed at Nossa Senhora da Ajuda. He was appointed to the post once occupied by Gaspar Figueira de Cerpe, who retired to the city.

When the King of Candia saw him gone from the camp, he collected all the men he could in the short space of time, and advanced to threaten it, but instead of attacking he seized the roads leading to Columbo, thus cutting off communications and supplies, and held him as if he were besieged. Now Antonio de Mello de Castro had no knowledge of the tricks and stratagems of the Chingalas nor any experience of the country, and he would not make up his mind to give them battle. This led to a general complaint in Columbo regarding the removal of Gaspar Figueira. When this reached the ear of the Captain-General, he sent for him and begged him by his affection for himself and because it was to the advantage of His Majesty's service, to start as soon as possible with the companies which were available from the garrison of the city and the others which he had ordered from Caliture and to raise the blockade ; after doing this he was to continue in that post.

He had already ordered Antonio Mendes Aranha to retire with his army within the fort and to send him four companies which he selected for the purpose. These started on the road with all the speed the urgency of the case demanded ; but when they arrived at the Hill*, they found another order for them to return. For Gaspar Figueira, as soon as he had

O Morro, the Mount Lavinia of to-day.

taken leave of the Captain-General, did not return to his house, but started with five companies which formed the garrison of the city, and some friends of his among the residents who volunteered to accompany him, and had already routed and dispersed the forces of the King, who retreated to Candia leaving in our hands a large supply of provisions and arms such as are the usual spoils of war, and a great number of slain.

Gaspar Figueira took over the command of that camp and ordered that the companies from the garrison of Columbo and the residents who had accompanied him on this occasion should remain with Antonio de Mello de Castro. Many compliments were exchanged between these two and then all started, the latter for Columbo and the army to re-subdue the districts which with the arrival of the King had risen in revolt. It had some skirmishes with the Candian Dissavas, who retired in confusion leaving a large number of slain and four hundred prisoners ; though it was not usual to give quarter between us and the Candians but always to cut off the heads of all on both sides, yet the previous year the King had given orders to his men not to kill the Portuguese who were captured in battles, assaults, or by their *bagueas*, but to bring them to him alive without killing them. And so they did, and all that were captured were given over by his orders to the Mayorals of the villages in his kingdom with a command that they should be well treated; and they were accordingly treated with respect.

Bagueas are the same as brigands among us. The King would usually send them into our territory to kill any Portuguese they found in his village, or any soldier who was going to or returning from the camp, or the priests who were administering the sacraments to the Christians in their parishes, several of whom lost their lives in this service. In consequence of the King's order Gaspar Figueira directed his men to spare the lives of those who were captured in the jungles after the rout, and they were employed in the magazine and powder factory. This he did so as not to seem less humane, though the King's intention was different, as we shall see later.

1655 When the King saw how many times he and his Captains had been defeated by Gaspar Figueira de Cerpe, and that for all his exertions he had never succeeded in dealing him the least reverse—a matter which caused him great annoyance—he proceeded to assemble all the forces he could, being determined to defeat him this time and to win back the prestige which he considered lost. With this object he ordered his Dissavas to bring to Candia forty thousand men at arms, including three thousand with foot-muskets, nine thousand with espingards, thirteen thousand with bows, fifteen thousand with pikes, with a company of fifty Carbineers from Holland as his personal guard ;* all his noblemen also accompanied him on this occasion ; with this great armament he started from Candia on the 21st of March 1655.

Gaspar Figucira was at the time on the boundaries of the Four and Seven Corlas, checking from there the King's inroads on those districts. He had no notion of the King's plan, when he received information of the forces and the resolve with which he was marching on him. He saw that a retreat would involve in ruin not only those districts but also all the others subject to the jurisdiction of this Crown, which would submit to that King, and that it would not be possible to save them without great trouble and a large force, while we had only the army of Caliture, which, as it was not sufficiently strong to meet the Hollanders, had retired to that fortress. If the King became master of those districts, Columbo would be soon involved in absolute ruin in consequence of the famine to which it would be exposed ; for while the natives gladly rendered allegiance to the King, it was only under compulsion that they did so to us. For these reasons he determined to give battle ; even if he were defeated, the damage consequent on a retreat would be still greater ; by a battle he would preserve at least the prestige of the Portuguese arms, which, with their lands, would be lost by a retreat ; while by fighting he placed the matter in the hands of God.

Many thought Gaspar Figueria careless of the lives of others, but they were wrong, for he was very charitable,

*Twenty-four Hollanders, with their officers, were sent on 12th May, 1653, as a body-guard for the King.

careful, and devoted to the interest of the King ; he was tireless, brave, and very resolute in anything he undertook ; he treated with disrespect and contempt the man who failed in his duty, but to the one who worked with zeal and gave satisfaction he was a devoted friend, open handed, and keeping his house and purse, which was never large, as free as if he were the master of great riches. He was accordingly hated by the bad and adored by the good.

CHAPTER XX

The battle which the Captain-Major Gaspar Figueira de Cerpe fought with the King of Candia in our Territory, and the siege which the Hollanders laid to Caliture

Gaspar Figueira had eight companies of two hundred and forty Portuguese and one company of thirty-seven *topazes* while the Dissava of the Four Corlas led four thousand Lascarins. With such limited forces not only did he decide to meet the King, but also to push forward and save him some of the trouble of marching. In order to discourage their men, who expected us to retreat owing to our forces being too small to meet such a great army as theirs, not only did he wait for them but also advanced with great resolution to meet them on the road ; and it cannot be doubted that often boldness is the chief factor in victory.

As soon as this experienced and brave Captain was informed that the King of Candia was coming with such forces, he paid those spies in whom he had confidence heavily and warned them under penalty of death not to tell any one in the army of what they knew, nor would he inform any of his own friends ; for though they were men of valour, some of them might not have the requisite discretion, and so they might chance to intimidate the army. When it was time to give the password, he issued orders that they were to march at daybreak and that their food should be served out to the soldiers at three o'clock. There was nothing strange in this, as that was the usual hour for distributing their breakfast whenever they intended to march.

They started at daybreak, and by seven o'clock in the morning our Lascarins encountered those of the enemy, who were also on the march.* As the Captain-Major was aware of the state of things, as soon as the first shots gave him warning, he advanced quickly to the front between the companies, appearing as if anxious to find out the cause, and

*At Kotikapola, in the Beligal Korale.

making all hasten their pace he joined the vanguard. They saw a valley a short way off covered with innumerable enemies, and without halting he commanded them to sound the charge so as to encourage our men, being himself the first to dash into that vast crowd, as if he considered their numbers nothing.

The King had advanced on our front, and on the two flanks they showered the balls from their foot-muskets and espingards; the arrows were so thick that they looked like clouds. All would have been horror and confusion if they had to deal with a nation without the experience of similar fighting which we had, for we hurled ourselves on them with repeated volleys, Figueira in the forefront of everybody sword in hand, doing more in his own person the work of a thunderbolt than of a Cerpe; for death was the only refuge of those who received his strokes. The fight lasted more than an hour; the enemy could not withstand us and in their great fear everyone only looked for some means of saving himself without being influenced by the affection and respect he owed his King; who seeing matters in this state, in despair attempted to throw himself in our midst, but as he was prevented by his nobles he took more sane advice and hastily retired with his company of Hollanders, hiding himself in a dense marshy jungle between two mountains till night-fall, when he was able to make his way to Candia.

Our Lascarins cut off eleven thousand heads and took alive one thousand six hundred prisoners, with seven hundred foot-muskets and innumerable espingards. This was the greatest victory we had ever obtained over the natives. All the arms and prisoners were sent by Gaspar Figueira to the Captain-General, and throughout the city great thanks were rendered to God for his singular mercy, and the Host was exposed in all the Churches for three days, which were observed with rejoicing and illuminations.

The Captain-Major rested his troops for some days and then advanced and took up his quarters on the frontiers of Candia, the remotest district belonging to us, in a village called Motapali, from where he protected the Four and Seven Corlas. The King retired to his palace and would not show himself to any one for eight days; after that he gave audience dressed in mourning, which he continued to wear till we had surrendered and been driven out of Columbo; nor during the whole of that period would he allow his Dissavas to invade our territory or escort him with the white rods which are the principal insignia with which they accompany their Kings when they go out of doors.

At the very time that the King descended on our lands with the forces we have described the Hollanders laid siege to Caliture, as they had arranged to attack us simultaneously from both sides; for if the King met with the success they expected, they would have found no difficulty in capturing the position. With this object they came with nine hundred soldiers and all the Lascarins from their territories, and posted at the mouth of the harbour which the river formed, three ships and two *sumacas*, landing from them seven heavy pieces of artillery with which they formed two batteries. They also sent into the Reigan Corla four hundred Lascarins supported by a Company of their own Carbineers, to ravage those lands; there our black folk succeeded in capturing two of their Lascarins, whom they despatched to the Captain-Major Antonio Mendes Aranha who was within the fortress, and there they gave him the information I have related.

In order that the enemy might realise that the siege would not prevent his checking their raids from the fortress itself, he prepared some *tones* and by night placed the Dissava on board with some Lascarins and a company of infantry. They sailed upstream in the shadow of the trees so as not be noticed, and by dawn reached the enemy's position where they disembarked and made all haste, but were only in time to find their fires in the huts; for they had hastily retired the previous night on the orders of their commander, who had received notice of the result of the battle with the King. The same day they removed their artillery on board, and in the afternoon raised the siege, which had lasted for eleven days, withdrawing to their quarters at Bentota. They had killed five of our soldiers and wounded eight in the course of the siege, but they did not fail to receive heavier loss, as our arms were not idle.

On the 18th of May we learnt that Antonio de Sousa Coutinho, who had been appointed Captain-General of the Island in succession to Francisco de Mello de Castro, had arrived from Goa with two hundred and fifty soldiers in nine galliots. By the force of the current and the carelessness of his pilot he was taken to the point of Galle, from where two ships sallied out with a fresh wind and with their guns easily scattered the galliots which were only driven by oars and were soon disabled. Antonio de Sousa Coutinho was forced to make good his escape round the point with seven of his boats, for the remaining two could not follow him as they had the majority of their crews killed and themselves almost destroyed by the artillery. Their only chance was to run on shore at Gindure, two leagues from the fort, where those who escaped were taken prisoners ; the remaining seven made a circuit of the Island and reached the Kingdom of Jafanapatão.

Antonio de Sousa Coutinho immediately landed and sent word that on the 15th of June some companies of infantry should be at Aripo, where he would arrive on that day with some men from that Kingdom. On the receipt of the news, a large number of men at arms and of service to carry his baggage were hastily despatched, and the Captain-Major Antonio Mendes Aranha offered to go with four companies from the garrison of the city as his personal guard. All reached Aripo on the day fixed, and without delaying there in a few days the new Captain-General entered Columbo, where he took over the Government. With the money which he brought from Goa he paid the soldiers one quarter day's pay, for they had received none for one and a half years and were consequently badly off for clothes.

CHAPTER XXI

How the Hollanders came with a powerful fleet and laid siege to Caliture which they captured

At the end of September a fleet from Holland reached Galle with their General Giraldo Holfot* who had full powers and supervision over all their possessions in that State ; this fleet consisted of eighteen ships and two *patachos*† and conveyed six thousand soldiers. After a few days spent in the fort in learning the state of affairs in the Island from experienced men, as to where it would be best to begin the war, he decided that the first position to be attacked was Caliture, so as not to have it on their rear and also as it contained the best troops we had employed in the war. Taking five hundred men from Galle and his General Master of the Field, he started with this force of six thousand and five hundred, leaving Adriano Uvandremed‡ in charge of the fort with a garrison large enough for its defence. On the second of October he reached Caliture, and the fleet which anchored off the estuary landed some artillery with which they planted three batteries, posting three thousand five hundred men on the Columbo side of the river so as to prevent our sending any relief.

The garrison of the fort consisted of twelve companies of four hundred and seventy men ; for the new Captain-General had strengthened it with a hundred of the men he had brought with him and five cannon of eight pounds. The enemy pressed it hard with their batteries without however much effect owing to the strength of the walls which they themselves had built of the clay they had dug out of the moat, and consequently its defences and garrison were such as to make it capable of sustaining a prolonged siege ; and there is no doubt that had they tried to carry it by assault, as was their General's intention, the enemy would have lost, did not

*Gerald Hulft, Director General of India, at one time Secretary of the Town of Amsterdam.

†Pinnaces.

‡Van der Meyden.

his Captains who had experience of the Island persuade him to change his plans.

But since as a rule we kept in our forts in this State but scanty supplies, in eleven days the want of provisions and ammunition compelled the besieged to ask for a parley, and they surrendered on the following terms :—

They were to march out of the fort in military order as was our custom, carrying their arms, matches lit, flags flying and drums beating, with two pieces of artillery loaded and on their carriages ; in this order they were to march to the General's quarters where they would be disarmed ; the soldiers and petty officers were to be taken to Batavia and sent from there in their own ships to Holland ; the Captains were to be sent to Persia that summer, and the Captain-Major Antonio Mendes Aranha, since he was a *casado* of Columbo, was to remain in Galle till they concluded the war that year : if they failed to take the city, they would send him to his house; otherwise they would send him wherever he wished.

On these conditions the fortress surrendered on the 14th of October 1655. The terms of the capitulation were punctually carried out, for they also calculated on the difficulty the men would experience in returning to Ceilão.

CHAPTER XXII

The battle which we fought with the Hollanders on the shore of Moroto

When the Captain-General learnt that the enemy were besieging Caliture in such force, he ordered Gaspar Figueira de Cerpe who was with his army at Motapali, to abandon the country and to go and relieve the fort, moving by way of Columbo so as to provide himself with necessaries; immediately on receiving this order Gaspar Figueira started. The King of Candia had been speedily informed of the arrival of the fleet at Galle, and he was also told of the forces it had brought. When his nobles heard of this, they tried to persuade him that it was a good opportunity for His Highness to invade our territory, and take his revenge for the past as soon as the army had withdrawn. But the King checked them and said. "Let us leave them alone, for they have quite enough to occupy them, and I will not agree to attacking them on the road." Our territory was accordingly left unmolested and quiet—a rare incident whenever we had to make a retreat.

On the 13th of October Gaspar Figueira entered Columbo with his army, and found ready some men from a fleet which convoyed some *champanas* of provisions: these were going to form the cinnamon galliots and to convey back the Captain-General Francisco de Mello de Castro. This fleet consisted of ten rowing vessels or *fustas* as they were called, with two hundred and forty soldiers under the command of the Captain-Major Nicolao de Moura. On the 15th Gaspar Figueira was ready to start for the relief of the fort, when seven galliots arrived with three hundred soldiers who had been despatched from Goa by the Conde de Sarzedas, who had arrived as Viceroy of the State. He accordingly delayed another day to allow these men to disembark and rest. With these reinforcements he had a force of nine hundred soldiers in twenty-four companies, none of the men being above thirty-five nor under twenty years—the finest troops that had been seen in the Island for many years.

On the morning of the 16th Gaspar Figueira started on his march and halted at the *Morro*, when he was informed by the people of the country that the fort had surrendered two days before. He immediately sent word to the Captain-General, who replied that the spies were not speaking the truth, but that in any case he should take the relief force there, and if the fort had surrendered, post them at the passage of the river to prevent the enemy approaching Columbo. By the time this order arrived the latter had already crossed the Panature river, which is two leagues from the *Morro*. On sending information of this, he received a final order from the Captain-General to start the next morning and give battle to the enemy wherever he found him.

At six o'clock on the morning of the 17th, which was Sunday, the Captain-Major broke camp. He had not advanced more than a league when on the Moroto shore the two forces came in sight of each other, and without either reducing its pace they charged with great courage. The Hollanders had a very large force, which exceeded six thousand four hundred soldiers and a fair number of Lascarins from the district of Galle, men who were in no way inferior to the best in the Island ; but to our men the whole of Holland seemed a trifle, since they found themselves with an army larger in numbers than any that had encountered the Hollanders on any previous occasion. The fight was carried on furiously at the point of the spear for an hour nad a half without either side getting the advantage, though they caused us heavy loss with four field pieces. But as our numbers were not sufficient to cover the whole shore, the enemy seized the opportunity to advance with a large squadron by our right flank, thus hemming us round in such fashion as to compel us to turn our backs on them. We lost in this battle five hundred and twenty men, and those who escaped had to trust to their heels, for they gave no quarter to any one who fell into their hands. Our loss included the best Captains we had in the Island and some fidalgos.

CHAPTER XXIII

How the Hollanders besieged and assaulted the City of Columbo

That day the enemy came and encamped at Nossa Senhora da Vida, a little more than a cannon shot from the city, and on the next day, which was the 18th, the Captain-General formed those who had escaped from the battle into companies. And since the Bastion of S. João was the one most exposed to the enemy, and its extent was very small, as it was an old-fashioned eight sided one, and not strong enough to resist their bombardment, he ordered it to be overlaid on the outside with earth and fascines. In order that the enemy might not prevent the work by occupying the houses which were on S. Thome, from where they made a commencement, he selected a Captain to be stationed on that very bastion with five companies to man it, the gate of the city, and the casemates. They occupied the shore which lay between the enemy and the fort, and sinking pits in the sand they maintained such a continuous fire from them, that the enemy not only found it impossible to prevent the overlaying of the bastion, but they also worried them at their battery. Our men were engaged at this work for five days, in the course of which the overlaying was concluded as designed. On the morning of the twenty-sixth the enemy's battery was completed and armed with five demi-cannon and one of thirty-eight pounds, and from there they bombarded us the whole of that day, inflicting some loss on us at that same bastion, more however through the fall of the parapets which were of stone, than from their balls.

To return their fire we erected as speedily as we could a platform on the shore at the foot of the bastion of S. João, a very convenient spot, arming it with two demi-cannon and also one of thirty-eight pounds. With this we knocked down the houses which were close to their battery and in which they were lodged, compelling them to protect themselves with an entrenchment. Both sides kept up their firing for some days ; on one occasion both the thirty-eight pounders were fired at the same moment and the two balls met in the mid distance, the enemy's turning back and entering the mouth of its own cannon, which it broke to pieces.

By the beginning of November they had pushed forward their trenches a matter of thirty paces, and here they erected a battery with six twenty-four pounders and two borers, and they kept up a hot fire from both till the twelfth. When their General Giraldo Holfot saw that with such delay he could not obtain the fulfilment of his hopes for a long time, he determined to assault the city the next day, and arranged his men as follows.

He ordered two large ships to be prepared and manned by a considerable body of good infantry ; these were destined to enter the harbour simultaneously with the land assault, and after bombarding the breastwork of Santa Cruz, they were to seize it in the middle of the fight by means of their *lanchas* ; for the spot was a very advantageous one to them, and as it stood sheer over the sea on a reef, it appeared likely to have no garrison. He also sent within the lagoon a large number of small boats, with which he had come prepared for that purpose. That night he ordered one thousand foot to cross the bridge which stood on an arm of the same lake and served the road which ran to the Queen's Gate. He also posted two thousand others close to his batteries ; of these one thousand were to cross the stockade by the sea shore, one-half advancing to the casemates, the gate of S. João, and the platform, and the other half to a breastwork which was on the shore in front of the College of the Society, the remaining one thousand being destined to attack the bastion of S. João and the line of wall which ran from there to the bastion of S. Estevão. Their preparations were not made so secretly but that the whole city was aware that they intended to assault it on those sides where we found their forces stationed in the morning and so we had the opportunity of making our preparations to receive them.

At eight o'clock on the morning of the 13th of November 1655, the sea made it possible to cross the stockade by the shore. On the signal being given by the firing of three shots from one of the batteries, they all advanced simultaneously in excellent order, giving us the chance of firing two volleys before they reached us. The ships spread their sails to a fresh breeze, making short tacks, and immediately on seeing the signal they steered for the harbour, one entering and casting anchor alongside the breastwork of Santa Cruz, the other standing a considerable distance to sea to avoid danger. Each squadron reached the position which had been assigned it, and only the one thousand who were going to the bastion of S. João and the wall failed to do so as they fell in with the trench : however they divided, some going to the bastion of S. Estevão, the rest along the shore to lend a hand to the five hundred who had reached the platform and casemates and who had extended along the line of wall which stretched as far as the breastwork. All placed their ladders and swarmed up them with great courage, throwing a large number of grenades in their attempt to obtain possession of some of those positions. But after a fierce struggle on both sides they were all repulsed by our men at all points ; those whom we hurled down the ladders climbed again with the greater determination, undeterred by the crowds who fell dead by our sword strokes and musket shots.

Nor did the one thousand who went to the Queen's Gate and the bastion of S. Sebastião have less to do. The Captain-Major Gaspar Figueira directed the defence of the gate of S. João and the casemates, and in the middle of the struggle he was informed that the enemy had carried the breastwork on the shore. To avert this danger he ordered a trusted Captain to hasten to its relief, which he did ; and when he thought that the soldiers would follow him in effecting an entrance, he found himself with only one follower and the post abandoned by its garrison who were residents of the place. These two fell on the enemy who were within and compelled them to rush out to the shore, turning back the great number who were entering; and as they thought that a large reinforcement had arrived they threw several grenades within, which set fire to the pans of powder with which all our bastions were well supplied ; our Captain did not escape being burnt. On seeing the fire, a few soldiers and some of the residents who had abandoned the position hastened back to its defence, through shame at seeing two men alone fighting with the enemy. At the same time a cry was heard that the enemy had entered the city ; this made them all frantic, but no one left his post, for they had enough to do to defend it.

Antonio de Mello de Castro was stationed in the middle of the fort with one hundred soldiers to assist wherever it was necessary. As soon as he was informed where the enemy were, he hastened there with all speed, being followed also by some of the residents and a company of topazes. Coming upon a body of three hundred men who did not know in what direction to move and who were only kept in check by one priest, our men at once set on them, putting all the three hundred except sixty-two to the sword. These men had effected an entrance by a low wall which girt the city on the side of the lagoon and which neither had nor required a garrison, reaching it in the boats which they had brought for that purpose.

The enemy were repulsed by our men with great courage at every point ; and when they saw their heavy losses and our stout resistance, they were obliged to withdraw at midday leaving the foot of the walls and bastions covered with corpses. The ship which had entered the harbour opened fire at the breastwork of Santa Cruz, which however sent it to the bottom in a short time ; a few who did not go down in her tried to escape in a *lancha*, but were also sunk by a cannon shot ; and of all she had on board only the Captain and two others effected their escape by swimming. The rest came on shore, and we employed them in dragging from the ship thirty-eight pieces of artillery which we mounted at some of our posts, as well as three pipes of Canary, some barrels of meat, and a stock of ship's shrouds which we used as matches for maintaining a continuous fire at our stations.

The enemy's loss in this assault exceeded two thousand of their best men, and had our soldiers not been new to the Island and consequently little accustomed to such fighting, not a Hollander would have escaped. In the middle of the struggle a woman, hearing it said that the enemy had entered the breastwork, was driven by her grief to seize a halberd and march bravely to that post, and there she remained so long as the enemy did not withdraw ; and I have no doubt that had she found anyone within, she would have played the part of a gallant soldier. She was the wife of a brave citizen, Manoel de Sousa Bigodes by name, whom the gout had rendered almost useless.

We sent to bury the dead, and in consequence of their great number we dug outside the walls where they lay pits to receive several each ; we did this to prevent their causing a plague among us. After withdrawing, the enemy remained for some days without making any movement, so much so that we thought they intended to retire ; and there is no doubt that if we did not give them battle, losing a large number of brave men, and if we had a force for sallying out with, not one would have escaped being put to the sword ; but we were so few that we did not have even guards for our posts, and in the fight they killed and wounded ninety of us.

After a silence of ten days they recommenced their bombardment and pushed on with their trenches, forming new ones—and there were six already—all against the bastion of S. João, some of them alongside the moat, on which in the course of the night they threw a gallery with the intention of mining our bastion by its aid. But in spite of the intense darkness they did not escape notice, and immediately some of our men jumped into the moat, killed eighteen whom they found working there, and broke up the gallery. In the morning we set about raising within the same moat a mound on which we erectd a six pounder to reply to any device the enemy desired to introduce there ; but when they saw that we had anticipated their plans, they went on with their trench in the face of the same moat, and in spite of our numerous and continuous assaults, burning them with fire itself, we were unable to stop the work.

To protect their workmen they erected three little forts here to keep us in check, but we neglected no chance, and replied in every possible way in view of the peril which menaced us. In this fight we lost several soldiers of great distinction ; and in spite of all exertions, which were far greater than our small numbers admitted of, we could not prevent their continuing the trench. When it reached the point where we had destroyed their gallery, they piled a large quantity of earth inside the moat and soon filled it up, after which they broke through the protecting wall and went on mining below that earth, raising such difficulties for us that we could make no offensive movement against them either from the mound or the bastion of S. Estevão.

Thirty paces in front of the Queen's Gate they raised a battery of eight demi-cannon with which in seven days they laid low the wall which ran from that point to the bastion of S. Sebastião. The destruction was so complete that not a vestige of it remained, for it was made of *taipa* like the rest which protected the city. Everyone accordingly busied himself in overlaying the stretch from the bastion of S. João to that of S. Estevão with earth and palm trees, a precaution which was not unnecessary, as it was here that the enemy pressed on with greater vigour. To prevent the city being left unprotected on that side we erected a stockade of pointed stakes secured by cross beams at two places, and made it all so complete and defensible that it took the place of a wall ; and at the flanks which met at the gate, at the foot of the bastion, we mounted four pedreiros. The enemy had decided to make an assault at this point, but the soldiers who frequently fled to them from us dissuaded them from the plan.

During the whole period of the siege they fired into the city a large number of bombs of great size, and wherever they fell on a house, the least that they did was to destroy the roof and leave it exposed with the walls alone ; but they caused more disquiet and fear than casualties. They made another kind of bomb, which were much smaller and were covered over with a large quantity of tow and other combustibles, and made in such proportions that in their lower part in the midst of the tow they carried from twenty to twenty-five tubes like little pistols, charged to the mouth with two balls. These were put into the mortars and fired with such careful calculation that when they reached the height of a *braca* or a *braca* and a half above us, they would discharge their tubes in all directions, the tubes themselves causing as much havoc as the balls, and finally the bomb would explode. With this invention they killed several people.

But what caused us the greatest trouble—and only the devil himself could bring such an invention to light —was that they used to fill their mortars with wedges and large stones and fire them at the same angle and aim as the bombs : this was usually done at night, and with this infernal device they killed a large number of our men. For as they showed no spark, no one was safe even if he walked about ; and so each one commended himself to God, waiting in apprehension for his fate; indeed one shot from a mortar killed seventeen of us in the bastion of S. Estevão. Following their example, we brought out of the magazine where it stood the mortar which Dom Filippe Mascarenhas had ordered to be cast and taken to Negumbo from which we used to fire the coconuts into that fort ; and though it was small, we did not fail with our stones to cause considerable loss among the men who manned their fortlets and batteries, for we would not give them an hour's rest any night and they were always kept disturbed.

We could not get outside the island, nor could any vessel come to us without being taken, for eighteen ships were anchored in a long line in front of the harbour. As soon as it was night the *patachos* came and anchored closer to land, and the *sumacas* did the same, followed by the *lanchas* which came quite close to the shore, all forming a half moon, while the armed *chalupas* performed their rounds outside ; at break of day all returned and cast anchor alongside the ships.

CHAPTER XXIV

The story of the Siege Continued

As we could not prevent the enemy digging below the mound 1656
which they had piled up in the moat so as to undermine the bastion of S. João, which was so escarped that it was not half its size owing to the way we had cut it down to erect parapets and to repair those which the incessant bombarding had ruined, we dug at the foot of the same bastion with the utmost rapidity a countermine through which we went to meet them. In our opinion this was a step of no little advantage, as we checked what they had worked at so assiduously and destroyed the hopes which they had formed. One afternoon we encountered them and had a fierce fight ; and as the passage which they had made through the earth was two *bracas* in breadth, many hastened to its defence and a large number of them were killed ; while the hole which we had made being small and dark, they could do us no harm. The only arms which could be used in this position were bacamartes and pistols.

The fight ceased at nightfall, and the enemy protected themselves with some planks secured to beams in which they bored loop-holes. We rapidly dug a pit in the interval between us and them and buried in it a cask of powder six palms long, leaving the round touch-hole projecting a palm and a half outside ; and it was a miracle that with such continuous firing going on there for such a length of time a spark did not fall on it. After doing this we broke down the passage, leaving sufficient room for one man to squeeze in from breast to shoulder. In order to have people specially set apart for its defence, the Captain-General sent for some retired Captains of good reputation to whom he said that as the post was one of the greatest dangers, it was not desirable to entrust it to any chance people but only to themselves ; he therefore begged them to take its defence into their own charge for it was of the greatest importance to His Majesty's interests, and he would richly reward them ; it was only thus, by having such honoured cavaliers to defend them, that they could all be free from anxiety : for the longest that that duty and the siege could last was one month, as when the proper season came the following March, reinforcements would arrive.

Eight accepted the invitation with alacrity, and two by two they maintained two watches there, one by day and the other by night; for there was only room within for two people, and these had to be separate. Inside the fort at the mouth of the countermine they set up a wicket through which a man could hardly creep; and when the two whose turn it was to go on guard reached there, they disarmed themselves of all their weapons before entering; for their presence would have been merely a hindrance, and therefore each of them took with him only a bacamarte. When they passed the wicket, it was locked with a key which was handed to the officer commanding the bastion.

The two advanced some distance below the earth, where they could hardly drag their bodies through and the darkness was so intense that they lost their sense of direction. Close by on their left side was a recess made of the broken pieces from the bastion; here one of the two climbed up a height of two palms and hid himself under some planks which chanced to be there, and should have been employed when that bastion was overlaid. There that sentinel remained, while the second advanced a further distance of two *bracas* to the point where we had broken in upon the enemy who sheltered themselves behind the planks, leaving only seven palms of earth, where the cask of powder lay buried, between that sentinel and the enemy.

Twenty-five of the latter's Carbineers kept guard there and they usually exchanged words with this sentinel, for they were unaware of the one stationed at the first point. These were sometimes insults and sometimes they were more rational, according to the humour of the speakers; frequently they threw in fruits, tobacco, and similar articles; but as a rule one man stood with the mouth of the carbine placed on one of the peep-holes in the planks and through the carelessness of our men some were killed, serving as a warning to the rest to be on the look out; for whenever they saw the peep-hole darkened the shot was sure to be prompt.

Where the sentinel stood a man could not lying on a side, crawl more than a foot, and with his right eye he had to watch the peep-holes. His companion at the first post kept his watch lying on his breast, as no other method was possible, from among those planks, as that place was on a higher level than the enemy. Their orders were that if an advance were made from that side on the bastion, they were to fire their bacamartes in such a way as to set the touch-hole of the powder cask alight. The post was one of such terror and peril that the boldest did not fail to be dismayed and the stoutest heart sank, not only because of the greatness of the danger, but also because they were locked in, and on most nights they were not relieved, for then their task was awful. Accordingly some of the very Captains in whom they had confidence could no longer endure the strain, and deserted to the enemy abandoning their post ; thus the risk became so great that they did not trust one another through fear of being killed by their companions or betrayed to the enemy, for the one in the first station could easily do this. For this reason not only the first roster of those who were invited to this task was exhausted, but even up to the fifth ; and out of the whole number only three went through with this fearful and unbearable ordeal till the end, a period exceeding three months. Of these one was Manoel de Sousa, a native of Villa Vicosa, who was called Sousinha owing to his small size : the second was Francisco Pereira, a native of the Isle of Terceira : and the third was a native Captain of this city.

As the enemy was at the foot of the bastion, its capture was an easy matter ; and with the possibility of this occurring, we raised close to it on the inner side a counter-bastion of timber and earth, arming it with two six-pounders, so as to oppose them from there. We ran entirely short of matchcord, whereupon the soldiers tore up their shirts, and those who had none utilised rags of white cloth to remedy the deficiency. And because the enemy had made no trenches nor placed guards on the Mapane side, as the ground here was stony, and the bastion, moat and wall of modern design, one morning two hundred of us sallied out with the slaves of the residents and a supply of axes and entered the jungle of Nossa Senhora dos Milagres, half a league from the city. Here we cut down as many trees from the bark of which matchcord is made, as all of us could carry, and returned unchecked ; on learning of this sally the enemy erected a massive stockade, placing in it a guard strong enough to prevent our repeating our exploit.

CHAPTER XXV

THE SAME CONTINUED

SEVERAL large volumes would be required were I to narrate in detail the particulars of this awful siege; I therefore only set out at length some of the more important incidents which time has not wiped out of recollection, as is the case with all things in the world; what presents itself to us is matter for no small wonder, and only serves to rouse us to a consideration of the great misery of our frailty, true mirror of what we are in life.

On the 17th of October, as I have stated, we fought the Hollanders on the shore at Maroto, and on the 18th the Captain General carelessly and without consideration allowed all the people who lived in the seven parishes which formed our suburbs, to enter the city during two days. This is a matter to which Captains in charge of forts, especially those beyond the sea, should pay great attention so as to prevent a similar occurrence again: for they were a useless crowd who were of no advantage to us.

We did not realize this serious blunder till the beginning of March, when the provisions which had hitherto been abundant and which had been publicly sold for a price a little higher than usual, but not excessive, began to run short. As this took place suddenly we looked about for a remedy, and we turned out of the city by night a large number of those people of both sexes and all ages, so that they might make their way inland. We turned out one thousand five hundred to two thousand on four occasions. But as the enemy had guards at every point, they immediately turned them back, and would not allow any of the poor wretches to go and relieve the pangs of hunger from which they suffered, merely to destroy us by consuming the little that we had. When they returned to the city-gates we would not let them enter, and seeing themselves repulsed so that they could find refuge with neither side, they took the only remedy available and threw themselves into the moat, where their continuous cries and lamentations were of no avail and they were all destroyed. When we surrendered nothing was left of all this crowd except their bones lying close to the lake, the most horrible sight the world could see, for they were almost all Christians, brought up among us, and living under our protection.

A fearful plague followed the famine, attacking not only the poor, but making no distinction of rich and high born. Some of those who were attacked by it swelled out as if with dropsy, while others fell down dead without any pain or illness. From the 15th of March, 1656, when it first broke out, till the 20th of April, up to which the dead were buried, there were counted twenty-two thousand and thirty persons. Nor need this surprise us, for there were households consisting of sixty, and the small ones had twelve or fifteen. After that date men were wanting even for burying the dead, and so great was the horror and misery that all longed to be buried ; for not even the few soldiers had anything with which to satisfy their hunger.

Crowds walked about the streets begging for a little hot water for the love of God, for they well knew that they could not help them with anything else. The misery became beyond endurance, and one hundred and twenty of our soldiers including some of our guards, deserted to the enemy. These gave a true account of our position, but they were not believed as the story appeared impossible to the listeners, and it was also related by men who were looking for an excuse for their behaviour. In honest truth the state of things was far worse than they could describe. And God in His wisdom so ordained that though it rains here three or four times a day as it is so close to the equator, yet during the whole period of the siege it never rained, and this caused such intense heat that it was not possible to walk even with shoes on through the streets, for these were covered with dead bodies full of noxious flies, and emitting a horrible stench. There was a public butcher of dogs, and anyone who obtained an *arratel** considered himself very fortunate. The elephants which died were eaten up to their skins, and they stealthily killed some of them to get the chance ; out of the fifteen we had in our service none escaped save Ortela, for the affection all had for him. There was no kind of unclean

*A pound weight.

animal which escaped being eaten : entire families of Portuguese of position were found dead in their own houses.

A woman, a native of the country, whose husband had been killed by the enemy, was driven to this extremity by the hunger which all suffered. She had her little infant at the breast when her milk began to fail her, and thinking that it was sure to die, the wretched woman planned to use it for her own support. She accordingly killed it and was opening it to take out the stomach, when a woman from a neighbouring house chanced to enter in search of a light. Surprised at what she saw, she demanded what she was doing with her child ; and just as a thief who is found with the stolen article in his hand has usually no excuse except necessity, so did this poor woman and acknowledged what she had designed. The neighbour ran out of the house horror-struck and made the matter public; it was at once reported to the Captain-General who sent an Adjutant to arrest her and take her to the bastion of Mapane and tie her to a cannon. The city was full of the incident and the punishment which had been ordered, whereupon some pious priests went and pleaded with the General to remit the sentence. They urged that the woman could have no greater punishment than being compelled by hunger to kill her own child, the greatest misery that is possible in life, and an act which is so abhorrent to nature itself. He accordingly pardoned her so as to avoid creating a scandal in our perilous condition. Rumour has it that other similar cases took place at this crisis, but I mention only that of which I am sure.

The enemy kept up a heavy fire, using against the bastion of S. João alone, as I have said, six batteries, some of eight demi-cannon. At the Queen's Gate they had the one with which they threw down our line of wall as has been related. By the 4th of May they had raised here another battery for six guns, and that night they intended to mount it with artillery so as to destroy the bastion of S. Sebastião ; and as this was small and in a condition of great dilapidation, they would have been able to effect their object with little trouble.

During the siege there was in the city a priest of the Society of Jesus, a man of energy and remarkable courage. Realising that if the enemy continued his fire from here he would in a few days have the whole city exposed and easily make himself its master, as it had so few to defend it now, he took into his confidence some of those who he thought would follow him in every undertaking, just as he had done in others. Without revealing his plan to any one he passed the word to thirteen to be ready at mid-day, and having successfully asked for the Captain-General's permission, he sallied out at the head of those few and entered the battery unperceived ; and there the edge of their swords gave the alarm, so that a few succeeded in saving their lives. In one hour he destroyed the battery, which was made of palms and fascines, and placing the whole on fire he succeeded in withdrawing his followers without any loss behind the dense smoke, leaving the enemy astonished and confused ; and I have no doubt that if he had three hundred men with him, he would not have left a Hollander alive.

At eight o'clock on the morning of the seventh of May, being Sunday, while the Captain of the garrison, one guard and an artillery man alone were on the bastion of S. João, the enemy appeared above it : and this was no difficult matter, as the batteries were in such a state of ruin and so escarped that they could do it easier than if they climbed up a hill. They killed the three men and made themselves masters of the place without opposition. The alarm was immediately sounded and all hastened to their posts, for they were absent at Mass. About thirty made their way there, and finding the enemy descended to the road, they set on them with such courage that by their deaths they sought to save their lives : and so fierce was the struggle that seventy-six of the enemy were killed, including three Captains ,while the rest retired to the bastion leaving behind five flags and without daring to descend again to the street.

As the enemy were masters of that position, the small garrison we had at the rest of the posts, making a total of one hundred and fifty, got together and made three assaults in the course of the day to dislodge them from the bastion. We used a large number of pans and goblets of powder, and some of us occupied the counter-bastion which we had made of wood and mounted with two cannon. We threw a large number of pans and goblets without any of them catching fire, but as soon as one did, we created great havoc ; for as the powder stood in the midst of them without their noticing it they were burnt in such fashion that we could see hats and pieces of flags flying ablaze through the air.

Towards evening, as the enemy could no longer face our heavy fire and the great flame by which they had lost the majority of the men they had in that force, they abandoned their position and stationed themselves outside to defend it, the parapets themselves sheltering them ; for as it was so badly escarped they were enabled to do it very well. In consequence of the large quantity of powder which we used to supply our want of men, the flame could not avoid falling on something, and this caused a great fire which killed some persons of rank among us and attacked the timber of the counter-bastion ; and as the earthwork had no support, the cannon tumbled to the ground.

We lost this day more than eighty soldiers and Captains, every one had shown marvellous courage and devotion in the defence of the post : nor was that small which was displayed by the Captain-Major Antonio de Mello de Castro, Gaspar Figueira de Cerpe, Diogo de Sousa de Castro, Ruy Lopes Coutinho, Dom Diogo de Vasconcellos, and other fidalgos and Captains who lost their lives bravely in the siege. It is impossible to name them and mention in detail what each one did ; but the Padre Damião Vieira of the Society of Jesus deserves no less praise, for during the whole of the siege his behaviour was that of a most careful and zealous Captain than of a professed priest. There was not an assault in which he was not the first, and several were planned by him, all with success ; he it was who kept in check the three hundred who had made their way by the lake at the first assault, and it was he who destroyed the battery at the Queen's Gate ; in conclusion I declare that the Society may be proud of such a soldier and the soldiers of such a Captain.

By nine o'clock at night we had no more men to fight with them ; and had they come and followed us into the street, without doubt they would easily have killed the few we had. That night they brought a quantity of fascines and earth with which they made parapets towards the city, and by morning they had turned the artillery ; when we saw this, a Council was held to decide what should be done under the circumstances. Some voted for sending the few women and children we had into a church and setting it and the whole city on fire, while the few men who remained should die sword in hand in the midst of the enemy, so that the very memory of the people of this city might not be left, and the enemy might not boast of his conquest. The Prelates of the religious Orders who were present at this meeting vetoed the suggestion, declaring, that such would be the work of Gentiles and utter barbarians, and one condemned by all laws human and divine : our duty was to resign ourselves to the will of God and not to oppose His divine decrees : for though His Majesty had laid special importance on the defence of the Island, yet it was his Ministers who would be called upon to explain why no relief was sent for this length of time.

In view of these reasons and with some tears everyone agreed that the circumstances admitted of no other remedy but that we should parley with the enemy and ask for honourable terms of capitulation ; the ninth of the month was fixed for this, and till the departure of the Commissioners we continued fighting. The terms they allowed were that all the men of war should leave the fort with their arms, matches lit, flags flying and drums beating, and march with four pieces of artillery as far as Nossa Senhora da Vida, the General's quarters, where they should give up their arms, the Captains being left with their side arms, and that they and all the infantry should be sent to some fortress of ours in the State ; the soldiers were to leave their property in the houses of the residents, so that each could take away his own when he embarked : the two Generals with their servants and movables were to be sent to any fort they desired, and the same concession was made to all the residents and their families ; they were also permitted freely to sell in the space of one year all the movables which they could not or would not take away: passage was to be found for all in their ships within this space of time. Similar terms were allowed to the priests, and they were permitted to remove all the appurtenants of divine worship ; but they requested everyone not to take in public jewels, gold, silver or similar articles, so as to avoid outrages at the hands of the soldiers. These terms were entered into with Adriano Uvandremed, the General who had succeeded Giraldo Holfot, who had been killed by a carbine-shot in the course of the siege.

CHAPTER XXVI

The surrender of the City of Columbo and the transfer of the soldiers to Negapatão

At three o'clock in the afternoon of the 12th of May, 1656, we came out of the city, seventy-three very emaciated soldiers, all that remained there, including some with broken arms and minus a leg, and all looking like dead people.

We marched in single file through a crowd of natives who looked on from either side, showing in their faces their feelings at seeing us in this condition, for they were almost all our enemies from Candia. We had to leave the four cannon at the city gate through lack of men to drag them, and on reaching the General's quarters at N. Senhora da Vida, we gave up all our arms to the guard, the Captains and Officers retaining their swords. We then entered the house, where we met the General and the Major, who received us very warmly and gave us a toast in wishing us farewell, saying we must stay there and that before it was late they desired to go and receive the infantry and their lordships the Generals. We replied that their lordships could go to meet the Generals, but that all the soldiers were there before them. At this they changed colour, a great sadness following the cheerfulness with which they had received us. After exchanging a few words in their own language, they replied: "We were under the impression that your worships were the officers". And so it should have been, for whenever an officer of any position was killed his place was at once taken by another, and so out of the seventy-three as many were officers as soldiers.

As soon as they started for the city a Captain came and politely requested us to follow him. He took us nearer the fort to some good houses which had the advantage of a walled garden, placing a guard of a squadron at the gate; these soldiers attended to us very willingly and brought us whatever we required. Here we remained two days, at the end of which the Master-General of the Camp came with many apologies, because his engagements had not allowed him to attend to our comforts earlier, and he was sure we had had a bad time for want of necessaries. He took us slowly to the city by that road, telling us that we would have to render a heavy account to God for allowing the destruction of so many people by attempting what we could not accomplish : he had been over the posts which we had defended, and they needed a garrison of not less than one thousand two hundred men. He had read of many sieges which had taken place, but none of them could be compared with this : for though others might have lasted a longer time, they were not accompanied by the miseries and incidents of this one : every deserter had spoken of the sufferings within the city, but they would not believe them as the account seemed impossible.

He took us within their lines of attack, to show us their forts and batteries. His conversation gave us an opportunity of questioning him about the quantity of powder and shot they had consumed : he said he did not know the number of shot, for besides the large supplies they had received three times, they had also made use of ours. The quantity of powder which he named was so great that we were astonished ; but I do not mention it, as I would not rely on my memory. Including reinforcements eight thousand three hundred and fifty men, all Europeans, had taken part in that siege, and of these there remained one thousand two hundred fit to carry arms, and seven hundred wounded and burnt : all the rest were dead.

After this he led us to the city and took us to the Church of the Society's College where he left us with the message that we could bring our property there and transact any business we had, for we were to go on board in three days. One company was stationed as a guard at the door of the Church to prevent our being roughly treated by any of the soldiers ; whenever we desired to go outside the Church to transact any business, we were at liberty to do so, but not at night, for fear of anything happening to us. Once the Master-General of the Field discovering some soldiers attempting to enter the house of a rich citizen, cut down one with his sword and had the other two hanged ; he therefore appointed four patrols with strict orders against the ill-treatment of any of our men. Three days later we were ordered to embark, and were sent on board two ships with some of the residents and poor widows, but they would not allow us to take boxes or trunks so as not to overload the vessels ; accordingly every one took his property in bags and sheets. Thus we embarked, and in a few days reached Negapatão, where they had set at liberty all those who had been taken prisoner at Galle and been distributed among the ships. The terms of the capitulation were punctiliously carried out as regarded the Generals and residents, all of whom were treated with the utmost courtesy.

When we surrendered there was not left a piece of brass cannon uninjured, for they were all either without their gudgeons or had a ring missing, or they were gaping and it was possible to introduce an arm through the fire-hole. Several of the iron cannon were in pieces and there were only a few undamaged, including three mortars on the flanks ; for although several parts of the city had no batteries, the cannon in those positions were changed and accordingly none that was fit was left unemployed. We used in the siege three thousand seven hundred and twenty-nine quintals of powder and surrendered with only twenty-four and two *arrobas*.

As soon as the siege was begun the King of Candia had come and assisted at it with forty thousand men of war and service ; and when we capitulated, he sent some emissaries within to persuade us with great promises to go over to him. The majority of those who were born in the country, and some Portuguese with their families, did so ; they were accompanied by some priests, and to all of these as well as to the prisoners he had at Candia he allotted villages in the territories which had belonged to this Crown, to live there in comfort in the exercise of their religion, without being compelled to perform any other rite. He repeatedly urged the Hollanders to give him Gaspar Figueira de Cerpe, and promised a large sum of money for him. This matter was brought before the Council where they decided not to hand him over, and sent a reply to the King that they were unable to comply with his request, as their religion forbade them to do so ; for apart from our having surrendered on terms, it was a grave crime and abomination to entrust a Christian to one who was not ;

in truth the crime of raiding cattle was heavily punished among them.

As a matter of fact their refusal was not due to their respect for religion, but because they knew that the King wanted him to be his Captain ; they therefore arranged to send him on board at once, and maintained a guard of a squadron during his stay there, and would not allow him to go outside his house, making a great boast about not delivering him up. The King had ordered them to attempt to persuade Figueira himself ; but he would not listen to their promises, although he was well aware that he only desired to have him to command his armies, and not to take his revenge for the victories which he had obtained over him ; indeed, after the last victory, the King went about in mourning till we surrendered.

On the 19th of the same month the King broke the peace with them, and offered them battle at the Great Stockade. Here he was victorious and would no longer admit the treaty which they sought ; for the war left him unquestioned master of the whole of Ceilão, while the Hollanders had only the forts and some villages close to the shore and they could obtain nothing from inland ; whereas if the King has to enter into a settlement with them, he will be compelled to surrender all the districts which had appertained to the Crown of Portugal ; so that for the King to be lord of Ceilão he has to fight with the Hollanders, while what they received will be an expenditure greater than their income ; all that they gained is that the little cinnamon which is collected in the Island is under their control, and they can transport it by sea, as the King does not trouble about it.

CHAPTER XXVII

How the Hollanders captured the Island of Manar and laid siege to the Fort of Jafanapatão, which they captured

The Hollanders saw that after the capture of Columbo we were sending large forces to strengthen the Island of Manar and the Kingdom of Jafanapatão where we had collected a fleet of rowing boats which had been despatched to the relief of Columbo by Manuel Mascarenhas Homem, who was Governor of the State on the death of the Viceroy the Conde de Sarzedas, under the command of the Captain-Major Francisco de Seixas Cabreira ; there was a further fleet of twelve *sanguiceis* which the same Governor had sent to Manar under the Captain-Major Manoel de Mello de Sampaio ; also the one hundred and ten soldiers and Captains who had surrendered at Columbo, whom the Hollanders had taken to Negapatão and who had gone as prisoners in their ships. The same Governor had appointed as Captain-General of Ceilão Antonio do Amaral de Menezes, who actually held the office of Governor of that Kingdom. They realised that if we kept these reinforcements we would give them trouble, and if we maintained them in the Island itself it would be a difficult matter to remedy the mistake : to escape
1658 this anxiety they arranged to drive us quite out of the Island.

With this object in the middle of February 1658 they came with ten ships carrying three thousand and two hundred soldiers and some brave Chingalas who had been our men in Columbo. They first of all made for Titicorim, as five rowing boats under the command of Dom Alvaro da Silva were on guard there ; and since the harbour is open they succeeded in coming so close to land that they could fire without hindrance, as the only artillery our vessels had with which to resist them, was one two-pounder each ; consequently they were helpless. The enemy were thus able to destroy them, sending two to the bottom, while the other three barely succeeded in reaching land with the greater part of their men killed or wounded. Unable to do anything else, the Commander ordered the boats to be set on fire and started for Jafanapatão with those who wished to follow him.

The enemy returned to the Island of Manar, where they found the Captain-General Antonio do Amaral de Menezes with twelve companies of a little more than four hundred soldiers, and some rowing boats and *sanguiceis* which he had formed into a fleet under the command of the Captain-Major Gaspar Corneiro Girão ; with the help of the companies on land he had also made for the distance of a league along the shore an entrenchment, which he occupied with them so as to prevent the enemy effecting a landing.

As soon as the enemy arrived with their fleet they made for the boats and *sanguiceis* which they dispersed with repeated volleys of artillery, sending some to the bottom and driving all the others without exception on shore, with the greater part of their men killed or wounded. Thus relieved, they were able to land wherever it was most convenient for them. And as there are two long leagues of sandy shore with a very clear bottom from Manar to Talemannar and the companies guarded the first league from their rampart as already stated, the remaining league was left defenceless ; he therefore steered his ships there and landed five hundred men from his *lanchas* unopposed, and drew them up in a squadron.

When our men saw this they sallied out from their entrenchment to attack them, just as they were, but owing to the fewness of the men in the vanguard they dared not do so ; one only, an Alferes named Sebastião da Costa, who was determined to show his valour, hurled himself on the squadron and was at once killed. The remaining companies left the entrenchment they held and formed up to attack the enemy ; but the bombardment from the ships was so heavy and continuous that they could not do so and some of our Captains and brave soldiers, including the Captain-General de Menezes himself, were killed. In the meantime the enemy had the opportunity of landing all their troops, and when our men saw this they retired, followed by them, and when they reached the fort it surrendered, as it had no means of defence and could not resist.

Our men crossed the river with the speed of necessity and started on the march of eighteen leagues to Jafanapatão, dead of hunger. They arrived there with the Captain-Major of the Field Antonio Mendes Aranha, who took steps with the Governor of that Kingdom, João de Mello de Sampaio, to form them into companies, for several of them had no Captains ; they were then stationed on the Rio Salgado to defend that passage against the enemy who came in a few days to attack us in our own camp marching by land, bringing up the river all their *lanchas* and a number of barques with provisions and stores. After fighting with them we had to retire to the first street of the town, where we threw up barricades. Three days later they advanced on that position, and as we found it difficult to maintain it, we retired by night to the furthest, which was nearer to the fort. There we sheltered ourselves and remained for four days, but they attacked us in the flank with their artillery and forced us to retire by night within the fort, where also all the residents and others from the town had gathered.

As this contained only the house of the Governor, the hospital, and the convent of St. Francisco, all took refuge in the Church and its cloisters, packed together as best they could. The fort was a regular square with four bastions ; the distance from one corner to the other was twenty-five paces, and in the middle of the walls there were lunettes or half oranges, all very small after the old fashion, the whole structure being of pumice stone. A river ran on one of the sides, and the other three were protected by a trench twenty-five palms in breadth, and a dozen deep. The infantry were posted between the trench and the wall, and in the course of that night they raised for their protection a rampart which served as a barbican.

The enemy set up three batteries with which they bombarded our two batteries on the river side, as the moat finished at their base ; these they broke down with ease, as they were crumbling like earth from a cemetery owing to the nature of the stone with which they were all constructed. They also threw a large number of bombs and a continuous shower of stones from their three mortars, thus killing several of our men. In the fortress there was only some spoilt rice and no other eatable, and there was not a grain of salt. We all underwent much misery through the want of these, and several of our people were consequently attacked with disease and died.

We made some sorties to stop the works the enemy had begun, and so prevented their continuing them. We had a fort at the entrance to the channel a little more than two leagues from the town, similar to the one *do Bogio* ; this was held by a company of infantry with fourteen pieces of artillery, a constable, and two artillery men. The enemy set up their batteries at the point of the Elephants' Quay, as this was where that fort approached the land nearest ; and as it was built of pumice stone they easily broke it down. In little more than a month it was compelled from want of food and ammunition to surrender.

The siege of our fort was vigoroulsy maintained, and after two months' bombardment, in view of the misery we endured and the lack of provisions and other necessaries, the enemy sent us a summons and offered us reasonable terms; we declined these and insisted on maintaining our defence from the 20th of March, when we first retired there, till the 22nd of June. But as we saw that we had no powder, rice, or any other kind of provisions, the majority of our men killed, our bastions in ruins, and that there was no possibility of help reaching us ; and as for some time the firing from the other fort had ceased—a sure sign that it had fallen—and seeing the great amount of sickness which prevailed, we held a meeting and agreed to surrender the place.

We invited the enemy to a parley, but as they saw that we were acting through necessity and that there was no possibility of help reaching us so long as they held Manar and the fort in the harbour where they kept five ships, they would not give us any honourable terms. They would not rob us of the honour of our arms, but in every other particular we had to submit to their mercy. They allowed us to leave with our arms, matches lit, banners flying and drums beating, but without our jewels, gold, silver, or similar articles. They undertook to send the Governor, fidalgos and Captains to one of our forts in the State, and similarly with all the Casados and their families ; while the soldiers would be sent in their ships to Batavia and thence to Europe. This condition was badly kept, for they were all taken to Batavia.

On the 24th of June, 1658 our men marched out to the number of one hundred and forty in terms of the capitulation. As soon as we had surrendered our arms at the appointed place, they first of all surrounded us with some squadrons and we were passed slowly on one by one to where the Fiscal stood, who stripped and searched every one, even examining his private parts, he himself removing the shoes, and taking away everything we had without overlooking even articles of little value; those who helped him were so zealous that they took away our clothes and very hats. To relieve us of everything, when we wanted to go out of the citadel, they had ordered us to leave our property in the Governor's house, where they placed an Adjutant to guard it so as to return it to us. We were greatly indebted to him for his care, for he guarded it so well that none of us ever saw anything of his again. After taking leave of this zealous officer, when the search was over, they sent us almost nude to the College of the Society of Jesus. The same process was gone through with the rest of the people without making an exception even of the women; for this scoundrel without any respect or shame searched the parts which nature had meant to be hidden, without their tears or fainting helping the poor wretches at all; not even the most noble escaped his scrutiny; for the thirst of avarice leads people to such disgraceful acts. We were all thrown into their ships, in which after bearing much hunger and suffering we were brought to Batavia, where we were locked up in a prison in the city.

The fidalgos and chief people who took part in that siege were the Governor, João de Mello de Sampaio, the Captain-Major of the Field Antonio Mendes Aranha, Diogo de Sousa de Castro, Manoel de Saldanha e Tavora, his cousin Manoel de Saldanha, Dom Alvaro da Silva, Alvaro Rodrigues Borralho, Dom Goncalo da Silva, João Botado de Seixas, Gaspar Figueira de Cerpe, Mathias Catanho, the Vedor da Fazunda Leonardo de Olivera, and others who bore themselves in that siege, each according to his position, without in any way disgracing the blood of their ancestors.

BOOK III

A DISQUISITION, WHEREIN IS SET FORTH OUR LACK OF FORESIGHT REGARDING THE CONQUEST OF INDIA, AND HOW IT WAS TO OUR ADVANTAGE TO OCCUPY ONLY CEILÃO.

CHAPTER I

The errors committed by us over the Conquest of the State of India

Our first book contained a description of Ceilão, and our second an account of the military operations therein. It is now essential for the end which we have in view, to make certain observations before we come to matters of proof. If our opinions are erroneous, other men of judgment, understanding and care have been guilty of the same weakness. Our desire is only directed to the satisfaction of the zeal which has led us to undertake this task; if it is found not acceptable many others too have been futile.

Would to God the Crown did not have to pay more for that policy which it had adopted for a hundred and eighty-eight years, in the course of which the bulk of the numerous heroes who lost their lives in that State were sacrificed in vain! Methinks if the world were emptied of people, it could to-day be filled by those men of ours. The greatest evil of all is that there is nothing left to us save some dim memories and the little-liked remnants of our zeal. I am clearly of opinion that what has overthrown our magnificent fabrics are the thunderbolts of our own sins and not the might of the enemy, which the Lord our God has employed as the instrument of our punishment. May he ever be praised, for even thus he has treated us as a loving father; He directs everything to our good, and his divine kindness permits all for his own glory.

Our Monarchs in their ardent zeal to spread the Faith of Jesus Christ throughout the world, spent what they could without stint—even more than their inheritance rendered possible—both by assigning revenues to meet the expenses, and by distributing territories and lordships among their subjects. The whole world must admire their devotion to the service of God in this sacred work, and also the zeal with which their subjects gave effect thereto, traversing so many climes, and undergoing such hardships, to convey their religion to lands so remote and unknown to Europe. Had the task been continued with the same devotion, it cannot be doubted that God would have been always found propitious, for the cause was his own. Human dispositions however are not always unvarying, times do not remain the same, and there set in a decline from these glorious beginnings, which led to the inevitable conclusion which we see to-day.

It is not our intention to lay blame on any particular individual, for it is beyond doubt that everyone desires to act with wisdom in the resolutions which he adopts ; but as a rule various opposing influences appear, it may be in the times or opportunities or forces, for they are not always of the same kind, or because judgment is not in accordance with desire. This may be clearly seen at any time in a Council, for though everyone there desires to serve his Prince with love and fidelity, yet he votes according to his opinion. We can attribute this same diversity to those who govern the State and the parts thereof,—though all desire to act with wisdom, they fail, owing to the reasons indicated, to attain their object. If they put anything into execution, it may not be the wisest ; therefore where the intention is good, all blame should be withheld. We do not include in this number those to whom fame is always a debtor and they are her creditors in glory ; they consulted with God and tested their desire by prudence.

Our object is only to set out the causes as we understand them which led to our total ruin in the State, as we see the ardour of our glorious Kings in the propagation of the Faith so ill repaid. I think if they were asked to-day where God in his mercy keeps those who formed these plans, they would say without doubt that they are repenting having ever undertaken this conquest, for the disservice which has been rendered to His Divine Majesty. The first reason which presents itself to us is that from the Cape of Good Hope inwards we were unwilling to leave anything outside our control ; we were anxious to lay hands on everything in that huge stretch of over five thousand leagues from Sofala to Japão. The worst was that we set about this without measuring our forces or thinking that even with the natives themselves this conquest could not last for ever. We needs must have expected infinite trouble at their hands ; we ought to have considered the fact that there are always avaricious people in this world : when the nations of Europe saw how with our limited forces we trod the world under foot, it was certain that envy and avarice would urge them to attempt the venture on which they found us embarked, for they would think that they were no less competent to undertake a like enterprise than we. No nation thinks that it is inferior to another in courage. Even assuming that their attempt was not meant to be hostile to ours, and that their only intention was to seek places which we had not occupied, yet we would always come into collision with them. Much more as there was not a corner which we did not occupy or desire to have subject to ourselves. This is proof of the little discretion with which we proceeded.

The second point is, that not only did we not overlook what was valuable out of the abundance found in those parts, but also what was petty, such as rice, coconuts, dates and the like. The reply will be that as our main intention was the spread of the Holy Gospel throughout the East, therefore we laid our hands on everything, so that all might be aware of that. This plea might be admitted, if the results bore it out ; but they are entirely to the contrary, and our experience points to other objects which compel us to assert that there were private ambitions for acquiring reputation which commenced and maintained so large a number of forts which were of no value, as that of Barbacena and the like. In some of these we kept a hundred Portuguese, in others two hundred, who had to live within four walls, many of which were only built of earth, forty and fifty leagues from each other, and with little or no defence. To render this service welcome they would advise His Majesty and say " Senhor, I have reduced under the Crown such a Kingdom, with such and such riches. "

There were witnesses who puffed up these worthless lands, which at most would produce a little rice which could be purchased from the natives with our money. I desire them to tell me in what manner did the long list of forts which I shall mention below assist Christianity or this Kingdom ? What about the others which we occupied on the coast of Africa ? How much of the abundant gold of Sofala, Mocambique, Quiloa or Mombaca, came to our Kings ? How many of our people did not the Islands of Querimba, Zenzibar, Monfia and S. Lourenco consume ? And all this for the discovery of wealth, for which our affections thirsted.

CHAPTER II

The same continued

We pass on to our third point. For the preservation of these forts—we are speaking of those of less importance and value—they were provided as the rest with Captains, men who had seen service in that State, and as such were experienced in war. On entering office it was open to them to examine minutely and to inform themselves as to the walls, artillery, munitions and whatever else was necessary for the defence of the place, so as to make as good as possible any deficiency. But this coin was not current. All the anxiety of each was to ascertain what his predecessor drew, and by what ways and means. These he would speedily put into operation, adding fresh methods which his anxiety for leaving the place a rich man indicated, and it was always the poor natives on whom the screw was brought to bear. If there chanced to live near some Prince or Lord of the country who was on terms of friendship and alliance with us, he would be the target at which all their bolts were aimed, and this with as much hauteur as if the Captain were a King, and the other his servant. The frequent result of this was quarrels which could not be set right without great expense and prejudice to the service of our King, while that Prince and his people would always have a grievance against us, and our nation would be ever held in hatred. I dare say among those who went out to govern these forts there were some who acted with humanity, but they could not set matters right ; for the evil done by one man remains deeper impressed in the memory than the good acts of a hundred.

The fourth point is that we ought to have kept our men together where a superior could remedy the injuries and hardships inflicted by them on the neighbouring inhabitants, and make up for what was lacking in them. We were scattered among so large a number of fortlets distant from each other, that even if no Europeans went to those parts, the natives of necessity tried to rid themselves of the oppression to which they were exposed. The Canaris, who live closer to Goa than any other race, have brought this truth home to us, for in 1653 they took from us the four forts of Honor, Bracelor, Cambolim and Mangalor, which our garrisons occupied in their ports. The Imam has just done the same in Arabia Felix, for he took from us a fort so strong and a city so well situated as Mascate, and the fort of Curiate, with the rest of the forts which we had on that coast. Both these acted without the assistance of the Hollanders or of any other race, and they did so as they saw themselves unjustly oppressed—a motive which will fill our hearts with the greatest courage. God our Lord, as is just, helps the humble even when they are not of his flock ; he punishes with the greater severity us who are. For we have his commandments and stray from them, while they are ignorant of them : the needle of his balance does not swing more towards one than towards another of his creatures.

For a clearer comprehension we have dilated on what we have said so that our reasons may point to what the results have made clear. It is easy to realise that a Kingdom however great which divides its forces cannot possibly last, for the portions which are separated therefrom not only weaken it, but are themselves doomed to entire destruction, both because of their smallness and also by the increased vigour of any hostile attack. For example where a number of cows or mares are feeding in a plain with their young, many herds of wolves would be powerless to attack them ; but if one is found straying a single wolf can do what it likes. If this is so clear, how can we find excuses for an error so obvious ?

We must necessarily attribute it to one of two causes—if it be not the case, as I fancy, that both are to be found. The first is that the maintenance of so many little forts points to the influence of private interests. The second is that all our treasure was wasted foolishly by our persistence in the face of all reason. Courage and zeal was displayed in the punishment of the infidel and treacherous towns of Mocambique, Mombaca, and the like ; but I should like them to tell me what was to be gained by occupying and maintaining them ? If they produced four grains of gold and a little ivory, that was purchased not only with our money but also with the lives of the King's subjects when he needed them to be expended in his service where they would have been of greater use, and not where the preservation of the land demanded the removal of such large numbers and such heavy expenditure. For one soldier who reached them alive, three had to set out from there. The very bells and artillery, though they were of bronze, could not withstand the effects of the climate. Indeed our ships which took those harbours are better able to speak to this, for it was rarely that the vessel which started with two hundred, returned with one hundred ; the rest were left buried behind. How many people were not lost in the rivers of Cuama in the thirst for the gold of Monomotapa ? Of a verity, these are matters which appear more like fables than the truth.

CHAPTER III

A disquisition on the whole of the State, pointing out the main resources of the Forts

As I found myself involved in a labyrinth of these forts, it seemed wise, though it involved much trouble, to visit all of them and find out what they were, what we obtained from each, and what they produced. We took with us as companion on this long journey such poor gift of discourse as God has endowed me with, some provisions and almost an entire absence of knowledge and began the voyage.

Leaving the coast of Africa we passed to Arabia Felix to commence our peregrination. We boarded a vessel and set sail, and the first port we touched at was the Island of Socotra. Here we did not land, for the ruins of a fort which we had there cried out to us and promised to guard us from such a desire. We passed on to the city of Mascate, Curiate and the other forts which we had on the Persian Gulf. These told us, "Friend, if the Moors have not become Christians, at least these lands produce horses, incense, and dates ; but, Portuguese, it has cost you your money. It was open to you to carry on your trade without wasting on our occupation so many soldiers and settlers ; for the duties and rents which you obtained were not sufficient for the maintenance of your armadas. Our regret is that the sacred temples where the word of the Lord used to be preached, have been converted into Mosques, where the abominable Al Corão is expounded." I remarked to my companion, "These forts speak the truth."

We diverged from our route to avoid the complaints of Dio, and reaching the coast of India, landed at the city of Damao. We did not stop here, but proceeded by land through S. Gens, Danu, Aserim, Tarapor, Mahim, Quelmc, Manora, Agasaim and other places. We reached the very noble city of Bacaim, where there reside more than two hundred families of highly honoured fidalgos. We pressed some of the chief people to tell us in detail what riches they had, and what those cities, forts and settlements produced, for thev could not fail to be great in view of so many people and nobility sent by Portugal with so much zeal. We addressed our question to two people of authority both by their position and age, and they reply "We shall satisfy your desire for knowledge so as to please you, as far as we can, in a few words. You ought to know that in this world too there is Limbo, and these lands as far as you have come and further on to Tana and Caranja and others of less importance, are that Limbo. None of them have either necessity or glory. They have no glory, for they have no kind of wealth. They have no necessity, for there is no lack of food such as rice, corn and meat, which we consume by themselves, as we have no spices. For the lack of this we give God great thanks, because out of a misfortune very often a great blessing arises. It is no small matter to escape the visits of the Hollanders to these parts ; as they eat nothing without spices, they have no desire to be our guests."

We rendered them due thanks for their courtesy and for revealing to us the true state of things, and after bidding them farewell we went on till we reached Chaul. We saw the walls of the city, which were complaining that they were squeezed in by the Moors on the land side and did not have a palm's breadth wherein to expand. The inhabitants on their part bewailed that they had no food for themselves, much less to share with the Moors. From here we pushed on to the great and noble city of Goa, the emporium of the whole of India ; although its situation had been badly selected, we found it had two very convenient harbours for the protection of our armadas, as well as other advantages which will preserve the memory of its Conquistador for ever.

We left this wealthy and noble city with regret, for we were now in the midst of the entire Indian Ocean and had to go off to the other side to see what we had there. A few days journey brought us to Honor, Bracelor, Cambolim, and Mangalor. In these we find rice purchased from the Canaras, as well as some pepper. The complaint in the mouth of every one was that while a single Factor could attend to the trade, our men were engaged in peopling, fortifying and maintaining four military forces which had no other attraction than this trade ; and here they were entirely wiped out at last by the natives ; many lost their lives seeking wealth and those who escaped are going about begging. We were moved by these misfortunes and continued our journey without delay. In a few days we arrived at Cananor, where we saw a fort and settlement crowded up to the walls by Malavars and Moors. We questioned them as to what they had, because we saw so many enemies threatening them. The reply was that there was some cardamom and ginger which we purchased from them, and which they were very anxious to sell to us: we kept up that fort there without any further benefit. We proceeded to Caranganor, a fortress with a garrison and settlers. From its position, as it is far from the sea, we thought that it was not suited for commerce, and we inquired what trade was carried on there. We were informed that it was kept up because at the commencement of our conquest the gallant Duarte Pacheco had obtained there some victories over the Zamorim, and therefore this was maintained as a memorial of the same.

The following day we arrived at Cochin, which is the foundation and beginning of our empire in that State. It is our second city in point of size and is occupied by numerous Portuguese, all as poor as it is possible to conceive. On seeing us some of them come to inquire into the reason of our arrival ; when satisfied as to the real object of our pilgrimage they delivered a harangue on the miseries to which they were subject. I thought this was to avoid extending hospitality to us, so I turned to my companion and said " I see from the safe-conduct which they have brought that we are not likely to find a lodging among them, though the reputation of Cochin promised us otherwise." Among the numerous complaints they made was the following : " Senhors, the want in the city is so great, that if we were to relate to you but a very small portion, you cannot fail to be scandalised. We have nothing with which to bring up our daughters, and so we allow them to do what they can for themselves. There is a quarter in the city called Caloete, where formerly loose women used to reside ; to-day for our sins the whole of the city is a Caloete ; for all our women share the same fate. We have no trade, and at most there are two *patachos* which go to Sinde and Cachanagana. When one of these arrives in safety it is no small matter, but the owner gets the sole benefit of it. The owner of the other, which is captured by the enemy, has joined the rest in their misery. May God pardon the man who built this city. If it was meant for the defence of its King, as a mark of gratitude for the kindness which he displayed to our first Conquistadors, the fortress which we then had was sufficient. Though there were in India not more than a hundred and forty Portuguese, they were sufficient not only for the defence of the fort and of the King, but they also obtained many victories over the Zamorim. Thus we would have been able to-day to have this land populated, and at least we would have escaped famine and not committed so many offences in the sight of God."

We were grieved at hearing all this, and as we had nothing to offer them nor they to entertain us with, we bade them farewell and went on to Coulão, which we reached very weary. We entered a settlement with more than two hundred Portuguese families and a fortress which is small and in view of its fortifications incapable of defence; for its walls are single and it has no garrison. The inhabitants entertained us with coconuts and the liquor of the palm trees, and we accepted their hospitality as we were pressed with hunger and also did not wish to appear churlish, for they had nothing else to offer us. He who offers what he has, does all that he possibly can. In the course of our conversation we inquired from them as to their means of living. They replied that they depended on the four palm trees near the town, and they had nothing else on which to maintain themselves. They purchased some pepper from the Malavars for the King, and the fort and settlement were kept up for this object, when one Portuguese would be able to do this without the expense of supporting so many inhabitants who were suffering continuous hunger without rendering any service to God and the Crown.

We spent the night here and at dawn started on our journey, as we had already bid our hosts farewell. We traversed the entire coast of Travancor, and doubling the Cape Comorim crossed the Seven Coasts and reached Teticorim. Here we found one Portuguese who was living in the town, which belongs to the Native Paravas. On seeing him we were informed that he was the Captain-Major of the Fishery Coast. We saluted him with all due courtesy, and he asked us the object of our coming there. We told him our desire, and that we wished to know where the fort was so as to go and see the rest of the Portuguese and ascertain from them the trade on which they depended. He replied, pointing to what was little more than a hut, "The fortress is that house in which I live. All the Portuguese consist of myself; so that, friends, you have seen them all. I hold this government for three years, and it has been given to me as the reward of many great services. My regret is that I see no other white man in this port unless it be some traveller." On hearing this we were astonished and said to him "Senhor Captain-Major, your honour is a fortunate man, seeing that without soldiers you are the Captain over such a number of blacks. In good truth this might be called the eighth wonder of the world, for it is opposed to all other modes of government which we have seen anywhere." He answered "The Government depends on the will of these people, and they tolerate it as this country produces a great quantity of rice, and there is a large manufacture of cloth, both of which we purchase from them at a high price."

CHAPTER IV

The same continued

Wishing the Captain-Major farewell we went on board a *champana*, and after a voyage of four days reached Manar. Here we entered through a narrow canal which separated the Island from Ceilão. We did not wish to delay at the fort, as it had little to note and it belonged to the jurisdiction of that Conquest. Two days later we reached Negapatão, a city well peopled by Portuguese and which in 1642 submitted to the King of Portugal. Up to that time they were living according to the law of Nature, in an open settlement subject to the Naique of Tanjaor; in consequence of some quarrel with him, the origin of which I do not know, they appealed to us for assistance at the happy juncture when we had lost Malaca and nearly the whole of Ceilão. We therefore relinquished the protection of our own in order to assist people who had never shown a desire to submit to our Crown, but rather to retain their independence till forced by the hostility of the Naique. It was open to us to transplant them to Ceilão, but this we failed to do. Instead, his Majesty went to the expense of an armada under the command of the Captain-Major Domingos Ferreira Beliago in erecting a city well fortified with bastions, walls, trenches, artillery, soldiers and every thing else, at a time when the royal patrimony was at Extreme Unction.

We viewed this city, which is situated on a point of the main land were the Xoromandel Coast begins. Close to its walls there is a large settlement of the Gentiles, where the number of the pagodas, some of remarkable work, is not exceeded by that of the private houses. In one of the most revered temples they preserve with great veneration a column of black marble ten palms high, well wrought and polished, with the martyrdom of Christ our Lord engraved thereon. On this may be seen splashed some drops as of blood. The records of the idolaters narrate how they came by this. Many ages ago, before the Portuguese had arrived at these parts, on a peculiarly dark night, there occurred a great earthquake and storm of wind so violent that all were convinced that the world was coming to an end. Some scanned the sea, and there they discovered a great fire. They thought that it was a ship, and sent word to the others, whereupon all of them hastened to the shore. Suddenly the storm ceased, and the fire blazed out the fiercer. In a short while it reached land, whereon the flame died out ; and when the people came to see this strange thing, they discovered this column which they conveyed with great rejoicing and solemnity to this temple where they worship it as having come from heaven. When it is shown to any person of standing, there are great ceremonies ; but for the common people an exact duplicate is made and kept at the entrance of the temple. Everyone, our own people as well as the Gentiles, declares that its appearance is as I have described. God our Lord knows the object with which he wrought this marvel among the barbarians ; may he permit that it is for his glory.

The town is entirely occupied by people interested in trade from whom we purchase much cloth which is exported to various parts. From this a small revenue is obtained, which barely pays for the stipend of the Captain, and there is no other source of income. I therefore say to my companion "I am distressed over this nation of ours. Here every shoemaker thinks he has the wisdom to govern the world, yet we show so little statesmanship that at a time when we could not assist Ceilão, we wasted the little we had on new settlements which served no other purpose than to weaken our forces and to increase the expenses of the Royal Treasury. To send one soldier to India costs more than fifty thousand *reis*. Moreover for each one that enters service, five have to embark. Some die on the voyage, others discover kinsmen at Goa who take them to their houses, others join the religious orders, the younger are engaged as pages and large numbers are swept away by the fevers of that city. Those innocents who come from the Limoeiro* where they had been for their knaveries, join the Moors and at this I am not surprised.

*The prison.

The knave in Portugal cannot be a saint in India. What does surprise me is that all who serve in the State recognise this condition of things but gloze over the truth. The result is that out of the original five hardly a man remains not otherwise absorbed and of good character. To place him where he is wanted involves a cost of a further 20,000 *reis*. The consequence is that each soldier attached to the service of the King our Lord costs him 270,000 *reis*."

My companion added, "They cost even more, for you do not take into consideration the affection with which their parents bring them up and freely give them to the service of God and their King. Everyone to the best of his ability assists when they go on board, so as to relieve the miseries of their long voyage." I answer "I do not take that into consideration, as the bringing up of children is an act of Nature, and to assist to the best of our ability is a mark of our affection to our fellow men. I only refer to the loss incurred by the King, who does not know, at the distance where he is, what harm is being done here. The worst is that they think they are doing him a great service, and as there is no remedy for all this, let us go where there is more to see."

We passed on to the noble city of Meliapor, and visited the holy temple which is said to have been constructed by the glorious Apostle S. Thome, and where there are preserved as a treasure beyond price the spear of iron with which he was killed and some sandles which he used. On coming out of the Church we met some of the many noble inhabitants of the place, each of whom wishes to take us to his house. We went on with one who showed himself very kind and entertained us for the three days of our stay with great generosity, and we were visited by the chief residents. We learned from our host and others that at one time they had been all very wealthy in consequence of the great profits of the cloth trade of the city, as it produced the best material in the East. But the Hollanders have since their appearance in those parts robbed them of everything and now they were suffering from want, as they have nowhere to export their goods and no money for the trade. They told us of one of the principal ladies in the place who had been very wealthy and in a few days was reduced to such a condition of poverty, that she cut off her hair as she had nothing else to sell ; with what she realised by the sale of her hair she purchased some rice which she ate on the last day of her life.

We praised the name of the Lord with grief and continued our journey down the coast through the four Portuguese settlements of Pipli, Ogolim, Balacor, and Juncalão. Here they live according to the law of Nature, without a King to obey or a minister to supervise the government, all comfortably provided for and bloated with vice. They export their goods to various parts in vessels of the Moors and Gentiles who are masters of those lands, and from this they derive considerable profit which only serves to increase their vanity and presumption. We did not delay at any of these as we feared to see the wrath of God come upon them, consuming the green with the dry.

We had information that on one bank of the Ganges there is a kingdom the King of which is called the Mogo, and that there live here four hundred Portuguese, all of very exemplary life. We set out for this place with great satisfaction to behold this marvel, as we considered it a remarkable matter in this State where the boastfulness of man is great and even the least thinks his ancestors were sprung from the seven planets. At last we reached this kingdom, where we found these men—if brute beasts can be given that name—in the service of that King. They recognise no God, and all their devotions are paid to Bacchus ; anyone who does not make liberal offerings to him is not admitted among these servants of his. The Mogo has divided them into companies, and made Captains of the most fervent ; to these he has allotted villages to maintain their companies from their revenue, and they are employed in making war on his neighbours. Each Captain has to keep two Jalias, which continually move along the banks of the river which are covered with forest. At night they land and raid the open villages, robbing them of what they have and making prisoners of everyone they can lay their hands upon. All they capture is taken before the Captain and sold by auction in his presence along with the prisoners. The proceeds are divided among the company, the King taking nothing, as this is the pay he gives them. If any girl appear to a soldier suited for his purpose, he makes a bid for her, and as they are all very polite none of the others would take him from her. When she is thus knocked down to the bidder she is sent to his house with four of five others purchased in the same fashion and for the same purpose. This custom is common among them all, and he who does not live in this fashion is not considered a man. So they spend their lives in the state of penitence we have described, and their boast is that each of them has made more Christians than did S. Francisco Xavier the whole of the time he was in the East. And I do not doubt this, for they are always busy with their raids, and as these poor wretches are Gentiles, they baptise them as soon as they are captured. The King as he is a Moor, does not interfere, but sells them to the ships which come to these harbours for trade. We hurriedly retired to avoid meeting these people.

We went past some places where were others of the same confraternity, who, if they were not so zealous in making Christians, were at any rate similar to them in the rest of their lives. At last we reached Sião where lived a few others more civilised than those we left behind. These too lived by trade without law or a King. We proceeded to Macao, a city well inhabited by gentlefolk, and with good houses. Here they were full of complaints that they were very poor and in debt in consequence of business not being what it used to be. Since the Hollanders got to Cantam they spoilt the trade of the whole of China, and cheapened the price of European imports. Nevertheless it yielded the Hollanders handsome profits, for their goods were exported without expense, while ours which come from India were very dear on reaching China in consequence of the duties, freight and other charges. The result was that they were all very poor, cut off by distance from communication with the State, and exposed to every kind of disgrace.

After spending a few days at Macao and visiting the city, we passed on to the Malucas, and after a short voyage landed at Ternate to ascertain if the fortress which we had there was still in existence. A native who had known the Portuguese recognised us by our dress and accosted us saying "It is something strange to see you in this country, as your nation has been excluded from it for so many years—to tell you the truth, that was not without reason, when we consider the tyranny to which this people and all the neighbouring islands were exposed. You must withdraw as fast as possible, and not touch at any of them. If they recognise you as I did, it will be difficult for you to avoid death. You should thank me for this advice, which I give you owing to the affection which I had for a Captain of yours who was in this Island. All of us received as much kindness from him as if he were a father, and he behaved in the same manner to all the others. I always keep him in mind so as to show myself grateful, and it is for this reason that you receive this little favour. If you require anything for your journey, I shall share with you what I have, for affection does not show itself in words alone."

We thanked him for his advice as well as for his offer and we begged him to tell us who that Captain was, so that we might thank him too; as it was owing to him that we received all these favours. He replied "To the world he is now dead, but all of us in these islands keep him alive in our remembrance. Antonio Galvão was he; he had more virtue in him than all the crowd of tyrants and robbers who have been governors here." We thanked him again for telling us what we would never have known, and so great was his kindness that he accompanied us till we went on board a ship which was bound for Ceilão, in which he directed water and food to be stocked for our use. We bade him farewell and started with a favourable breeze.

Leaving Ternate we passed within sight of Tidore, Motir, Bachiam, Banda, Amboino and several other islands, which were there. We begged the pilot not to put in at any port, owing to the risk which that good old man had mentioned. The winds however became contrary and the voyage so prolonged that our stock of water ran short and we were forced to touch land to replenish the supply. God was pleased that we should come to the Island of Solor, and on our casting anchor they told us that some Portuguese lived there. We were very pleased with the news and were anxious to see these brothers of ours and their place of residence.

We disembarked and on the shore met some of them who had come to receive us, as they had notice of our arrival from the sailors who went with the casks. They embraced us with great joy and took us to the town, which consisted of about two hundred people, while near by was a small fort of earth.

To our question as to their trade, they replied that in exchange for their cloth they purchased sandal which they shipped to China and other parts, and also sold to the ships which came there for that trade. With these profits they maintained themselves ; their country produced some food-stuffs,—rice, millet, potatoes, meat and wild fruit—but it was very unhealthy. They also informed us that more to the west was another island and settlement of the Portuguese, who lived by the same kind of trade. We remained with them two days, being entertained as best the country permitted ; at the end of this period we set about continuing our journey, and after bidding our friends farewell we went on board and with a fresh wind behind us we sped through the entire archipelago, passing Maquaca within sight.

We told the pilot to touch there but this was not possible owing to the wind, to our great regret, as we were anxious to see a Portuguese settlement which was there. However a sailor who was a native of the country relieved us by saying "You need not trouble, as the settlement which you are anxious to see consists of two hundred and forty Portuguese who have their parish there. Though the King is a Moor he does not prevent them from celebrating their festivals with all solemnity, but even assists them with what is needed. Every one lives by trade, and there is no lack of foodstuffs in the Island as in the other islands. Everything is very cheap, and if this were not so, they would not be able to live there." We were pleased to find someone to give us this information, and we passed on within sight of Jaoa Major, entered the Strait of Sunda, and sailing past Sumatra in a few days reached Ceilão, by the blessing of God and with a favourable wind. Here we proposed to rest after our long journey, in the course of which we missed seeing little. There were some forts which the enemy had taken from us for some years, and in Japão the city of Nagacaque, which had been destroyed by order of the King of that Island, who had also given instructions that every Portuguese touching there was to be put to death. That was the reason why we were not anxious to see it : we preferred to be confessors for many years rather than martyrs for one hour.

CHAPTER V

In which is explained how at the commencement of our Conquest, it was to our advantage to have maintained Malaca, Ormuz, and Goa alone

The principal object of this imaginary journey of ours is to illustrate by these examples the very serious mistake we committed in spreading ourselves over the whole of the East. If our deliberate object had been to set up in that State a foundation which should prove our undoing, we could not have adopted a more effective policy than that which we followed when we occupied and strengthened so many little forts as pointed out. I know that some will disagree and assert that our policy was a wise one, and they urge many arguments in support. None the less the best of them are bound to be merely specious and without a solid basis. There are only two possibilities—what I say is either true or false : this is the answer to all the objections which can be urged. All concede that the prime requisite in the construction of a house is a broad and deep foundation, strong enough to support the entire fabric which it is proposed to erect : unless this is so all the labour will be in vain. As already stated, our wish is not to censure any individual, for all desire to act with wisdom. Those who find the result different from their expectations, lose their meed of praise and are styled unfortunate. Those who are favoured by Fortune, double their triumphs and are acclaimed as fortunate. Yet the object of both is the same, and the difference consists only in good and bad success. Often great victories are unexpectedly won with small forces, and again great armies are defeated by a handful of the enemy. Those who fail are blamed for attacking at the wrong moment or while the enemy had the superior position, or such like. This comparison however does not apply to our theme, for the bulk of these incidents were accidental and often could not fail to happen according to the chances of the moment.

But questions of conquest and occupation afford sufficient opportunity for discussion and mature deliberation.

I realise that these enterprises were started by those at the helm of government, and that they acted with a zeal worthy of all praise ; for they thought they were rendering the greatest service possible to their Prince. Others adopted the rules which they laid down. Nevertheless there ought to have been some to detect the mistakes in the line of policy, that new forts should not be occupied, and that the abandonment of some which we already held was the best service which could be rendered to the King and State. They should have seen those deficiencies which we have pointed out. If there were any such, they are entitled to the heaviest censure for recognising the failure and not doing anything to remedy the same. We ought to impute malice to them and innocence to the others.

We can imagine them replying "It is true we saw what you refer to. If we abandoned the forts which were the object of pride to all, what reason could we offer which would have found acceptance with the King and the people, who judge everything by appearances? They would see in this reason for punishment, and only double the praise given to the founders of the places." To escape the evil which threatened them so certainly, they adopted the same course as the men who founded those settlements ; for they not only did not abandon those which we held, but even added fresh ones. Thus they secured their own reputation and established a claim on their Prince for the acknowledgment of their services. We can see how rarely it was that those who had spent the best years of their lives in these parts, and who could have expected high rewards for their meritorious services to the Crown, failed to be thrown into prison. The reason God alone can understand : what we do know is that when he punishes it is for our sins, and the punishment is always less than we deserve. Their Most Serene Majesties the Kings D. Manoel, D. João the Third, and the rest who wore the Crown, did not fail to reward their subjects, so that we could blame them. We ought to reflect that Kings are the agents of God on earth, and that he inspires them to punish some and reward the others.

Some have governed the State and borne themselves with great purity, serving with devotion, zeal and courage, many even sacrificing their lives, without being infected with the poison of vile avarice ; if they will permit me I shall select for them a Captain of such parts, that if they were alive to-day I feel sure they would acclaim the wisdom of my choice. Not only the eminent men of our race, but all who are enrolled in the everlasting tablets of Fame, cheerfully acknowledge the innumerable claims of the unrivalled Affonso de Albuquerque—that glory of all the wise and famous leaders the world has procured This marvel of perfection lacked no virtue which another had, while he abounded in what was deficient in all. We shall compare the two most famous men of all ages..

Alexander the First, a miracle of courage and good fortune, achieved all his great designs, and even more than the forces of nature allowed ; yet his undertakings served more to immortalise his own person among men than to aggrandise the state of Macedon ; for had he lived for many centuries, at his death his kingdom was bound to be divided. Even time is never the same and his successors would not have been all Alexanders, and it was a certain fact that the loss would always fall on his country. What does a kingdom gain by being sovereign over the world, if in her decline her subjects revolt from her, and the glory she had won, the treasure she had lavished, and the lives she had thrown away are exchanged for the contempt and perpetual hatred of all ? And will those who envied her feel pity for her woe ?

Princes and Kings are the fathers of their countries ; as it is the natural duty of a father not to dissipate the property which belongs to his children, but rather to add to it by moderate profits, no less is it the duty of Kings to cherish and preserve their kingdoms, and every policy they adopt should be devoted to this end ; otherwise a King is a tyrant over servants, not a father to his country ; where his duty is to protect, he would destroy. The great Caesar was as kind towards the conquered as brave towards his foes—qualities with which nature appears to me to have endowed him without stint ; the one without the other cannot make perfection, but the two combined helped him gloriously to achieve the great victories which have placed him in the first rank among men. Nor did he lack the other virtues. The wise man chooses the beautiful and shrinks from what is hurtful ; but even he could not avoid being tainted with the terrible poison of ambition ; he grasped at what belonged to the State, he placed her under an everlasting subjection, and hence her ruin. Thus we see that the most renowned and distinguished men were found wanting ; but our hero satisfied all save the envious : the virtuous yielded him place : the vicious hated him.

The supreme command over our vast empire was entrusted to the incomparable Affonso de Albuquerque. On considering what was in the interests of the service of the King and would tend to the development of the Empire and the honour of his country, he realised that our forces were too small to establish a lasting dominion there ; for our enterprises were numerous and we could not succeed in and preserve all we undertook. Occupied in these plans, where many obstacles presented themselves, his wisdom enabled him to discover a line of policy by which he placed a strong curb on all the Kings of the East, his great courage assisting him and supplying everything which was lacking with energy. He resolved to establish three Emporia where he could concentrate all the trade of this extensive dominion ; by means of these he not only held those barbarous hordes in check, but they served as a protection ; when our enemies saw these great and formidable forts guarded by our armies, they no longer had any expectation of reducing them to their former condition. These were what were sufficient for us without dissipating our resources over others, for they were enough to keep all that great universe subject to us. They were the forts of Goa, Malaca and Ormuz, the wealthiest, strongest and most important possessions of the Portuguese Monarchy. Everyone knows in the face of what dangers and with what devotion he gloriously achieved his object ; these matters cannot be related here ; we shall only speak of what experience has shown to us by their results.

CHAPTER VI

Continued

Malaca was one Emporium, a fort strong by nature and every device of man, a Court to which all the islands of the extensive Southern Sea and the mainland looked up as the wealthiest and most imperial, crowded with the trade of every kind of wealth as being the harbour where the commerce of the rest of India was carried on. This was won and kept by our arms, and it gave us the sovereignty of the whole of the Archipelago as far as Japão and the mainland of China, without anyone being left to oppose us. Indeed all these monarchs were dismayed and sought our friendship and gave us all the privileges we desired, with free entry for our trade in their ports.

Goa also was a sovereign emporium in the middle of the coast of India where there met all the trade of Persia, Arabia, and the rest of the East ; for the city was large and the Island very strong with two safe and commodious harbours for the protection of our fleets ; and taken a second time, the Kings of all India were terrified and sought our friendship so as to have us on their side, granting us everything which was useful to us.

The Island of Geru was adorned with the city of Ormuz, situated at the mouth of the Persian Gulf, a wealthy emporium where met all the nations and riches of the East which were conveyed to Persia, Mesopotamia, Palestina, Natolia, the Arabias, Egypt and Europe. In these three emporia there lived three powerful Kings of that part of the East whose banners were replaced by the escutcheon of Portugal, by the valour of Affonso de Albuquerque.

On these three great and solid columns was built the new Lusitanian Empire, a foundation sufficient to bear the weight of these far-stretching realms. We can see from the reasons we have mentioned that our hero rendered by his policy the highest service that ever subject has rendered towards his Prince and the development of his country ; for he by his wisdom, courage, and high qualities acquired and held this wealthy empire, and that with forces so small, as we all know. If we wish to realize the grandeur of his spirit, we shall find that he commenced where the great leaders of the world left off their conquests ; for he won the wealthiest and most difficult by terrifying and reducing those regions, rendering the name of Portugal immortal and feared. But at the same time he did not show himself avaricious in anything : his sole desire was to serve His Majesty and to make the name of his people glorious and respected by all.

Experience has shown us that three colonies were enough to make our Empire everlasting. All our other forts and settlements only served to weaken their strength, thus rendering opposition easy. While we increased the number we had to defend and provide with troops, spending on them artillery, ammunition and other necessaries, objects of hatred to our neighbours, the majority of these forts were of no advantage to the Crown or the colonists. And even if all of them yielded great profits, we could have obtained the same without occupying them, merely by placing a Factor in each to carry on trade on His Majesty's account, the port being free to our nation, which all these Kings willingly would have granted us. This however became impossible when they saw us placing on them the curb of a fortress—a fortress of little substance, one might rather say, where the Captains quarrelled with them over their private interests, and the Crown had to pay heavily to support their actions. Thus in the case of Dabul, a Moorish city in the middle of the coast which runs from Goa to Chaul, there was a Factory of ours where there lived a Factor and his clerk, who collected half the revenues of the Customs ; we had another such at Congo, a city in Persia, where they made the same recoveries ; and I am sure we could have done the same in all the other ports without occupying them. And from these Factories His Majesty recovered half the dues without incurring any expense, as we have pointed out.

The forces we scattered over so many little forts on land should have been kept on the sea, and we should have maintained a fleet in the Southern Sea ploughing those waters with our keels and thus keeping in check those idolaters and Moors and holding them subject to the yoke of our arms ; and with the knowledge that these seas were occupied, no one would have dared to venture on them. Another fleet should have been stationed at Goa, guarding from there the Red and Persian Seas, visiting Ormuz, helping our friends and punishing our foes ; if we did so everyone would have been dependent on us, and we would not have been disturbed nor attacked by anyone.

Oh brave and wise Captain, the honour and pride of the Portuguese race ! For it was you who did plan and achieve what was to the advantage of your King and country, as if inspired from above, and thereby shed lustre on your race ; if you did not reap the reward of your toil and zeal, tell me I beseech you where is the good man who can avoid the poison of envy. How much more you who have given so much reason for envy ? Where men failed you sought your help in God, since only he who looks to Him for shelter obtains his reward in his glory, a treasure for all time ; and on earth among those who give proper thought to your virtues, you will be the crown of all whom Fame proclaims throughout the ages.

From what I have shown it can be clearly seen that to perpetuate our Empire, in India we need have maintained only these three forts ; and the rest of our colonies were the cause of our total ruin, as they could not be defended and we had to disperse our forces, thereby enfeebling them. It is also clear that all the trade of those parts was at our disposal without any opposition from their lords.

The Hollanders quite recognised the unwisdom of this policy ; they would not employ their forces in establishing cities and colonies, but kept them all on the sea, and thus obliged all the Eastern Princes to allow them to open Factories in their territories, where they collected their produce and supplied what they lacked. In Java Major alone, when they drove away the English from their Factory at Jacatara, they built a city to serve as a colony, naming it New Batavia. In view of their trade with Japão they built the fort of Taivana in Formosa, from which they were expelled by the Chincheo who deprived them of the whole Island by force of arms.

On the Choromandel Coast they established another small but powerful fort called Palicate, so as to obtain from there the cloth which is the whole of their trade with the Red Sea. They established no other fort, but maintained Factories on all the points of India. In 1639 they took from us Batecalou and Trequimale, and although these were in the Island of Ceilão which they were so anxious to acquire, we see that they razed them to the ground as they were of no use. All the others they occupy to-day belonged to us and they are only kept up to resist us, for their sole aim and object has always been to obtain the monopoly of the traffic in spice over the entire world ; and that is the reason why they did not try to take from us any of our forts on the coast from Goa to Dio, for no spice is found there.

I have no doubt that the maintenance of their possessions already costs them much more than they get from their duties and other revenues ; for they have all the pepper they require in the kingdoms of Jambe and Pera, and the islands of Sumatra and Borneo, wherefore they did not want the pepper of Coulão and Cochim ; for the maintenance of that great city would necessitate a large force and they could not get from it sufficient revenue to cover a fourth of their expense, although they cut it down to a third of its original size : Cananor, which requires a garrison of six hundred soldiers at least, and similarly with all the others they took from us. It is also true that the whole of their trade is maintained on account of the Company, and no private individual even if he were a high officer, is allowed to do so under severe penalties, hence all the profits go to the treasury ; but this was not the case with us, where as a rule every one looked to his own profit and the Royal Treasury supplied the expenses.

CHAPTER VII

How we ought to have abandoned all our possessions in India and occupied the Island of Ceilão

In spite of what we have related, some excuse might be urged on behalf of those who occupied so many lands at such distances from each other, and with little or no benefit. It might be said that they never considered that at some time some neighbouring Prince or State of Europe would desire to oppose our enterprises in these parts, both as they were so distant and because their discovery was the result of our labour : that for this reason they spread with such confidence over this large expanse, as their garrisons secured all the forts against the natives. But no excuse can be found for the men of to-day, who did not concentrate all on our own wealthy land and give up the poor soil of the strangers, as Ceilão was the heritage of our Kings. The answer will be, how was it possible to induce these people, who had become naturalised after a residence of so many years and who had been born in these lands, to abandon them and to settle in strange lands of which they had no knowledge or clear conception, in view of the inconveniences that such a change would entail?

To this we ean reply that when the good is common and the better is open to all, the dictates of prudence should be followed. For first of all the advantage of the State rather than of private individuals, should be studied ; and again, do we know of any of these colonies to which such a transfer was suggested, which opposed it with these and similar reasons ? To this latter question we answer them by reminding them that they and their fathers went from Portugal to these foreign parts to serve their King there as was of the greatest advantage to him ; they settled in those colonies temporarily while no better opportunity was available ; but the present occasion was one of urgency ; by remaining where they were they ran the risk of being easily hemmed in by enemies, as it was not possible to relieve them. In matters of this nature perseverance can effect more than force ; if a beginning had been made with the smaller settlements, the larger would have volunteered if they heard of the success of the former. Thus Ceilão would have been peopled, our forces united, our countrymen enriched and delivered from any one who could oppress them at any time, and our Kingdom become the most prosperous and wealthy the world has ever seen, as will be shown in the remarks I have still to make.

The first step to take would have been to enter into an arrangement with the Kings and lords of the neighbouring lands to whom we intended to hand over ours. If the trade of the port were of importance, a Factor should have been left there ; the price agreed upon should be divided among the residents according to the property which each left behind, and each colony informed of the place in the Island where it could establish its home, so that it could go to that harbour of the Island which would be most convenient, taking along with it the property of the Crown, the artillery, and all the other military fittings for guarding the colony. Those who settled inland would require only some small pieces, while the guns of heavy calibre could be left for the protection of the coast forts ; as much of the land surrounding their future home as was required for their maintenance should have been divided among them, the distribution being made with due regard to the position of the parties and what each had given up. The poor too should have been supplied, and all given sufficient for their livelihood ; for apart from there being quite enough to distribute generously among all, we see that the sun does not refuse to supply his warmth to any created thing. Thus all would have been satisfied, and our people avoided the miseries which are one of the causes of unrest in a country. For poverty is the parent of lying, theft and deceit ; they beget quarrels and other grave sins which only offend God.

Their houses could have been built where the site was suitable, and in the coast towns there should have been forts of greater strength ; on the very day of their arrival at their future home, houses could be built for all the families. Do not consider this an exaggeration ; when our army was on the march, every day in the space of one hour there was not left a person who had not finished his hut ; and this would last for three years if not for the rain ; this is due to the abundance of timber and covering material which can be obtained in every part of the Island.

At the start we should erect a shelter for which in the interior clay would be sufficient, till in course of time the people could complete the work; for there is no lack anywhere of lime, excellent stone and sand, and fuel in abundance. There is plenty of timber of every kind in all parts close at hand, so that transport costs nothing. We have mentioned the large supply of iron the earth produces, and it is sold very cheap: so that there is no deficiency of everything for building a house in the fashion we wish and all this at very little expense.

The course adopted in one settlement should be followed in all; similarly with the buildings, as the same advantages are to be found everywhere. If the King of Candia would see our eagerness in settling the Island, how we brought all our forces there and hedged him in with forts and towns, he would have given up his claim to the kingdom without our being compelled to have recourse to arms. Nor would we have treated him unjustly; for his claim to be King is derived from his mother, and she lost her rights in consequence of her apostatizing and becoming a Gentile after being a Christian. There are other reasons too which we can assert —the protection which this Crown has exercised over that kingdom, based on the will of Dom Filippe, the last and rightful King thereof, as we have narrated in the fifth chapter of the first book.

We must remember that in all our forts and settlements in that State there lived and are living other residents, natives of the country, with their families; these are of Christian parents and grandparents and they served and serve us with affection. We call them *Topazes*, and they form the handicraftsmen, traders, and merchants; their sons serve us as soldiers and have won an honourable record of service in war and have not been found wanting towards the State. We ought to have brought all of these and kept and protected them along with the rest and distributed some land among them; for they assist us in war, many of them sacrificing their lives, without any hope of advancement. If in their country they took up arms in our defence against their own people, they would do much more where there was no impediment of kinship or nature. For these reasons and because they were Christians brought up among us, it was not desirable to abandon them but rather to hold them in honour.

I do not say that the scheme I have proposed for successfully settling the Island, could have been carried out without the sanction of His Majesty : for that is the very foundation of the whole of this structure. He should have been consulted and the reasons set before him in detail, that this was to his true interest ; and when His Majesty authorised the scheme, a person should have been chosen with a comprehensive knowledge of the Island, a man of a good conscience, and he should have been charged with the task of distributing the land in such a way as to satisfy all ; for on that depends the well-being of the Crown, the enrichment of the subjects, and the preservation of the Empire, all which we shall see in the next chapter.

CHAPTER VIII

How the Island should have been utilised

We have shown that excluding the territories of the kingdoms of Candia, Uva, Jafanapatão, Triquimale, Batecalou, and those appertaining to Manar, which are the lands of Mantota; in the territory subject to the Emperor alone which we discuss later on our Lord the King is entitled to twenty-one thousand eight hundred and seventy-three villages. The jungle of more than sixteen thousand of these is covered with cinnamon as described above; the rest are situated on the plains where everything is marshy land producing an abundance of grain, three or four crops in the year of the same seed, and various other articles. Thus the bulk of the land from Chilao past the kingdom of Candia and the frontiers of Uva as far as two leagues beyond the pagoda of Tanavare, was all under cinnamon; the same lands produce an abundance of uncultivated pepper, as I have already said.

For the citizens to acquire great wealth, His Majesty should have conceded to them the privilege which the people had possessed, of each collecting all the cinnamon he could; this privilege was withdrawn in 1626 by King Filippe IV in consequence of advice, the only result of which was loss to the subject without any benefit to the Crown, though the chief strength of a monarchy depends on the wealth of its subjects. The privilege however should have been subject to the condition that a fifth of the total collection should go to His Majesty, and I am of opinion that all the cinnamon collected should have been purchased on account of the Crown at a fixed rate, to prevent its going through many hands.

We know that this spice is found nowhere but in Ceilão; what is named Coulão cinnamon comes from the jungles of Porca, and I have already described what it is like, and it is well-known in this kingdom. Some would maintain without any reason that cinnamon is found elsewhere: but that is not true. I have seen some stuff in Jaoa Major which resembles it in shape but not in taste or colour, for it is very yellow and extremely bitter ; and that is what they call cinnamon. The Ceilão article is highly valued throughout the world, and it can be all shipped and sold on His Majesty's account. By reason of the little trouble involved in collection, the people would sell it very cheap ; and so our Lord the King could furnish cargo of this alone for, not a hundred, but two or three thousand vessels a year.

Every one should also have been obliged, each on his own plot of land, to plant pepper-vines at the foot of the trees. These grow without any cultivation owing to the climate, and if they received a little attention they would do even better ; for when once planted they would last for ever, and from the two crops gathered yearly, they should pay a fifth to the Royal Treasury. With this alone without purchasing any they could send to this Kingdom many shiploads, obviating the necessity for our spending money thereon, while the inhabitants should be free to sell their share to Persia, the Arabias, the Mogor and the other parts of the East. As it is of the best quality, it commands a higher price than what is produced in the whole of India. The people need pay a fifth of these two commodities alone to His Majesty ; they should be permitted to take everything else the land produces for themselves, as has been always the custom. Thus the Island would have become very powerful, and the King would have had the greatest treasures within our discoveries by securing these products in such abundance without the expenditure of a *real*. The Customs duties would amply suffice for the maintenance of the garrisons in the forts. It is easy to see that had the Island been settled a great trade would have grown round it.

Besides cinnamon and pepper, His Majesty had two commodities which were not inferior and which were always collected and sold on his account, namely, elephants and precious stones. If we were unwilling to keep the natives of the country continuously at this occupation, we could have engaged blacks and Kaffirs for the work. But the Chingalas themselves would have worked at this. When the treaty was ratified and we had nothing in the Island save the city of Columbo, as Dom Filippe Mascarenhas saw that the greater part of the cinnamon lands in which the Chalias who collect it lived, fell to the Hollanders, and as he realised the enormous loss His Majesty sustained thereby, he found a remedy for it in kindness and good words ; he persuaded the *Pachas* to collect yearly the amount by which the crop fell short of the three thousand two hundred *bahars* which according to the Tombo the Chalias had to collect, and he paid them a *pataca* the *bahar*. Thus the one thousand nine hundred *bahars* were distributed among that caste and they collected it annually, and so made good the deficiency without the King losing a stick of cinnamon, at a time when the Hollanders held the greater part of the land where it was found and where the peelers lived. If when we had such small forces in the Island we could induce them to do this by fair words alone, what could we not have done when the whole country was occupied by us ?

Of the precious stones alone, namely, rubies, sapphires, topazes and catseyes, sufficient could be found to send to this kingdom several shiploads a year in which would come stones worth ten thousand cruzados. Do not think I exaggerate in this, for in everything I rather state less than the truth which I can enlarge upon without hesitation. Several thousands could be continuously employed in collecting them without any deficiency arising, for they are found in such abundance everywhere, and the sixty-seven leagues within which they are found teem with them. In searching for them they do not dig more than a *braca* and a half at most, till they reach a very blue sandy soil ; this is washed in baskets and a large quantity of gems is found among stones of less value. I would point out that where one variety is found the others too appear, and although they are of different kinds, they are not discovered separately. Hence we can infer that the whole of India and the whole of the world cannot have such great treasures as Portugal. I make no mention of the pearl fishery, which under our protection and care would have become an important source of revenue.

Apart from the products and wealth which I have described we could have built great fleets at little expense, as there is an abundance of timber and iron and resin, all articles which are largely employed in such work. There is in the Island a plant* which produces something like our linen thread, out of which the native fishermen make their nets ; from this we could manufacture ship shrouds similar to those of Europe, without the coarseness and thickness of coir.† In what words should I speak of the harbour and bay *Dos Arcos*? It is the best in the whole of India, with a bottom between sand and clay, and is protected from every wind save the East, which however does not blow except occasionally and then too gently ; moreover it contains several inlets, which are protected from this as well.

The chief winds which blow during the year are the North and the South, called respectively *Vara* and *Cachão*,‡ and they create in the Island two wet and two dry seasons. The longest and most beautiful river in the Island falls into this bay ; its water, which comes from Adam's Peak, is very good, and on its banks are found an abundance of trees remarkable for their size and variety. A dock could be made in the bay itself, and fleets of numerous ships of any tonnage that is required built there, especially as we had that large river for conveying all the material without any expense ; for as we have shown in the tenth chapter of the first book, it is the duty of the woodcutters to fell timber, and of the iron-smelters and smiths, carpenters, turners, pike and gunmakers, and all the other craftsmen in the Island, to serve His Majesty without any payment.

The weapons for arming them such as muskets, arquebuses, carbines, bacamartes, spears, pikes, swords, and gun stocks, would cost almost nothing ; all these are made in the Island in great abundance and of excellent workmanship. With these our forts and armies would be supplied without the expense which the Royal Treasury would have to meet everywhere else. Their carriage too costs nothing, as it is the duty of the *culles* to convey them, just as all the other craftsmen have their own duties to perform. So that we can see the great advantages we had for making fleets : a splendid harbour in which to keep them, with liberty to go

* *Crotolaria Juncea.*

† The fibre of the outer husk of the Coconut.

‡ The North-East and South-West Monsoon.

out and come in without danger at any season of the year, and an abundance of provisions for their use. Yet we never thought of utilising this harbour for building fleets, which were always the essential requirement in that State.

I should wish all who have travelled over the world or have read of its greatness, to tell me if they have seen or heard of any part which produces the treasures which as we have shown, are to be found in this Island? If we take the whole of Africa, we would not find there more than a little gold obtained by purchase, together with some amber and ivory. America produces gold, silver, pearls, emeralds, some amber and numerous drugs ; but we ought to remember that so vast is the extent of this country, that it is named the New World, and that it stretches from Pole to Pole, including numerous kingdoms and provinces, and that the majority of them lack most of the articles we have described. Those which have some, have not got the others. Brazil produces sugar and tobacco ; in Arabia there is incense, myrrh, dates and horses ; in Persia, silk and some drugs, while pearls are found in the Gulf ; in Gusarate, cloth and drugs ; in Canara, rice and pepper ; in Malavar, pepper, cardamom and ginger ; in the Xoromandel Coast, cloth ; in the Kingdom of Carnate which is subject to Golconda, diamonds ; in Bengala and throughout the Kingdom of the Mogor, cloth, rice, sugar, and wax. There are also numerous provinces which have some products and not others. In Pegu are found rubies and lacre; in Sumatra gold, copper, tin, benzoin and pepper; in Champa, ebony, *calamba* and *aguila* ; in Borneo, camphor, diamonds and pepper ; in Siam, benzoin and drugs ; in China, gold, silk, musk and drugs ; in Japão, silver and copper ; in the Malucas, cloves ; in Banda, nutmegs and mace ; in Timor and Solor, sandal. The products of each kingdom of Europe are well known, but they are more the result of cultivation than the gift of nature ; accordingly we do not refer to them.

We see that several of the lands which we have named include numerous large kingdoms, and they cannot fail to have a reputation for great wealth. What then should we say about an Island, the greatest length of which is not more than seventy two leagues, and which produces the five commodities we have described, in such store? Its cinnamon is the best in the world; its gems are in such abundance, and only diamonds and emeralds are wanting; its elephants are the most prized of any within our discoveries, its pepper is the finest in the East, the pearls and seed pearls of its waters are considered very excellent. I do not speak of the numerous other drugs which the Island produces, and of which we take no account. Some amber is found on the coast. Methinks that those who declared that this Island is the terrestrial Paradise, did so not in consequence of its fertility or the profusion of every kind of dainty to support life, nor for the blandness or healthfulness of its climate, nor for the footprint two palms long which the Gentiles have fabricated to attract veneration to the spot; but because while its extent is so limited, it produces such an abundance of riches.

Let us look at the inhabitants of Sofala, Mocambique, and Mombaca, where the trade consists in a little gold, amber and ivory, all purchased, and made the monopoly of the Governors and Captains of those forts. Instead of living in these lands devoid of all that is needed for the maintenance of life, and entirely unhealthy, it would be better for our people to live in a healthy land, which is provided with everything, and pleasant for the life of man; where all would be wealthy, and have something to sell without being obliged to buy; all our forces united, and not living in continual fear of defeat or attack; holding the entire East in submission so that their Kings would be compelled to court our friendship; serving God, and having in that immense tract a firm rock on which to build the Faith of Jesus Christ; while our King would have a wealthy Empire founded on those same forts, with which the deserving could be rewarded, with different revenues from what they yield now.

The same could be said of Mascate, Curiate, Damão, S. Gens, Danu, Aserim, Tarapor, Manora, Quelme, Mahim, Dantora, Agasaim, Bacaim, Tana, Caranja, Chaul, Morro, Honor, Bracelor, Cambolim, Mangalor, Cananor, Caranganor, Cochim (where the Hollanders only found, when the city surrendered, more than 10,000 abandoned white women, without parents or husbands), Coulão,

Negapatão, Meliapor, Macao, the Malucas, Timor, Solor, and all the others which we held in that State. Here all would live rich and content, and avoid the necessity of scattering among so many settlements such a large number of Portuguese, who live without law and with only their vices as the guide of their consciences, in the midst of Gentiles and Moors whom of necessity they have to obey. We would certainly not have failed to obtain the produce of those lands where we had those forts, for the lords thereof would not desire to be on bad terms with us when they saw us with sufficient forces with which to administer rigorous punishment to them. Moreover it would be an advantage to them to sell their fruits and drugs to us. We had good experience in the time of King Filippe IV ; when there was such a bitter war with his rebel Hollanders, he granted passports for them to come freely to this kingdom to load salt and other goods, as all are anxious to benefit by what its provinces produced.

CHAPTER IX

The rest of our errors in modern times

Everything has a commencement, growth and decay. In the commencement there is either wisdom or error, and we committed the grave error of spreading over so many parts. During our growth, while we were in that State, Ceilão became ours without any expense. We have already discussed all the excuses which have been urged, and now there are different ones ; but these are of such a quality that it is impossible for us to admit them. The suggestion is that those who governed the Island never realised the wealth which we have indicated, and had no clear knowledge thereof. It is a common tendency to make a fuss of what is petty, and to ignore what is of importance. They only guessed at or imagined the existence of any portion of this wealth, but that was not sufficient to compel them to attach proper weight thereto, nor had our Most Serene Kings information such as would have led to the discovery of the truth. It is beyond doubt that if they had the information, they would have sent to the Island at least sufficient forces for its defence. We realize this from the zeal with which they opposed the Belgae in Brazil, and Angola ; how much more would they have done in Ceilão, where without all these results the fact of its being their patrimony would have compelled its defence? We should also add that in view of its large outturn of cinnamon alone they attached much importance to Ceilão. In proof of this is the fact that His Most Serene Majesty Dom João IV made a treaty with the States of Holland for a period of ten years in India, and it is certain that had he known what Ceilão was, he would while the treaty lasted have ordered everything which was in the State to be diverted to that Island—an undoubted consequence, which was not noticed.

Here the thought, or rather the complaint, occurs to us, though those who governed the Island were men of great wisdom, versed in affairs, whose duty it was to know what there was in the parts they governed, so as to give an account thereof and of themselves, as everything passed their hands ; yet they were so careless and remiss that they failed to report what it was their duty to have done in order to provide a remedy. If His Majesty or his Ministers would have failed to provide the remedy, yet they had done their duty. It was not for them to wait till the evil was beyond remedy, so as to afford the opportunity for a soldier of little talent and less fluency ; for his only duty was the service of His Majesty ; he could not overcome the never-ending toil of that terrible war, marching by day and night for eighteen years, barefoot, covered with the *bloodsuckers* of the forests, and always living in the thickets.

The worst is that in spite of everything, some one who reads or hears this might say—and with a certain amount of reason—that these are exaggerations and falsehoods, to ascertain if I can obtain some reward and acquire some reputation for myself. I therefore protest before Jesus Christ that I have set out no matter which is fictitious, but the pure and simple truth. I also renounce for ever any reward which the generosity of the King our Lord, whom God protect, should desire to confer on me not only for this labour which I have undertaken, and which is the fruit of my zeal and love of country, but also for everything which I have rendered in his service for more than forty and a half complete years, without failing a day, from 21st March 1640 till 4th October 1680 when I came to this Capital by order of the same Lord. Though it be the case that I have no wealth, yet thanks be to the Highest God who grants to all his creatures what is sufficient, if only they knew to accommodate themselves. Therefore they can undeceive themselves, for in neither case will their criticism be valid. Our only object is this, that if at any time this Kingdom should find itself with great strength, these matters should not remain buried in forgetfulness.

In the decay of that State is clearly revealed how greatly we lacked foresight, and how we failed to discover a means for our self-preservation. Reason alone demanded that, when we saw opposed to us two powerful enemies, the Hollanders and the English. Though at the time we had all our forces, the latter with the Persian took from us Ormuz, the best fort we had, and we were unable to prevent it. We were unable to drive the Hollanders out of the Southern Sea ; assisted by the shallows of those waters, they infested that great archipelago and appropriated the trade of all those islands as well as of the main land. They accumulated such wealth that the Company was able to double the number of their vessels without let or hindrance, and they made themselves so much the masters of those parts that we were prevented from sailing those waters. Matters reached such a stage that if one vessel in five of those engaged in the China trade escaped, it was regarded as a marvel ; and because India at the time was as full of vice as of wealth, the valuable cargo which they found in one ship incited them recklessly to seek for all vessels which we despatched to various parts, as if they were the inheritance and birthright which we enjoyed there. Thus the bulk did not escape, save perchance some vessel on the coasts of Pegu, Bengala, Xoromandel, Sinde, Basora, Mocambique, or Mombaca. They did not trouble to look for them in any of these parts for they would fall into their hands as they occupied the mouth of the Straits of Singapura with powerful ships ; because that was the passage from Malaca to the Southern Sea.

In this fashion they went on wearing us out year after year in every part, robbing us of all we had save wretchedness, till finally seeing themselves so well off they, to finish the business, used every summer to place a fleet of twelve vessels to ride off the harbour of Goa. This left the rest of them free to move about as they liked ; and though our galleons fought with them more than once, yet they persisted in their blockade. And because they recognised that Malaca was the Emporium of the South, where was centred all the trade in the spices and drugs of those waters, they blockaded that too, maintaining five or six ships within sight of that fort. This kept the place as it were besieged and prevented all trade, till they had quite decided to drive us away from there. With the object of rendering it impossible for us to send any assistance, they entered into a treaty with the King of Candia, and in 1639 captured from us Batecalou and Triquimale. In that winter they entered with some vessels the harbour of Marmugao, a strong fort under the protection of which we maintained a guard of three galleons and a flotilla of rowing boats. In spite of them the galleons, which were all we had on those seas, were destroyed by fire. Having achieved this, at the beginning of the following year they landed in Ceilão and took the forts of Galle and Negumbo, while they also laid such close siege to Malaca by land and sea that after six months, early in January 1641, it was compelled to surrender.

Elated with this success they hoped to make themselves masters of the entire State and pressed on the war in Ceilão, while the armada which rode off Goa every summer, continued its tactics, till the end of 1644, when as we have narrated the eight years' treaty was ratified. This settlement relieved us to such an extent and left us so free from anxiety, that it seemed to us not only that the eight years could have no ending, but that there were no Hollanders at all in the earth. Yet wise Captains exert themselves to exercise greater care and vigilance in times of peace than during active hostilities; wherefore, in view of our peril, everyone should have shown greater care and forethought. If that were not so, I should like them to tell me what was the reason or object of our Most Serene King D. João IV in entering into a treaty with the Hollanders with reference to the State, when they had taken from us two forts in Ceilão as well as Malaca, and everything was so reduced with their uninterrupted success? It would have seemed reasonable to send all possible assistance to those parts, at least to wrest back the two forts in Ceilão, which was the royal patrimony, and to put a curb on their progress. But in his great discretion, when such a powerful enemy was knocking at our doors, he saw that it was undesirable to scatter our forces for the protection of what was so remote; he therefore arranged the treaty, for he thought that ten years was sufficient for that State to take thought and discover some means for its own protection. We should recognise that this treaty was as much in favour of this Crown as prejudicial to the Hollanders; for they had to suspend an invasion in which they had progressed so successfully, while it gave us the opportunity to increase our forces, rectify our mistakes, and provide what we lacked, so that at the expiry of the period our position would be so strong that they could not even with a considerable force, find it easy to resist us.

In consequence of all the reasons I have urged, we can find no excuse, for necessity compelled us to preserve ourselves. I am not referring to Ceilão, though it is such as I have pointed out; we ought to have chosen whatever part was suited for settlement so as to remedy past evils and to obviate those which threatened us, before they arose. But we took no trouble about all this and instead went to sleep, as if the war would have no beginning nor need the end thereof be dwelt upon. We ought to have realised that it was not possible for us to preserve the Island, while the Hollanders held a portion of it greater than we did, and that their sole design was to exclude us from every part of the State which yielded spice, so that they could have the entire trade in the article throughout the world. The consequence was that we not only failed to profit by those eight years to bring to that Island everything we had in the State, but we even let it continue with the same garrisons as it had before, carelessly wasting the time till war was declared, with the results which we have seen.

In 1656 they took Columbo from us, and with the arrival of some fresh forces they in 1659 also captured Manar and the Kingdom of Jafanapatão, and drove us entirely out of the Island. Subsequently they took from us Negapatão, and Cochim, and made themselves masters of Meliapor and the forts of Coulão, Caranganor, and Cananor. If the Canara had not taken from us the four which he had on his coast, there is no doubt that they would not have left us there, just because they produce a little pepper which we used to buy from the natives, and which is to-day sent to this country. As the Canara is now master of these places he cannot be prevented from selling us the stuff. I have reached the end of my story, and I have only to record the regrets which this notable disaster has left to us; for where the remedy is difficult, most of the chief ones survive.

CHAPTER X

THE END OF THIS WORK

SINCE my return to this Kingdom I have from time to time heard rumours to the effect that Ceilão was going to be retaken, that its King was earnestly begging us and trying to persuade us to go, saying he would help us to drive the Hollanders outside the Island, and others to the same effect. These are merely the offspring of our regret, for we all know how little or almost nothing we hold in that State. The Arabs seeing us thus weakened ventured to place armadas on the sea in opposition to us, and they have with great boldness offered us battle many a time. They crossed those seas and landed at Dio on two occasions, and plundered the town; they did the same at Bacaim; they subsequently laid siege to Mombaca twice, and to Mocambique once, pressing both of them hard, and showing themselves bolder than any other nation in the East. These were a people of whom a few years back we took no account. Their success of Pate would prove this much better; seeing our scanty forces they plucked up courage, and by continuous training in arms they are the people who cause us to-day anxiety in the East. Thus it is possible to realise that not even in imagination can we think of an enterprise of this nature.

Suppose that we had in India not the small force which is in our forts, but those which we maintained in our palmiest days; the success would not consist in winning them back from the Hollanders, for the main point would be their defence and preservation, and this is not only difficult but almost impossible. While we were there they had on those waters not less than 400 vessels, all fitted for any contingency that might arise, and engaged in trade from port to port. To-day they have in addition the cities and forts which they have taken from us, all garrisoned with good infantry; the number of their vessels is much greater; they have cut down the city of Columbo by a half, reducing it in size so that every portion should be covered by a powerful fort which they have constructed on the hill where the Convent of Santo Augustinho used to stand. At the point where they cut off a portion, they have erected three bastions and a wall all of the latest fashion, and they have dug a moat which is always kept filled with the water escaping from the lagoon into the sea, together with a covered passage. The result is that it is to-day the most strongly fortified position in India. They serve as an example to us, as we could not in the course of four years get together in the whole of that State a force sufficient to enable us to take Galle, when we had so many good men in the Island as well as the rest of the forts which they subsequently took from us. How will it be possible, when we have not got these, and their resources are doubled, that we could drive them out? All of us who take part in this enterprise should have wings so as to reach the light without any loss. From where will we have the resources with which to resist the impetuosity with which they are bound to set about regaining what we take from them? I am certain that he alone can talk of these matters, who has little knowledge of such things; we have other reasons too, but they are not for this place.

If it is the fact that the King of Candia has offered to assist us to enter the Island, I cannot help being firmly of opinion that he must be out of his senses; unless it be that he has turned Christian and confession has compelled him to unburden his conscience, and he therefore seeks to restore to Portugal the territories in Ceilão of which he is in possession and where he is obeyed as the King of the whole Island, as it was always his object to drive us out of it and make himself absolute lord, because with us he never could be master of his own. There was no mountain to which he fled but we followed him there. We entered Candia and set fire to the city and the palace itself, after which we withdrew without delay by one side of his kingdom to our own territory. Our tactics were such that he could never be forewarned nor could he hinder our retreat. It is thus clear that with us he could never be at rest, while he is not exposed to all this trouble at the hands of the Hollanders. They are not the people to march in single file among the forests, shoeless, through marshy fields and morasses, covered all over with the *bloodsuckers*. These are matters to which we gave no heed.

In proof of all that I have urged one should note that we are Christians, the King and his people are Gentiles ; we are white, they are black ; we are Portuguese, they Chingalas ; with us in the Island they were slaves, without us its lords. Can anyone tell me if he has heard mention of any race in the world which voluntarily subjected itself to the dominion of another, and not where it could no longer resist ? Our Kingdom realised that during the sixty years of the oppression of Castella, when nature created such opposition among the nations that we longed to drink the blood of everyone who belonged to that nation. Are they not our neighbours, and white like ourselves ? Do they not belong to the same flock of the Lord ? All this was so, but our hostility created such antipathy between the nations that it grew into deadly hatred, till the teaching of Christ our Lord, "Love your enemies" was denied.

It is quite true that the King of Candia as the result of the upbringing, intercourse and education which he secured among the Portuguese, has a great regard for us ; he recognises the high breeding, courtesy and gravity with which we conduct ourselves, and above all our good faith. But this disposition is as regards individuals and not towards the nation, regarding whom he has much to complain of. Accordingly he gave orders to settle them at Ruanella in a handsome city in a strong situation, and there seven hundred of them live with their families quite comfortably, as he allotted to all of them villages belonging to this Crown ; and with them there live the priests and the members of the religious orders to administer the Sacraments. This was his far-sighted plan when he ordered his people not to kill us but to take us alive, as I have pointed out in the nineteenth chapter of the second book. If a few of us are sent to the Island, I have no doubt they will be hospitably received by the King ; but we would deceive ourselves if we expected a similar reception for a force under officers. I think he would prefer to lose his life rather than consent to such a thing, for he has thoroughly learnt that all our plans were designed towards the conquest of his country.

It was for this reason that he allied himself with the Hollanders, a people regarding whom he never feared that they would ever be in a position to give him trouble ; for he knew that they could not undergo the same hardships as the Portuguese. So much is this the truth, that as soon as we had surrendered at Colombo he declared war on them and made himself master of all the territory which belonged to this Crown, without leaving them any out of those lands which they were in the enjoyment of during the period of the truce. Nothing in fact was left to them save the forts—for it could not well be less—and some villages on the sea-coast which he could not prevent being subject to them, and from which they obtained four sticks of cinnamon, and that is what the King himself never cared for. On the contrary his great regret was that the Island contained these forests, and had he been able to destroy them all he would have done so. As it is the Hollanders find it impossible to collect cinnamon at a distance of more than a musket shot. In the same way the King does not consent to the mining for gems, and when he desires to present them to his friends among the Kings of the other Coast, or to his relations, he selects them out of the large stock which he has in his treasury, thus avoiding searching for them in the earth. He thinks that by not trading with them, the existence of this source of wealth in the Island will escape notice. We are compelled thus to realise that there is no necessity to import anything to enable his people to live in comfort, and it will be difficult to find any Kingdom or Province which can boast of such a state of things.

It can be seen from what I have stated that the Hollanders are not making much profit out of Ceilão, and from what I learn the revenue will exceed the expenditure but slightly. If we should be able to arrange with the Company that they should give over to us the forts which they hold in the land, under whatever conditions they wish, we could take them back to occupy and deal with them in the way I have indicated. For them as business men it is incumbent to seek where the greatest profit lies. Many States and monarchies which had no other remedy acquired great wealth, and in a short time returned to their original condition, for God our Lord places no period for change. A time may come when this advice will be our salvation. In His divine hands are all Empires, and in ours amendment with repentance for our sins. These will be the most effective instruments which we can obtain against our enemies. By this means we may continue the government of this Island, in following with better wisdom the Captain-Generals who had presided over that Conquest up till now. The first who occupied that post was Pedro Lopez de Sousa. After him came in order D. Hieronimo de Azavedo, D. Francisco de Menezes, Manoel Homem Mascarenhas, D. Nuno Alvarez Pereira, Constantino de Sa e Noronha, D. Jorge de Alboquerque, Constantino de Sa e Noronha for the second time, D. Jorge de Almeida, Diogo de Mello, D. Antonio Mascarenhas, D. Filippe Mascarenhas, Manoel Mascarenhas Homem, Francisco de Mello de Castro, the fifteenth and last in Ceilão being Antonio de Sousa Coutinho. In addition Antonio de Amaral e Menezes, who was the sixteenth, held that position in Jafanapatão and Manar.

THE END

Praise be to God, and to the Immaculate
Conception of Maria, Virgin,
Mother of God.